"Every company – and every count[...] [...] to compete successfully in the 21st ce[...] [...] are book that is both an outstanding s[urvey of a fast-changing and] vitally important economic landscape and a delightful 'field guide' that will enrich your understanding of what's really happening on the ground."

—Dominic Barton, Global Managing Partner, McKinsey and Company

"Winston has written a first of its kind – a timely, insightful and eminently readable analysis of the world's fastest growing mobile economy. A must-read for anyone interested in China, the mobile economy, or technology, more broadly. Eye-opening and thoroughly enjoyable."

—Reuben Jeffery III, President and CEO, Rockefeller & Co., Inc.

"China is determined to make innovation an engine for the next stage of the country's development, and no sector has been more creative or dynamic than the mobile economy, which in some areas has surpassed even the United States. Winston Ma's deep dive into this fiercely competitive, constantly evolving industry dissects the companies, personalities and forces that are transforming China and that will inevitably influence commerce far beyond its shores."

—John L. Thornton, Co-Chairman, Brookings Institution

"As the world moves to mobile technologies, and with China now the world's largest market of Internet users, all stakeholders have to think about China's economy, market, and society from a completely new perspective. This is an indispensable book for understanding the emerging shape and scale of opportunities in the Middle Kingdom and beyond."

—Rod Beckstrom, Co-Author of *The Starfish and the Spider*, Former President and CEO, ICANN

"Chinese society is experiencing a rapid transformation, becoming increasingly industrialized and digital-based. The Chinese internet population has officially entered into the age of mobile internet. This extraordinary book explains how the internet has been the engine that catapults commercial activities from offline to online and towards ubiquity."

—Xiaodong Lee, President & CEO, China Internet Network Information Center (CNNIC)

China's Mobile Economy

China's Mobile Economy

OPPORTUNITIES IN THE LARGEST AND FASTEST INFORMATION CONSUMPTION BOOM

Winston Ma

This edition first published 2017
© 2017 John Wiley & Sons

Registered office
John Wiley & Sons Ltd, The Atrium, Southern Gate, Chichester, West Sussex, PO19 8SQ,
United Kingdom

For details of our global editorial offices, for customer services and for information about
how to apply for permission to reuse the copyright material in this book please see our
website at www.wiley.com.

Wiley publishes in a variety of print and electronic formats and by print-on-demand. Some
material included with standard print versions of this book may not be included in e-books or
in print-on-demand. If this book refers to media such as a CD or DVD that is not included in
the version you purchased, you may download this material at http://booksupport.wiley.com.
For more information about Wiley products, visit www.wiley.com.

Designations used by companies to distinguish their products are often claimed as
trademarks. All brand names and product names used in this book are trade names, service
marks, trademarks or registered trademarks of their respective owners. The publisher is not
associated with any product or vendor mentioned in this book.

Limit of Liability/Disclaimer of Warranty: While the publisher and author have used their
best efforts in preparing this book, they make no representations or warranties with respect
to the accuracy or completeness of the contents of this book and specifically disclaim any
implied warranties of merchantability or fitness for a particular purpose. It is sold on the
understanding that the publisher is not engaged in rendering professional services and
neither the publisher nor the author shall be liable for damages arising herefrom. If
professional advice or other expert assistance is required, the services of a competent
professional should be sought.

Library of Congress Cataloging-in-Publication Data is available

A catalogue record for this book is available from the British Library.

ISBN 978-1-119-12723-9 (pbk) ISBN 978-1-119-12725-3 (ebk)
ISBN 978-1-119-12724-6 (ebk) ISBN 978-1-119-32139-2 (ebk)

Cover Design: Wiley
Cover Images: © Bloomua/Shutterstock

10 9 8 7 6 5 4 3 2 1

Set in 12/14pt NewBaskervilleStd by Aptara Inc., New Delhi, India
Printed in Great Britain by TJ International Ltd, Padstow, Cornwall, UK

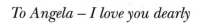
To Angela – I love you dearly

Contents

Foreword

Some authors are good at spotting and analyzing trends. Others go in deep and provide detailed explanations of how an industry ecosystem or specialized sector is evolving. But in *China's Mobile Economy*, Winston Ma delivers the rare book that is both an outstanding survey of a fast-changing and vitally important economic landscape and a delightful "field guide" that will enrich your understanding of what's really happening on the ground.

Start with the headline: even those generally aware of the scale of the country's ongoing digital transformation may have missed this news – 2014–15, Ma insists, marks "the most important inflection point in the history of the internet" in China. Almost overnight, the world's largest digitally-connected middle class went both mobile and multi-screen (smartphone, tablets, laptops and more), with huge implications for how consumers behave and what companies need to do to successfully compete.

How have China's Big Three, the group known as "BAT" (Baidu, Alibaba, and Tencent) responded so effectively to the shift to a mobile platform and how are their business models converging as the lines between e-commerce, social media, and entertainment blur? What does the swift rise of more than 600 million mobile consumers and the rapid merging of online-to-offline shopping (O2O) mean for Western multinationals in traditional industries such as autos and beverages, as well as for digital stalwarts like Apple and aspiring newcomers such as Uber? (Quick quiz: guess which three cities are now Uber's most popular in the world, measured by rides per day? Answer: Guangzhou, Hangzhou and Chengdu.) What role has government policy played in helping drive China's digitization and how will future regulation shape the fates of fast-growing sectors such as online banking?

Ma offers rich insight into all these macroeconomic and industry questions, making a convincing case that, as next-generation mobile devices and services take off, China's strength in this arena will transform it from a global "trend follower" to a "trend setter." At the same time, in a delightful array of boxes and sidebars, he supplements his analysis with a depth of cultural reporting and definitions of popular terms that would make a social anthropologist proud. Are Chinese consumers "shai"-ing your products in social media, as they have express-delivered fresh Canadian blackberries purchased online? Well, good for you. But be careful that they truly view your goods and services as "gao-da-shang" versus dismissing them as "tu-hao-jin." Understanding these phrases and the behaviors behind them, Ma rightly suggests, is no less critical than understanding what your next round of Big Data market research may be telling you.

As befits a successful investor, deeply grounded in both Western capital markets and in local equities, through his distinguished career at the China Investment Corporation (CIC), Ma strikes the right balance between enthusiasm for the opportunities that China's mobile marketplace offers and a clear-eyed assessment of potential challenges ahead. At McKinsey and Company, we too believe every company – and every country – must succeed at digitization to compete successfully in the 21st century. In many of our recent reports we have cast a bright light on some of the themes explored here, from China's growing capacity to innovate to the role the internet can play in its next wave of productivity-driven growth.

As Ma concludes, "The development of China's mobile economy is one of the most important trends that will reshape the future of business, technology and society both in China and the world." We couldn't agree more. From our work with leading global private and public sector clients across many industries and regions, we know just how keenly they are following the next phase of China's economic evolution. This independent, richly reported and highly readable book is a welcome addition to our understanding of this exciting, continuously unfolding story.

Dominic Barton
Global Managing Partner, McKinsey and Company

Preface

For China, the years 2014 to 2015 were the most important inflection point in the history of the internet, as the Chinese internet population officially entered the mobile internet and multi-screen age (with smartphones, tablets, personal computers and more). During this incredible period of change, the mobile internet in China gave rise to a dynamic tech sector, thriving social networks and the world's largest digitally connected middle income class. The development of China's mobile economy is one of the most important trends that will reshape the future of business, technology and society, both in China and the world.

Of course, the mobile transformation of China's economy has also had profound implications for global stakeholders dealing with the Chinese market. During China's digital boom, foreign investors are richly rewarded, and consumer goods companies see an emerging market filled with opportunities from an expanding middle class. Overseas users are cautiously adopting smartphones and mobile apps created in China, but Silicon Valley tech giants are taking notice of new competition arising from Asia. This book intends to provide a cutting-edge overview of this digital transformation in China as well as its global impact.

Chapter 1 will provide an overview of China's macro economy and the important government policy drivers behind the digital economy growth, such as urbanization, information consumption, smart cities, as well as internet plus, which is essentially the sum of it all.

This opening chapter will also introduce the big three "BAT" companies, Baidu, Alibaba and Tencent. These companies have respectively dominated the three strategic areas of the mobile market, namely the online search, e-commerce, and social network and messaging service in China. At this time of market inflection, these three key players are becoming more open-minded and proactive in moving into new areas through expansion, acquisition and strategic cooperation. Their impact can also be felt overseas by foreign investors, consumers, products users, start-ups and industry companies across the globe.

While the BAT companies strive to maintain their dominance over the digital high ground, many other Chinese firms are becoming strong players in the mobile market as well. Some of them have reached a significant size, and they come to the battlefield with unique strengths from different origins, such as Xiaomi (smartphone/hardware), LeTV (media content), Lenovo (PC/smartphone), Huawei (network/smartphone) and ZTE (telecom/smartphone). In addition, there are countless start-ups being formed every day by entrepreneurs eager to become the next Robin Li, Jack Ma or Pony Ma (the three founders of BAT, respectively).

The partnership, competition and cross-investments among these players of different traditional strengths, corporate scales and market focuses have made the mobile market extremely active and dynamic. As illustrated by the online shopping extravaganza and digital retailing revolution, the successful business models in the mobile era aim to integrate the four "Cs" seamlessly: Context, Community, Content, and Connection (see Figure P.1). As a result, the mobile internet and social networks are making a profound impact on productivity and growth in many parts of the economy. This chapter will briefly list some examples in the entertainment and media, retail and finance sectors, which will be discussed in detail in later chapters relating to corresponding business areas.

Chapter 2 will cover the various global stakeholders and the new opportunities and challenges they are experiencing. In particular, the "going mobile" and "internet plus" trends are critical for the foreign companies heading to China in search of their slice of the digital economy pie. In this fast-changing market, even for multinational corporations that have done

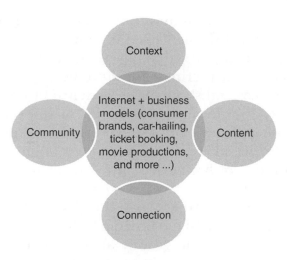

Figure P.1   The Four "Cs" in the Mobile Economy

business in China for many decades, a comprehensive rethink of their strategies in China may be necessary. Meanwhile, the mobile infrastructure opens up new opportunities to foreign merchants who do not have or need to have, a physical presence in China. To a large extent, mastering mobile internet strategy will separate the winners from the rest of the pack in their competition for Chinese customers.

Chapter 3 is centered on Xiaomi, the highest valued start-up in China. Focusing on a niche passed up on by premium brands like Apple and Samsung, the Chinese brands like Xiaomi, Huawei and Lenovo have mainly offered low price, high performance devices, which have played well into the general Chinese population's desire to own a smartphone and to access the internet for the first time. As China's smartphone market started showing early signs of saturation in 2015, Xiaomi (and its competitors) is striving to innovate its business model and product offerings to become a true "internet company" instead of a pure "smartphone company".

Chapter 4 starts the "internet plus" discussion with digital retailing. The online retailers have expanded so rapidly that the shopping malls, also a recent development in China, have already had their business disrupted by the new technology. The traditional retailers need to move away from the perception that e-commerce is merely another sales channel for their products, as it is critical for customers to get the same products, services and shopping experience in every channel where they choose to make purchases. As illustrated by the Alibaba/Suning alliance and the JD/Yonghui investment, the mobile era retailers have to integrate their online and offline channels, instead of having separate systems to sell products online and offline.

Chapter 5 carries the digital retailing discussion into mobile e-commerce territory and the broader online-to-offline (O2O) service consumption. The growth in "experience" consumption, such as movie-going, dining out, taxi-hailing and so on, is at the core of the O2O trends in China. The future e-commerce model – if the term e-commerce still applies here – is likely to be a seamless platform that links customers across multiple screens of mobile devices, providing standardized products as well as specialized goods and experience offerings, and connecting online content with offline activities.

Chapter 6 explores the mobile entertainment sector, which is of strategic importance for the internet giants' digital empires. This is because entertainment content and services are not only an important revenue source by themselves, but also a distinguishing factor that draws users to any specific e-commerce ecosystem and keeps them hooked. For a large part of their time online, young netizens play online games, watch videos of TV programs and movies, assume online personas in the virtual world and form online communities to have fun together. As smartphones are becoming the top channel for internet access in China, they enjoy themselves whenever and wherever they are during their "fragmented time" throughout the day (i.e. the time they spend online while outside of their homes).

It is important to note that "fragmented time" creates a different and additional demand for entertainment content. For example, online novels can be read on mobile devices any-where and anytime, which not only leads to a disruption of the physical book market, but also creates a different experi-ence from traditional book reading (hence new readers). As such, the mobile internet provides a new avenue for market-ing, advertising and brand building, with the biggest growth potential from people in smaller cities, who may not have PCs but are now engaging with online entertainment content using their smart devices.

Chapter 7 discusses the application of the O2O model in the movie business, which has added an online DNA to the tradi-tional film industry. To meet the quest for high quality content, the tech giants are not only betting on set-top boxes (devices that provide contents over the internet and bypass traditional distribution) to convert TV and theater viewers to online view-ing, but also creating their own blockbuster movies for the big screen at offline cinemas. The mobile internet has empowered young movie fans to get intimately involved with a movie, from the beginning to the end of a movie's life cycle. While tradi-tional production companies face new competition, the indus-try has experienced soaring movie box office receipts thanks to the new social network, crowdfunding and big data. The so-called So-Lo-Mo trends ("Social-Local-Mobile") are bringing new challenges and opportunities for both Hollywood and Chi-nese movie studios in the digital age.

As one would expect, the internet giants have quickly evolved into media companies. The same has also happened in dining services, car-hailing and other sectors. Because every major firm's goal is to create a "closed loop" of its own, the companies are increasingly in competition with one another. As many players race to offer services at below cost to compete for users, the market is starting to have doubts about the sus-tainability of such businesses. In fact, internet firms are tak-ing huge bets by spending heavily on subsidies because the repeat customers may not stay when the subsidies end. The cases addressed in this book will examine whether a profitable model will eventually arise in those markets.

Chapter 8 will examine the huge impact "internet plus" has on the traditional finance sector, most notably in commercial banking and asset management. The rising integration of internet and finance is closely linked to the two imperfections of the existing financial system and the potential solutions from the internet. One is the difficult access to credit by small and new businesses, because banks focus their attention on bigger and more established companies for their perceived lower credit risk. The other is the lack of investment channels for individuals, as the public stock market and real estate require large sums of investment capital and high levels of risk tolerance.

For instance, internet firms have offered short-term deposit products online that provide more convenience and liquidity, essentially making the financial system more efficient. Similar innovative products include crowdfunding for movie productions, where young people with limited disposable income can nevertheless make an investment and enjoy the experience of being a mini financier for film productions. In the P2P (peer-to-peer) lending area, China has surpassed the level in the US (where the model was first developed) to become the world's largest market. The internet giants Alibaba and Tencent have set up internet-only banks, which can potentially provide microloans to individuals and small businesses more effectively than traditional banks due to their big data capabilities.

Chapter 9 will discuss the broad trend of major internet and tech companies in China moving beyond the saturated domestic market to compete on the global stage. Their presence has been felt abroad as they send their products and services overseas. For example, China's smartphone brand ZTE has obtained a sizable market share and has a top three Android phone-maker ranking in the US market, only behind Samsung and LG. They also actively partner with or directly invest in foreign companies to accelerate their expanding reach. However, as will be seen in the examples in this chapter, it is not an easy task for a Chinese company to break into the US and other markets that are external to China.

Chapter 10 examines the opportunities and challenges that foreign firms are facing in the Chinese market, which they have to tackle in order to win the battle for global domination. For example, the San Francisco-based car-sharing app company Uber has been an undeniable hit in China, and its rapid growth in China so far may be the best performance by a US tech company in years. Going forward, the Chinese market is poised to be a trendsetter, rather than a trend-follower, in next-generation mobile devices and services. The story of China is rapidly transforming from the old "Made in China" to the new "Innovated in China".

Acknowledgments

Compared to my previous book *Investing in China*, published in 2006, this book on China's internet-based "mobile economy" was a much more challenging project. For one thing, China's economic model had transformed from decades-long double-digit growth into a more sustainable growth model based on innovation and consumption. For another, the explosive growth of smartphone users, e-commerce and online content consumption and creation led to a digital revolution in almost all industries and business sectors.

A book on such a complex and fast-moving topic would not have been possible if I had not been blessed to be able to work with and learn from an amazing group of mentors in business, law and investments.

My deepest thanks go to Dr. Rita Hauser and Dr. Gus Hauser and the New York University (NYU) School of Law. My private equity investing, investment banking and practicing attorney experiences all started with the generous Hauser Scholarship in 1997. At the Hauser Global Law School program, I encountered a broad range of perspectives and viewpoints, which was the basis for my future career as a global professional working in the cross-border business world.

Sincere thanks to John Sexton, the legendary Dean of NYU Law School as I was pursuing my LL.M degree in Comparative Law. During his decade-long tenure as the President of NYU, he kindly engaged me at his inaugural President's Global Council as he developed the world's first and only GNU – the "global network university". John's dream for the NYU Law School as well as NYU is as audacious as his personality. From him, I picked up the spirit of entrepreneurship and risk taking, including launching an ambitious project like this book.

Special thanks to Frank Guarini ('50, LL.M. '55), the seven-term New Jersey congressman and a long-term friend from the NYU Law School community. With incredible vision and generosity, he continues to give me invaluable guidance, even while he is in his 90s. The time spent with this admirable leader has reshaped my way of thinking as well as shaping me as a person. He has been a tremendous mentor, and I thank him for continuously being a great cheerleader.

My sincere appreciation to Mr. Lou Jiwei and Dr. Gao Xiqing, the inaugural Chairman and President of China Investment Corporation (CIC), for recruiting me at the inception of CIC. One of the most gratifying aspects of being part of CIC is the opportunity to be exposed to a wide range of global financial markets' new developments. This unique platform has brought me to the movers and shakers everywhere in the world, including Silicon Valley projects that linked global tech innovation with the Chinese market.

Special thanks also go to Chairman Ding Xue-dong and President Li Ke-ping, whom I have been reporting to at CIC in recent years. Similarly, thanks go to Linda Simpson, senior partner at the New York headquarters of Davis Polk & Wardwell, and Santosh Nabar, Managing Director at the New York head-quarters of JP Morgan. My two former bosses on Wall Street gave me a firm foundation on which to develop a career in the global capital markets.

Many thanks to Mr. Jing Liqun, President of Asian Infra-structure Investment Bank (AIIB) and the former Supervisory Chairman of CIC, for educating me about the works of Shake-speare, as well as guiding me professionally. The readings of *Hamlet, Macbeth* and *King Lear* improved my English writing skills, and hopefully, the writing style of this book is more interesting and engaging than my previous finance textbook *Investing in China*.

For such a dynamic book topic, I benefited from the best market intelligence from a distinctive group of entrepreneurs and investors at the World Economic Forum, in particular, the Young Global Leaders (YGL) community and the Global

Agenda Council (GAC) on long-term investing. I would especially like to thank my fellow YGLs in the TMT areas, including Xiaodong Lee (CEO of China Internet Network Information Center), Calvin Chin (co-founder and CEO of Transist Impact Labs), James Lee (Chairman of Stoic A/S) and Haidong Pan (founder and CEO of Chinese online encyclopedia Hudong).

My gratitude goes to many other outstanding friends, colleagues, practitioners and academics, who provided expert opinions, feedback, insights and suggestions for improvement. For anecdotes, pointers and constant reality checks, I turned to them because they were at the front line of industry and business practices. I would particularly like to thank Ishan Saksena (CEO of B4U Network), Sean Yang (Canada CEO of Huawei), Denson Xu (North America terminal device CEO of ZTE) and Alan Cole-Ford (President of eChinaCash).

Many chapters of the book began, in some sense, with my blog series at the World Economic Forum (WEF). I am enormously grateful to my friend Karen Seitz for giving my complete manuscript the first read. As the founder of Fusion Capital and a former partner of Goldman Sachs, she was extremely busy in the global financial markets, yet she generously took the time to expertly edit my initial draft.

On its journey from a collection of ideas and themes to a coherent book, the manuscript went through multiple iterations and a meticulous editorial and review process by the John Wiley team led by book editor Thomas Hyrkiel. As the content development specialist, Jeremy Chia's careful editing contributed substantially to the final shape of the book. Special thanks to Gladys Ganaden for her help in getting the components of the book cover together.

And last in the lineup but first in my heart, I thank my wife, Angela Ju-hsin Pan, who gave me love and support. You are a true partner in helping me frame and create this work. Thank you for your patience while I wrecked our weekends and evenings working on this book.

About the Author

Winston Wenyan Ma

Winston Wenyan Ma is a managing director of China Investment Corporation (CIC), the sovereign wealth fund of China, with a focus on long-term investments in large-scale concentrated positions. Since joining CIC in 2008, he has held leadership roles in major direct transactions involving natural resources, financial services and high tech sectors. During 2011–2015, he was the Managing Director of CIC's North America office in Toronto, the only CIC office outside of China.

Mr. Ma is one of a small number of native Chinese who have worked as investment professionals and practicing capital markets attorneys in both the United States and China. Prior to joining CIC, he served as the deputy head of equity capital markets at Barclays Capital. Previously, he was a vice president at J.P. Morgan investment banking, and a corporate lawyer at Davis Polk & Wardwell LLP and Freshfields. He is the author of the best-selling book *Investing in China: New Opportunities in a Transforming Stock Market* (Risk Books, 2006) and has been widely quoted in global financial media. Mr. Ma was selected as a 2013 Young Global Leader at the World Economic Forum (WEF) and in 2014 he received the Distinguished Alumni Award from NYU.

Mr. Ma can be reached at WinstonWMa@gmail.com for comments and feedback on *China's Mobile Economy*.

Introduction

I was very pleased when Winston asked me to write this introduction for his new book on China's development in mobile internet and the new economy related to it. In my capacity as the President and CEO of the China Internet Network Information Center (CNNIC), I have been watching the development of the internet market closely. The China Internet Development Statistical Report published by the CNNIC over the past several years is one of the most authoritative data sources for studies on the development of the internet in China today. I am glad to see that this book has made references to many of the CNNIC's statistics and observations.

According to CNNIC data, at the end of 2015, China had 688 million internet users, and the number of mobile internet users reached 620 million, accounting for 90.1% of total internet users. This mobile internet population is incredibly large and continues to increase at a remarkable pace. As this book explains, the Chinese internet population has officially entered into the age of mobile internet. As more and more people use their mobile devices to chat with their social network, to find and share information, and to have fun anywhere and anytime, a new context of creating, delivering, and marketing content – and profiting from it – is emerging. Consumers want it, businesses demand it, and entrepreneurs are creating it. The migration of internet services to the new mobile environment is therefore inevitable.

The excellent analysis in this book should help the reader understand the latest revolution of the internet in China, and, in particular, the emergence of mobile internet and its architectural impact on the broader economy. This extraordinary book explains how the internet has been the engine that catapults commercial activities from offline to online and towards ubiquity.

With an outstanding background in finance and investing, Winston has based his analysis on a very solid foundation by drawing on examples from a wide range of contemporary situations in China and beyond, and conveying his ideas using simple but powerful statements. Important questions asked in this book include: In what ways is the internet empowering the economy? By fostering new types of business models and redefining existing business relationships, how, in turn, is the ever-growing mobile economy reshaping the future of business, technology and society in China? If you are looking for answers to these questions, you will find this book very informative and inspiring.

The author's reflections on China's public policy and internet strategy are also presented here. The rapid growth of the internet has been enthusiastically embraced by the Chinese government. However, with increased efficiency and productivity, as well as tremendous business opportunities being brought about by the internet revolution, many challenges in the public and private sectors still remain. As China's global online presence increases, some of these challenges include the management of cyber security risks and keeping balanced relations with the rest of the world. Winston and I have been fortunate to be involved in several forums, like the World Economic Forum, where related policy issues have been discussed, and I am excited to see that this part of our work is also reflected in his book.

Chinese society is experiencing a rapid transformation, becoming increasingly industrialized and digital-based. The uniqueness of China's experience deserves a close investigation from policy-makers, technology start-ups, internet companies, corporations and organizations facing an upgrading challenge due to the ongoing internet revolution, as well as other global stakeholders who are interested in entering the Chinese market. It is especially noteworthy that discussing the internet and the mobile economy in this case is not an easy job. This field of study is usually fraught with both theoretical and practical errors, and it is thus extremely valuable that many of them have been addressed in this book.

I expect quite confidently that the author's effort will contribute to a universal understanding of the Internet-based digital revolution in China. Therefore, I believe that for many of you reading this book should prove to be a worthwhile investment of your time.

Dr. Xiaodong Lee
President and CEO, China Internet
Network Information Center (CNNIC)
Research Professor, Chinese Academy of Sciences

The World's Biggest Mobile Economy

What is the most celebrated Chinese holiday globally, by the Chinese and by everyone else? Here's a hint: It's not the Spring Festival, also known as the Chinese New Year. It is November 11, known as Singles' Day. Not only is it the largest online shopping day each year in China, but it is also the largest in the world in terms of the total value of transactions.

Started by China's e-commerce giant Alibaba in 2009, the November 11 holiday has become an annual 24-hour online shopping extravaganza. **(See the "Singles' Day" box.)** It is the single most important day each year for online vendors to target young, tech-savvy consumers who are accustomed to buying online and using their mobile phone wallets to pay for almost all goods, services and entertainment.

In 2015, during the run up to the shopping holiday, Alibaba hosted a gala celebration titled *Double-11 Night Carnival.* The four-hour TV variety show was directed by a top Chinese film director, Feng Xiao-Gang, and held at the Water Cube, a landmark structure built for the 2008 Beijing Olympics. Aired on the satellite channel Hunan TV, the variety program was also streamed on China's major video streaming site Youku Tudou, which was acquired by Alibaba only days before the Carnival.

Just like China's annual Spring Festival variety show carried by the state television network CCTV, the 2015 celebration included an 11.11 countdown, "to celebrate the potential for limitless innovation that technology has provided for all of us", according to Alibaba's promotional statement. To ensure the 2015 holiday was a "Global Shopping Festival", during the televised extravaganza Alibaba's founder, Jack Ma, rang the opening bell for the New York Stock Exchange remotely from the Water Cube, while the program featured western celebrities including the actor Daniel Craig, who played James Bond in the latest 007 film *Spectre*, as well as the singer Adam Lambert.

Employing China's social networks, Jack Ma had announced prior to the event that even the US President would appear at the Carnival. And as the celebration reached its climax, actor Kevin Spacey appeared as his character in the web TV series *House of Cards*, US President Frank Underwood. Thanks to the explosive growth of video streaming sites in China, *House of Cards* and Kevin Spacey are both famous in China. From an Oval Office set, Kevin Spacey addressed Chinese shoppers in a two-minute video. In his trademark Southern drawl, President Underwood expressed his disappointment that the White House firewalls blocked him from shopping online to take advantage of the "amazing deals" on that day.

This November 11 online shopping event in 2015 illustrates several important trends of China's e-commerce in the mobile internet age.

First of all, while e-commerce has disrupted retailers worldwide, its boom in China is unprecedented both in terms of pace and scale. In 2013, China overtook the US as the world's biggest e-commerce market. Today, this annual shopping festival generates more sales than "Black Friday" and "Cyber Monday" in the US combined. On the basis of gross merchandise volume (GMV), Alibaba is now the largest online and mobile commerce company in the world.

For the 2015 Singles' Day, Alibaba Group announced that $14.3 billion GMV was transacted on its online marketplaces, an increase of 60% from 2014, making the 2015 Global

Table 1.1   Singles' Day gross merchandise volume (GMV) growth 2012–2015

Year	GMV ($)	Year-on-year growth
2012	3.3 billion	–
2013	5.9 billion	80%
2014	9.3 billion	58%
2015	14.3 billion	60%

(Data Source: Alibaba)

Shopping Festival the largest shopping day in history. It is worth noting that the GMV numbers in recent years have enjoyed steadily increasing growth (see Table 1.1). Also, the actual number of shoppers is increasing as additional buyers from smaller Chinese cities are using e-commerce, primarily through Alibaba's marketplaces every year. Although their purchases are smaller than those placed by buyers from first-tier cities, such as Shanghai and Beijing, they are an important driver for growth in the future.

Second, Chinese customers are migrating to the mobile internet rapidly. Because China has the largest smartphone user population in the world, the trend of "going mobile" has taken off with greater speed than anywhere else in the world. As the wired infrastructure has not yet fully covered the country, for many people in China, especially in rural areas, their first internet experience is often mobile instead of PC-based – from the moment they start using a smartphone. Since 2014, the number of people in China who surf the internet via mobile devices has exceeded the number of people doing so via their computer, with smartphones becoming the primary device of access for Chinese internet users.

On Singles' Day 2014, 43% of all transactions through Alibaba were made through mobile devices, up sharply from 2013 (21%). Even more remarkable, in 2015 Alibaba's consumers made the majority of orders (68.7% of total GMV) through mobile channels. The total mobile GMV was approximately \$9.8 billion, an increase of 158% from 2014. In fact, 2015's mobile GMV alone exceeded the total GMV in 2014.

Third, this latest shopping festival has also highlighted Chinese consumers' strong demand for international products. In 2015, Alibaba specifically made "globalization" a critical priority for the group's strategy, and it was committed to making the 2015 shopping festival "a truly and unprecedentedly global shopping experience for consumers".

According to Alibaba, more than 16,000 international brands, including Burberry, Apple, and Uniqlo, took part in the 2015 sale. During the Carnival TV show, western brands such as Columbia, Levi's, Budweiser and Corona bought time slots for advertisements. Buyers and sellers from 232 countries and regions participated. 33% of the total buyers made purchases from international brands or merchants, with the United States, Japan, South Korea, Germany and Australia as the top countries selling to Chinese consumers.

Finally, the inaugural Carnival show in 2015 illustrates the seamless fusion of online shopping and mobile entertainment. The main use of mobile internet in China is skewed towards fun and entertainment. Moving to align with this trend, Alibaba has recently been establishing its own movie and television production subsidiaries, launching a film crowdfunding financial product, and fully acquiring the online streaming video site Youku Tudou. The movie unit of Alibaba made its first direct Hollywood film investment in Paramount Pictures and actor Tom Cruise's blockbuster *Mission: Impossible — Rogue Nation*.

By integrating the shopping event with a televised show, Alibaba successfully created a continuous feedback loop of online consumption of both merchandise and entertainment. The Carnival show kept people up until midnight, when the sales began. During the program, online viewers were prompted to check their smartphones periodically, as discount coupons were distributed through their mobile shopping apps. Viewers could also play along with the game show portion of the event. When the hosts of the show greeted "Mr. Bond" and asked viewers to "support 007", consumers were guided to online ticketing services for the latest James Bond film *Spectre*.

Singles' Day (November 11)

November 11 was first known as the "Guangun Jie" (Bare Sticks Festival or "Bachelors' Day") in the 1990s. It was celebrated by students at Chinese universities because the numerals that form the date, 11/11, looked like four solitary stick figures. Over the years, this loosely defined holiday has become a celebration for all singles. The day has also become much more gender inclusive by becoming known as "Singles' Day" which is the name used today.

Gradually, as the Chinese economy continued to flourish, the event started to feature shopping as an intrinsic part of the celebration. When Chinese internet giant Alibaba provided access to e-commerce through their website, Singles' Day became a virtual festival for everyone, single or married, local or a part of the diverse Chinese diaspora overseas.

Alibaba launched the Singles' Day shopping festival in 2009 as a promotional event to raise awareness of the value of online shopping. Initially, having just 27 merchant participants, in just a few short years Singles' Day has exploded into the largest shopping day in the world. Each successive year's event breaks the previous year's record. And because of the vast size of the participating population, its transaction volume has exceeded Cyber Monday sales in the US by multiple times.

Whereas Singles' Day is a day of celebration for Chinese consumers, it is a day of fierce competition for e-commerce players. In 2015, Alibaba's main rival JD.com, in partnership with the social network and messaging service giant Tencent, hosted a singing contest show filled with famous singers and movie stars, which aired at the same time as Alibaba's *Double-11 Night Carnival*. The rivalry may further escalate as Alibaba has even tried to trademark the festival and prevent other companies from using the signature "11.11" slogan.

However, it would be premature to conclude from this event that e-commerce is taking over entirely from traditional retailers in China. In mid-2015, just a few months before the online shopping festival, Alibaba spent $4.6 billion to acquire a stake in Suning Commerce Group, one of the largest retailers in China. At the time of the transaction, Suning had a network of more than 1,600 outlets spread across 289 cities in China, selling electronics, appliances, and other products.

The two companies announced a partnership in online sales and offline logistics by breaking the information wall for products, services and memberships between the online and offline channels.

Not to be outdone, in August 2015 JD.com, Alibaba's primary e-commerce rival in China, also bought a 10% stake in Yonghui Superstores – another major domestic supermarket – for $700 million. Founded in 1998, Yonghui Superstores ran 364 supermarkets on the Chinese mainland, with ambitious expansion plans for hundreds more in the coming years. Similar to Alibaba, JD.com also aimed to leverage Yonghui's existing networks of bricks-and-mortar stores to boost its supply chain and diversify its offline offerings.

The marriage between the e-commerce giants (Alibaba and JD.com) and traditional retailers (Suning and Yonghui) illustrates a new retailing model that fully integrates online and offline channels, which is frequently referred to as "omni-channel". To enhance the digital consumers' experience, the internet firms strive to use both online and offline touchpoints to cover the full search, decision and purchase journey, including researching and comparing prices online, trying products at offline shops, paying online or at an offline outlet, and arranging delivery online for pick-ups at physical shops.

In fact, one of the two key themes of the Alibaba 2015 shopping festival is offline-to-online (O2O) (the other being globalization as mentioned previously). Approximately 100,000 brick-and-mortar stores in China, such as Suning and Intime (another Alibaba-invested retailer), will establish strategic O2O collaboration agreements with Alibaba Group, which in turn will cover marketing, customer management, post-sales management, logistics, and more, for the physical stores.

Interestingly, this new "omni-channel" trend provides some answers to the debate on the future of the e-commerce model as represented by the competition between JD.com and Alibaba. Alibaba operates the largest marketplaces for e-commerce, while JD.com is the largest online retailer in China.

Alibaba is more akin to a combination of eBay and PayPal, and its marketplace serves as a platform to connect buyers and sellers and provides services like online payments. JD.com is more like Amazon which deals with inventory, sales and distribution directly. Their growing integration with traditional offline retailers, however, makes their business models increasingly similar to one other.

Of course, the online shopping extravaganza is but one example of the explosive growth of China's digital economy. For China, the years 2014 to 2015 were the most important inflection point in the history of the internet, as the Chinese internet population officially entered into the age of mobile internet and multi-screens (smartphones, tablets, personal computers and more). During this incredible period of change, the mobile internet in China has given rise to a dynamic tech sector, thriving social networks and the world's largest digitally-connected middle income class.

At the same time, the integration of e-commerce with offline retailing is a case in point for the "Internet Plus" strategy promoted by China's central government. In his public speeches, President Xi Jinping emphasized that innovation, economic restructuring and consumption should be among the top priorities of China's next stage of growth (the 13th Five-Year Plan for 2016–2020). The "Internet Plus" action plan seeks to drive economic growth by integration of internet technologies with manufacturing and business. The term "Plus" is a reference to the internet as an enabler of new developments and higher efficiency, as in the case of the new "omni-channel" retailing model above.

Urbanization, Mobile Users and Information Consumption

Delivering the government work report in March 2016, Premier Li Keqiang noted that China's development is at a critical stage and new growth poles should be created through incessant innovation to transition to a "new economy". This was the first time the term "new economy" has ever been mentioned in the government work report. Meanwhile, the government's 13th Five-Year Plan (2016–2020) placed strong emphasis on household consumption and industrial innovation as the economy's new growth engines.

As background, after decades of staggering growth, China has entered into a stage of moderate growth and has put more emphasis on the sustainable quality of growth in the future. In the 35 years between 1978 and 2013, annual growth of the economy averaged close to 10%, and over 11.5% between 2003 and 2007. That growth rate slowed to 7.4% in 2014, and it dropped further to 6.9% in 2015 as the government focused more on the transformation of the economic model than on a high GDP growth rate per se. For the upcoming five years (2016–2020), the 13th Five-Year Plan set an "above 6.5 percent" average growth target.

The new administration has referred to the moderate growth in the new era as "the new normal". The new economic model is a consumer-driven growth model, where China shifts the balance of its economy away from government-led investment and import-export business and towards domestic household consumption. To achieve this goal, Premier Li Keqiang has written that "urbanization has the greatest potential for boosting domestic demand". In China's urbanization plan, the central government aims to boost domestic consumption by increasing the proportion of urban residents to 60% by 2020 (approximately 800 million people).

What makes this ambitious program unique is the government's parallel effort to promote information-related consumption as a related new growth engine. In late 2013, China's State Council issued a blueprint to officially promote "information consumption" – a term that includes both "consumption based on information technology" (such as e-retailing and online banking services) and "quality information products for consumption" (such as movies and online videos). For example, as shown by the shopping sprees on Singles' Days in recent years, the rapid expansion of the middle class and the exponential growth of the e-retailing industry have created an important catalyst for consumption growth in China.

To help implement this, the central government launched a "Broadband China" strategy in 2013 to significantly improve the country's information infrastructure, which equates internet networks with traditional forms of public infrastructure, such as highways and high-speed rail services. Also in 2013, the Ministry of Industry and Information Technology (MIIT) officially granted fourth-generation (4G) mobile technology licenses to three domestic telecommunication operators, marking the beginning of China's 4G era. The 4G network coverage is expected to include all the cities in the country within a short period of time. With such an infrastructure in place, China will see the development of "smart cities", with much improved Wi-Fi coverage in public places, FTTH (fiber-to-the-home) capability, HD cable subscription and so on, each of which will drive development and consumption.

According to the official data from the China Internet Network Information Center (CNNIC), by the end of 2015 China had 688 million internet users (just above 50% of the total population), which was by far the world's biggest internet population. While the internet-enabled business and innovation are set to play a major role in fueling China's economic growth, it also has profound implications for society, such as how people relate to and communicate with each other. One dramatic example of the internet gaining familiarity and popularity in China is a recent phenomenon known as "human flesh search". **(See the "Renrou Sousuo" box.)** Many similar new terms created by the internet culture in China will be examined in the following chapters in the context of their related business areas.

"Renrou-Sousuo" ("Human flesh search")

Although one might suspect a link to internet pornography, the term "human flesh search" actually refers to Chinese internet users mobilizing themselves voluntarily to collectively search and post information online publicly about specific people or events.

The searches usually involve individuals suspected of crime (such as corruption), of foolish acts, or simply of socially questionable conduct to the millions of netizens. This usually takes the form of posting photos of people and accusations of misbehavior, but a massive number of internet users can often collaborate to reveal a lot of information about an offending person very quickly.

The "bodily" aspect of this search term probably originated with a 2011 event involving a model's identity. In 2001, someone posted a photo of a pretty girl on Mop.com – a discussion website popular with teens and those in their early twenties, claiming that the photo was of his girlfriend. Suspicious visitors at Mop.com soon discovered that the beauty was a model and collectively posted her information as proof that the original poster was lying.

In the case outlined above, internet users penetrated beyond a person's facade to reveal that person's "flesh" so to speak. "Human flesh search" thus stands for performing a deep search on the internet. Another theory is that the name refers to the broad knowledge scattered across social networks and the collaboration involved in searching. In this context, "human flesh" stands for "people in general". With the amount of information that can be exposed on the internet, human flesh searches are very powerful, sometimes disruptive and very often controversial.

In some sense, the best example of a "human flesh search" was a fitting room sex video in July 2015. A young couple filmed themselves with a smartphone while they had sex inside the fitting room of a Uniqlo clothing store in Beijing's entertainment district Sanlitun. The video went viral on Chinese social media after it was posted online. It did not take long for the "Renrou-Sousuo" web users to dig up the porn enthusiasts' social network accounts and other details about them (although they denied that it was them featured in the video), which probably helped Beijing police arrest at least four people for their involvement in the sex tape.

Since the beginning of the 21st century, a large proportion of the Chinese population has stopped using landline phones entirely and moved to using mobile phones. The fact that usage of landlines was not as pervasive as in Western economies meant that for many the transition did not involve a migration from fixed-line phones at all, but was a transition to mobile phones directly. With their advanced and ever increasing technological capabilities, smartphones are also replacing personal computers (PCs). For many people in China, especially in rural areas, their first internet experience is often mobile instead of one connected with a PC – indeed, their first online experience is the moment they start using a smartphone.

In other words, the Chinese population has transitioned directly into a mobile-first mobile-only era. Focusing on a niche passed up on by premium brands like Apple and Samsung, the Chinese brands like Xiaomi, Huawi and Lenovo have mainly offered low price, high performance devices, which have played well into the general Chinese population's desire to own a smartphone and to access the internet, but at an accessible point of entry. It is worth noting the three domestic brands are neck-and-neck in terms of their sales volume in China, and they are now competing directly for the No. 3 position in the global market (just behind Apple and Samsung, the two undisputed market leaders).

The spread of low-cost mobile phones quickly reached all parts of this geographically vast country, and the large screens strongly preferred by Chinese customers from the outset, a trend driven by the mobile-only tendency noted above, made them great platforms for various types of transactions. For example, the lack of a developed credit card system in China means that mobile payment is the "first" and "only" non-cash payment experience for many users. Also, the Chinese users have adopted social network technologies comfortably. For them, the smartphone has not only become an extension of their daily routine, but also an indispensable link with the rest of society.

As a result, the percentage of mobile internet users (as a subset of all internet users) has risen steadily, a trend that has accelerated in recent years (see Figure 1.1). According to CNNIC's data, in mid-2014 more than 500 million people in China reported gaining access to the internet with mobile devices, exceeding for the first time the percentage who reported using computers to go online. By the end of 2015, China had the world's largest mobile internet user population of 620 million, representing more than 90% of the total internet population.

In summary, China's mobile infrastructure has developed with remarkable speed, marked by the exceptionally rapid penetration of internet access, the uptake of smartphones by users and the spread of digital social networks. In addition to

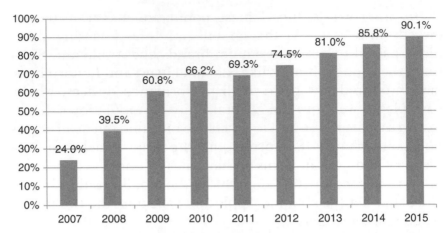

Figure 1.1   The Steady Increase of Mobile Internet User Percentage (2007–2015)
(Data Source: CNNIC, December 2015)

the unrivalled internet user population size, what also makes the market unique is the fact that China is the largest "mobile-first" and "mobile-only" market in the world. Backed by a huge middle class that is digitally connected, there are enormous opportunities on the horizon as China shifts towards a model of economic growth that is based on productivity, innovation and consumption.

More importantly, the development of the mobile internet has helped China develop more "smart cities" and a "shared economy" at a time the public goods and services supplied by all levels of government are stretched by the country's large population and fast growth. The mobile infrastructure also creates a new social infrastructure that is helping bridge the digital divide in China, allowing more Chinese people to benefit from the digital economic boom, enabling megacities to execute on their urbanization policies, and narrowing the income gap between cities and less developed areas.

For example, with daily subway commuters exceeding 10 million, the Beijing municipality increased subway fares to cut passenger numbers in 2014, which created substantial controversy. In an optimistic scenario for the future, more e-commerce and e-business opportunities may involve more

Chinese people in the growing economy, while reducing the number of commuters, and therefore traffic. In healthcare, advanced communication technologies enable China's first-tier hospitals, via regional health-information networks, to make high quality treatment available to lower-tier hospitals by linking patients to medical specialists elsewhere.

During the 2016 Mobile World Congress (MWC) in Barcelona, the GSMA (the representative body of the world mobile industry) published its findings, which showed that when compared to developed markets, China is more advanced in terms of consumer uptake of mobile data services. The transition from fixed line to mobile internet (from voice-centric to data-centric services) is happening all over the world, but China is leading the field with a strong uptake of mobile data services, such as "gaming, apps and video".

For example, there were 73% of Chinese mobile users accessing social media over their phones, compared to only 43% in the UK, where just 40% of mobile users have IP messaging apps, compared to 81% in China. GSMA concluded that "the ability to access a wide array of mobile data services in China – enabled by the country's rapid rollout of 4G networks and supported by strong local content players – is creating demand- and supply-side drivers". Indeed, with a 4G network capable of handling faster data-heavy applications than before, mobile service sectors such as video streaming and internet movies are making big leaps, and China's mobile netizens are becoming more sophisticated. The next section will introduce the internet giants BAT (Baidu, Alibaba and Tencent), their mobile apps and the Chinese customers that the internet firms seek to cover seamlessly.

Baidu, Alibaba and Tencent (BAT)

While the first wave of "open and reform" policies in the 1980s and 1990s created a large working class in China, the next wave of globalized growth in the 21st century has created a middle class that is already the size of the entire US population (and it is expected to double in a few more years). Collectively, these

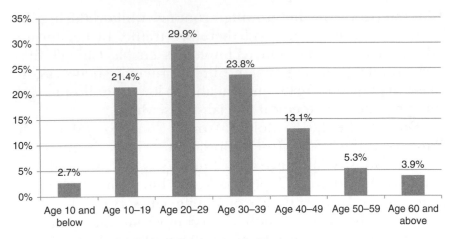

Figure 1.2   Demographic of Chinese Internet Users
(Data Source: CNNIC, December 2015)

new consumers have a significant amount of disposable income and they are also digitally connected. Mobile internet usage by this demographic is primarily focused on socializing, shopping and entertainment, due to the dominant composition of young netizens (below 39 years of age) in the internet population (see Figure 1.2).

According to demographic data from the CNNIC, by the end of 2015, more than 75% of internet users are between the ages of 10 and 39. Close to one-third of the internet population is between the ages of 20 and 29 (29.9%). As the mobile network speeds up and smartphone technology continues improving, the younger generation of Chinese netizens have shifted their entertainment habits online in record numbers. For the majority of their time online, they play online games, watch videos, assume online personas in the virtual world and form online communities.

This digitally-connected middle class is leading a seismic change in the Chinese consumer market. Not only is this new generation of consumers extremely comfortable with mobile e-commerce, they have enjoyed unprecedented exposure and access to foreign brands, with social networks having tremendous influence on their purchasing decisions. As a result, they have high expectations both of quality and of

Table 1.2   Top 10 most used mobile apps (June 2014)

Ranking	App name	Monthly active users (million)	Sector/Company
1	WeChat	383.17	Messaging app/Social network (Tencent)
2	QQ	316.69	Messaging app/Social network (Tencent)
3	Baidu	136.33	Mobile search (Baidu)
4	Mobile Taobao	123.48	e-Commerce (Alibaba)
5	QQ mobile browser	113.33	Mobile browser (Tencent)
6	Sougou Chinese character input	106.84	Chinese character input (Sougou)
7	360 Phone Guardian	94.431	Anti-virus software (Qihoo 360)
8	QQ Music	94.429	Online music (Tencent)
9	Qzone	90.61	Social network (Tencent)
10	Baidu map	89.10	Map services (Baidu)

(Data Sources: China Daily, Analysys International)

service that did not exist in China previously. In particular, the younger demographic consists of "conspicuous consumers" who like to share their experience publicly and for whom consumption is a social experience.

A list of the most commonly used mobile apps (as of mid-2014) provides a perspective on the new generation of consumers' preferences (see Table 1.2). The year 2014 is viewed as a "breakout" year for mobile internet in China, so the leading apps are a reflection of the important areas where internet giants have accumulated a significant number of users. The three most important areas – social network, mobile search and e-commerce, as represented by the three leading firms Tencent, Baidu and Alibaba – are discussed in detail below respectively.

Tencent's Social Network

As mentioned previously, two key themes of China's mobile internet usage are socializing and entertainment. In the mid-2014 report by the research firm Analysys International as summarized above, China's internet giant Tencent Holdings, whose focus is online games and social networking, owns half of the country's top ten mobile applications by monthly active users. Most notably, Tencent's two popular mobile messaging apps WeChat and QQ take the top two positions in the ranking.

QQ is one of Tencent's older applications for person-to-person communication. It was one of the earliest platforms in China where users could post pictures, videos and blogs. Its strategy is to offer entry-level services for free, then charge for added features once users are hooked. Users are willing to pay for "value-added services" such as weapons and costumes for their avatars, and it has proven to be a profitable model for Tencent. It is all the more remarkable as Tencent's peers are still primarily focusing on advertising revenue in their business models.

The newer version of WeChat is now the most popular forum in China. It started off as a messaging service similar to WhatsApp, and now it has evolved into a platform of integrated apps. For instance, many people find typing Chinese characters on a smartphone screen time-consuming, so WeChat has developed strong voice capabilities and has offered free voice messaging features. Chinese users can send text, links, videos and photos to friends more cheaply and conveniently through WeChat (by way of data package charges) than through traditional texting services offered by wireless carriers (with charges per text).

What is also remarkable is that Tencent has built an entire ecosystem of interrelated services and functions that can be integrated directly within WeChat. Alongside text, video and voice messaging, WeChat users can now shop and make mobile payments, play games, book hotels or flight tickets, order a taxi and do many other things without ever leaving the app ecosystem. Because Chinese shoppers are increasingly resorting to friends' reviews and recommendations online when they make a purchase, the WeChat platform becomes an ideal place to introduce offerings that can benefit from word-of-mouth recommendation and peer reviews, such as branded goods and experience consumption. From its humble beginnings as a messaging service, WeChat has become a full-blown, unified ecosystem for mobile commerce, content and entertainment.

Baidu's Mobile Search App

The main search engine in China, Baidu, has Google-like predominance in China's search and maps services. Today, urban residents mostly turn to their smartphones to navigate their daily lives as they commute in the cities, which explains Baidu's mobile search apps becoming the second most widely used apps after social messaging, ahead of traditional top activity e-commerce. According to Baidu, searches on smartphones have exceeded those on PCs since the second half of 2014.

However, from the advertising income aspect, searches on mobile phones are not as profitable as those on PCs, even though the market for these is growing substantially faster. The smaller screen of smartphones means less space for ads than on standard computer screens or laptops, and advertisers are still trying to figure out new strategies for driving traffic from them, as click-through rates tend to be lower as well. However, it is still possible for revenue from searches on the mobile platforms to catch up because they provide the merchants with additional information from the users, such as the context and location of their searches.

One of the most promising business opportunities is the growth in searches for location-based services. Traditionally, searches are considered as tools to connect people to information, but in the age of the mobile platform, searches can function as a tool for connecting people with services. Among Baidu's fast-growing mobile offerings is the Baidu Mobile Maps app, which integrates maps with related information of merchant partners, so that users are able to conduct searches for services close to their location.

The best showcase of Baidu's expertise in location-based services is an interactive heat map on its website at the Spring

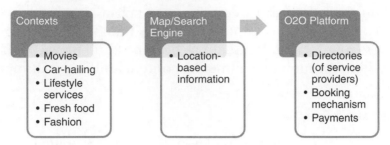

Figure 1.3   Location/Map Searches Are the Key to the O2O Business Model

Festival each year, which visualizes the movement of people during the one-month travel rush when millions of Chinese travel across the country for holiday family gatherings. In addition to the heat map, Baidu also releases the "Spring Festival Homecoming Tool Kit" on Baidu Maps. During the chaotic holiday travel season, the tool kit provides users with information on the cities' weather conditions, traffic conditions, railway timetables, flight schedules and locations of holiday train tickets sales agents.

The capability for location-based searches is the key to the growth of online-to-offline (O2O) transactions like the "Homecoming Tool Kit" example. O2O can be broadly defined as the integration of offline business opportunities with the activities on the internet. In its most popular form, O2O means attracting retail customers online, and then directing them to physical stores for actual goods purchases or real-life experiences such as seeing movies, dining out, hailing taxis and so on (see Figure 1.3). For instance, Baidu's investment into and partnership with Uber, the US car-hailing mobile app company, has been critical for the latter's rapid expansion in the China market.

Alibaba's e-Commerce Empire

As mentioned at the beginning of this chapter, Alibaba dominates the e-commerce world through two online marketplaces – Taobao and Tmall (the latter is specifically intended

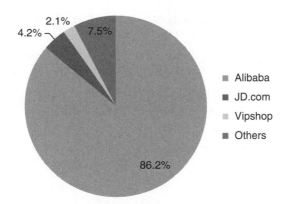

2.1%
4.2%
7.5%

- Alibaba
- JD.com
- Vipshop
- Others

86.2%

Figure 1.4   Market Share of China's Mobile Shopping Market in 2014
(Data Source: iResearch, 2015)

for high-end goods and luxury brands). Its leading position is further strengthened by the widely-used online payment system Alipay, which is affiliated with Alibaba Group. So far, Alibaba's e-commerce prowess has carried the momentum into the mobile world. As Figure 1.4 shows, in 2014 Alibaba owned an overwhelming majority (86.2%) of the mobile e-retailing market. (In fact, it had an even bigger share of mobile shopping than in the overall online retail market.)

Mobile e-retailing enables customers to place online orders anytime and anywhere, which aligns with Chinese consumers' desire for speed and convenience of "any time" shopping. Many of those purchases are ad hoc decisions arising from offline world advertisements, social conversations, or simply random thoughts. According to CNNIC data, in 2014 13.9% of Chinese customers purchased goods on smartphones while travelling on public transportation and another 10.6% customers did so while waiting in queues.

However, the wide usage of Tencent's social network platform such as WeChat, as well as Baidu's mobile search, indicates that popular mobile apps can potentially become primary mobile-commerce platforms in their own right. For example, in recent years Tencent has permitted merchants to set up "little WeChat stores" ("Weixin Xiaodian" in Chinese) by verified public accounts linked to the app's own payment system. Similarly, individual WeChat users can establish in-app stores to sell goods to their friends and followers. This type of "social distribution platform" based on social contacts has different dynamics from Alibaba's e-commerce empire. To maintain its leadership in mobile e-retailing, Alibaba has in turn invested aggressively in the mobile market, including social network and map services.

Competition for the Closed Loop

While the three internet giants that make up BAT come to the mobile world with different intrinsic strengths – search, e-commerce and social network respectively – all of them have an expansive vision to create a mobile world into which consumers can immerse themselves. This type of platform is expected to link every possible item or content with consumers who are looking for them, whether domestic or abroad, online or offline. The general belief is that the platform with the most users will eventually capture the biggest share, and therefore the highest profit, from the overall mobile economy in China.

This concept is often referred to as a "closed loop" (or "ecosystem"). In a closed loop, an internet firm has an important role throughout the online consumer's decision journey: generating demand, finding and comparing local merchants, moving customers from considering to making a purchase, paying and then reviewing or sharing with a friend and building loyalty. Similarly, in the O2O business, the firm delivers an end-to-end service, from taking an order to arranging for a service and collecting the payment.

Because the closed loop is so efficient, and because it drives revenues, all the internet firms – BAT and their competitors – are attempting to broaden their platforms through acquisitions and alliances with various online and offline businesses. In small and large ways, they are stepping into every possible corner of the mobile world. Compared to their peers, the BAT corporations have an enormous advantage from what economists call "network effects" – the more people use them, the more indispensable they keep getting. Their existing major networks create big data, which is also a rich source of information when these established players choose to pursue new opportunities or new market sectors.

Because of the advantages stemming from their existing platforms — the users, the data and the large amount of revenue income they generate, the BAT have extended their business development and acquisitions far beyond their core products. They're making waves in taxi-hailing, healthcare, and finance; they are creating advertisement business, building robots and connected cars and making blockbuster movies. In particular, the mobile entertainment business has strategic importance for BAT's "ecosystems". That's because entertainment contents and services are not only an important revenue source by themselves, but also a distinguishing factor that draws users to any specific e-commerce empire and further keeps them hooked. As shown in the list above, entertainment content consumption apps are among the top ten list. (In 2015, according to other research firms' rankings, the Tencent and Youku video apps have also joined the top ten most actively used apps.)

According to the CNNIC data by the end of 2015, 71.9% of users watched online videos on their smartphones, making smartphones the leading terminal for viewing videos, ahead of desktops or laptops (see Figure 1.5). The figure is expected to grow as Chinese mobile carriers adopt faster fourth-generation networks that are more suitable for video viewing. The young internet population is increasingly watching videos, reading books, sharing and having discussions about content on their hand-held devices while commuting on the subway or in their brief moments of spare time throughout the day. They may watch a short video or read an installment of an online novel for a few minutes while they are on the move or in between tasks.

As one would expect, these internet giants have quickly evolved into what might be viewed as full-fledged media companies. The same has also happened in dining services, car-hailing and other sectors. Because every major firm's goal is to create

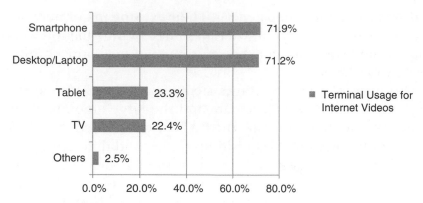

Figure 1.5   Different Terminal Usages for Watching Online Videos
(Data Source: CNNIC, December 2014)

a "closed loop" of its own, the companies are increasingly in competition with one another. As many players race to offer services at below cost to compete for users, the market starts to have doubts about the sustainability of such businesses. In fact, the internet firms are taking huge bets by spending heavily on subsidies because the repeat customers may not stay when the subsidies end. The many cases reviewed in this book will examine whether a profitable model will eventually arise in those markets.

Overall, the Chinese economy is going through a structural shift to more moderate, but more sustainable, growth. After becoming the second largest economy globally, its pace of expansion is slower and the course may be bumpier, but its consumption growth is undoubtedly still tracing a staggering trajectory. According to the data from China's National Bureau of Statistics, in 2015 the services sector surpassed the 50% share of GDP for the first time in history. In addition, the services sector grew at a much faster pace than primary sectors (agricultural, forestry, etc.) and secondary sectors (manufacturing, utility, natural resources, etc.).

In other words, China's expanding middle class has grown in importance as the country's traditional growth engines, such as manufacturing and exports, start to slow down. Under the new economic model, consumer spending on e-commerce platforms is meant to counterbalance the slowdown in other parts of the economy. The sophisticated and seasoned middle class shoppers – those able and willing to pay a premium for quality and to consider discretionary goods and experience consumption – are therefore emerging as the new pillar for economic growth. To some extent, internet firms like BAT, which connect and empower this huge swell of consumers, are a proxy for the prospects of Chinese consumption and the state of the Chinese economy itself.

Internet Plus in Business Sectors

China's "internet plus" strategy was unveiled in the 2015 government work report, which aimed to "integrate mobile internet, cloud computing, big data and the Internet of Things with modern manufacturing, to encourage the healthy development of e-commerce, industrial networks and internet banking, and to help internet companies increase their international presence".

Internet plus means the mobile economy is more than simply expanding the ubiquity of e-commerce through mobile platforms. On the surface, internet plus means incorporating today's mobile technology into the traditional industries to provide better consumer communication and transaction services. Chinese companies are thus investing heavily in internet infrastructures, such as cloud computing, wireless communications, new digital platforms, big data analytics and more. Many companies are looking to the internet for a new set of tools to engineer productivity improvements. As a result, consumers will benefit from lower prices and transaction costs, as well as better goods and services.

The more profound implication of Internet plus is growth and innovation by way of incremental consumption demand and new business models where traditional industries use the internet to run key aspects of their business. In other words, internet plus is more about "internet thinking" than "internet using". As mobile internet is leading the fourth industrial revolution globally, the "creative destruction" of traditional industry sectors is happening in all markets. Driven by the largest mobile internet population worldwide, the speed and scale of this transformation in China is unparalleled: immature industries such as retail and logistics leapfrog straight from the early industrial age to the internet one, and the growth and positive spillovers go beyond the consumer goods sector to services, entertainment, media, finance and other traditional industry sectors.

As illustrated by the Alibaba/Suning alliance and the JD.com/Yonghui investment, in order to fully serve and monetize digital consumers, the retail industry needs to use internet tools to get even closer to them and adopt more flexible business models. The traditional retailers need to move away from the perception that e-commerce is merely another sales channel for their products, as it is critical for customers to get the same products, services and shopping experience in every channel where they choose to make purchases. The new trend is for retailers to provide a "seamless omni-channel shopping experience" by integrating their online and offline channels, instead of having separate systems to sell products online and offline.

In addition to consumer goods, the growth in "experience" consumption, such as movie going, dining out, taxi-bookings and so on, is at the core of the O2O trends in China. However, even among the internet giants, no single player dominates in every area of the mobile linkages relating to the O2O market. If Baidu is understood to be the best link for people and information (search), Alibaba for people and goods (e-commerce), Tencent for people and people (social network), then O2O is the link between people and service, which requires the utilization of all three of the above connectors. That makes the competition in the O2O market extremely fierce and its outcome critical to each of the players involved.

Going forward, the Chinese economy will see internet business penetrate deeper into numerous traditional industries.

Among other things, the examples above demonstrate that the new value creation from the mobile internet can come from the following areas:

- Introduction of new competition. The internet lowers barriers to entry dramatically, making it possible for start-ups to launch quickly, scale up and compete. It gives entrepreneurs access to low-cost resources to start new businesses.
- Reduced transaction costs. The internet allows companies, consumers, researchers and the public sector to communicate and collaborate instantly. It facilitates productivity gains from e-commerce, crowdsourcing and internet-enabled supply chain management. It also allows manufacturers to connect directly with consumers, cutting out middlemen.
- The use of big data analytics. For instance, big data can lead to cost-efficient analysis of the credit risks of lending to small businesses and individuals. It also allows e-retailers to deliver personalized recommendations to consumers based on their past purchases.
- The ability to meet long-tail demand. For example, marketplaces like Alibaba have aggregated all the brands and offerings so that customers have a lot more choices online than they would in physical markets. In the fresh food sector, cross-border e-commerce provides customers with access to foreign offerings directly.
- The incorporation of social networks into purchase decisions. The information flow on social networks makes consumers more informed and active.
- Enhanced transparency, competition and efficiency can lower prices and improve the quality of products. The internet also empowers consumers to compare offerings from a wide range of companies easily.

In addition to business model transformation, internet plus has also stimulated "shared economy" applications that have led to broad social benefits. For example, as is the case in many cities worldwide, the demand for cross-town transportation is at the heart of an urban lifestyle in modern China. Although more individuals are buying cars, the demand for taxi services is steadily increasing as the population in many cities has exploded due to swift urbanization. The main issue is that demand is distributed unevenly because there are too few taxis during rush hour. Meanwhile, four-fifths of China's private vehicles reportedly remain idle for long periods of time, as the lack of parking spots in downtown areas forces most car owners to leave their cars at home – an enormous waste of resources.

As such, the mobile apps offered by the US car-service and pooling company Uber and its homegrown rival Didi Kuaidi (backed by Alibaba and Tencent) have been widely embraced by Chinese urban residents. These apps use the mobile internet to match demand and supply in real time, reducing information asymmetry between passengers and drivers. In fact, Uber's rapid growth in China so far might be the best performance by a US tech company in the country for a long time. The internet transformation of traditional industries and services like taxi apps is anything but trivial. It could ultimately make many modes of urban transportation cheaper, more flexible and more widely accessible to people across the income spectrum.

What's even more interesting is the fact that Uber's service has taken off in China much faster than it did in the US. For example, Uber's top three most popular cities worldwide – Guangzhou, Hangzhou and Chengdu – are all in China. The main reason, of course, is the large urban population and the high concentration of city residents. There are approximately 200 cities in China with more than a million people. As the growing Chinese economy brings personal wealth to more people, the Chinese urban residents have generated a strong, new demand for goods and services, and the cities need to adopt "shared economy" models as a result of their scale, density and simply because of the sheer rapidity of the transition. The related business implication is profound: new mobile applications can receive market feedback and achieve meaningful scale more quickly in China than elsewhere, because new technology based on "human infrastructure" tends to spread faster in China – this is because of the size of the mobile user market.

In that context, China is perhaps the best lab and market for "shared economy" applications. The mobile internet and smartphones have created a new social coordinating mechanism, and what the market sees is a seemingly endless potential to put goods and labor that are less than fully utilized to productive use. In the case of Uber and Didi Kuaidi, repurposing a fleet of idle private vehicles as taxis both cuts resource idleness and alleviates the shortage of rush hour taxis greatly. These mobile applications will help to create a more inclusive model of urbanization and economic growth because IT innovations intrinsically emphasize sharing over ownership. When more people are integrated into this new form of growth, everyone will get a piece of a smarter pie.

Innovated in China

The period of 2014 to 2015 was a time of inflection for the global competition between Chinese and US tech players. The blockbuster IPOs of China's two largest e-commerce companies, Alibaba and JD, were more than a showcase of the mobile internet boom and economic model transformation in the Chinese market. Their US listings – Alibaba at the NY stock exchange and JD at the Nasdaq exchange – also shook overseas capital markets as well as the global virtual world.

What is really interesting is that the challenges that Chinese companies now face in overseas markets are very much the same as those encountered by US companies such as Amazon and eBay when they ventured into China. More than a decade ago, those American tech firms were similarly intrigued by the Chinese market's large user base and fast market growth. Yet the cultural, language, political and technological elements turned out to be more complex than they expected. As a result, they swiftly retreated and chose instead to focus primarily on the North American and European market in the past few years.

The difference, I believe, is that for Chinese firms overseas expansion is a must instead of an option. While there is always more growth to be found within China, the fastest-growing market in the world will inevitably slow down, and the Chinese top tech companies must search and find their next billion customers in order to expand. And it is not only about expansion, any company that is strictly local within the context of a global economy is vulnerable either to competition or to takeover by a larger global player. For companies today, and this is not only true for Chinese companies of course, expansion into new markets is a question of survival. Their journey to the foreign markets is full of challenges, but with their overseas listing and significant foreign share ownership, one would expect Alibaba, Tencent and other Chinese companies to manage cultural differences better than the US firms did in China a decade ago.

While BAT and other Chinese firms are expanding globally to find growth in overseas markets, the internet companies in Silicon Valley such as Uber and Linkedin, are also focusing on China as the single largest market for growth after the US. Although the last decade saw Chinese and US firms establishing themselves in two isolated home markets, respectively, competition between them is set to heat up. In addition to fighting more directly in each other's territory, the Chinese and US tech players are also facing each other in other global markets, especially in the emerging markets in Asia and Africa.

Going forward, the Chinese market is poised to be a trendsetter, rather than a trend-follower, in next-generation mobile devices and services. Its unique strength is its unrivalled internet user population size, because data in the digital era is becoming a significant asset. With a population of approximately 1.4 billion and nearly 700 million internet users in China, the data in China's consumer market is primed for surging growth. It is the oil of the information economy and the foundation of upcoming Chinese-designed products and new business models.

Similarly important, and what makes the market unique, is the fact that China is also the largest "mobile-first" and "mobile-only" market in the world. Therefore, from the application side, China's market has evolved in a very different way from the Western equivalent, moving much more aggressively into mobile. A ride-sharing mobile app is a product which best represents the direction of mobile internet development in China: one can post the information of other shared resources on a PC, but one cannot carry a PC while hailing a taxi on the street. Nor can the driver install a PC in the car. As illustrated in the Uber China case, new mobile applications can potentially achieve significant scale more quickly in China than elsewhere.

Furthermore, with government endorsement in the background, a dynamic ecosystem of entrepreneurs and start-ups is being built up organically. The network of established internet firms and their seasoned entrepreneurs, endless eager talent, abundant angel investors and venture capital, and a sophisticated manufacturing system are collectively making China one of the most interesting centers of innovations in the world (see Figure 1.6). This innovation ecosystem is centered on a network of "graduated entrepreneurs" from established internet firms such as BAT. This development resembles the multiplying effect seen in the Silicon Valley ecosystem in the last few decades, where the generation of entrepreneurs spawned by Intel, Netscape, Google and Paypal have created waves of start-ups.

Not that long ago, China's tech industry was known primarily for low-cost, cheap knock-offs and copied internet business models. Fast forward to today and Chinese companies are moving to the forefront of global technology innovation. They can no longer be easily benchmarked against their Western counterparts. Alibaba at the very beginning might have been thought of as "China's eBay", but now Alibaba is more of a mix of Amazon, eBay, PayPal and Netflix. Although Xiaomi is often referred to as the "mini Apple", its business model is that of an "internet company" instead of a "smartphone company", and

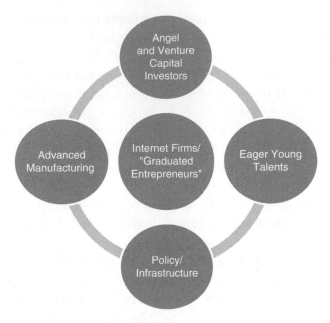

Figure 1.6   China's Innovation Ecosystem

its product offering has expanded into many different smart device categories.

As will be seen throughout the book, Chinese tech companies have already proven their mettle by catching up to global rivals in the smartphone and fourth-generation (4G) technology development process. They are now joining a fiercely competitive global race to become the first company to offer fifth-generation (5G) wireless networks and products to global customers. Many Chinese firms are moving aggressively into the future of an ultimate multi-device and hyper-connected world. For instance, Chinese players have invested heavily in the internet-connected and electric cars, which are considered to be the next key terminal for mobile internet after the smartphones.

Most remarkably, the new innovation ecosystem in China is creating more tech start-ups that cannot simply be described as the Chinese version of US firms. The new generation companies are more innovative in terms of products and technologies

Table 1.3   China's top ten highest valued start-ups (as of January 2016)

	Company name	Valuation ($ bn)	Latest funding (valuation date)	Business description
1	Xiaomi	45	December 2014	Leading manufacturer of smartphones and smart devices
2	Ant Financial	45	July 2015	Internet finance company covering mobile payment, cash management and wealth management
3	Meituan/Dianping	18	January 2016	China's Groupon and Yelp, covering both group buying and consumer reviews
4	Didi Kuaidi	15	July 2015	Dominant taxi-hailing app, Uber's biggest rival in China
5	Lufax	9.6	March 2015	Internet finance, one of the largest peer-to-peer (P2P) online lenders
6	DJI Innovations	8.0	May 2015	The world's largest consumer drone maker by revenue
7	Zhong An Online	8.0	June 2015	China's first online-only insurer
8	Meizu	6.0	February 2015	Smartphone and internet service company backed by Alibaba
9	LeTV Mobile	5.5	November 2015	Smartphone unit of LeTV, the internet and video conglomerate
10	Ele.me	3.0	August 2015	Online food delivery service for universities, offices and others

(Data Sources: Disclosures from fund-raising rounds; Approximate valuations) calibrated to local market needs, more willing to accept outside investors and have a more global outlook from the very beginning. (See Table 1.3 for China's top ten highest valued startups.) Their high valuation not only reflects their enviable scale in the world's largest mobile commerce market, but also illustrates the investors' optimism in the special business models or product features that they are pioneering.

Therefore, the innovation happening in the Chinese market is of strategic value to the leading tech firms in Silicon Valley as well as the global tech industry. Backed by the emerging ecosystem of entrepreneurship in China, Chinese tech and internet firms are very likely going to become a source of unique features, products and business models. There are also opportunities to cultivate cross-pollinated innovations between China and Silicon Valley, as well as other centers of entrepreneurial excellence. The story of China is rapidly transforming from the old "Made in China" to the new "Innovated in China".

2

Users, Partners, Investors and Competitors: Global Stakeholders

In 2014, PepsiCo launched a "Bring Happiness Home" campaign during the Chinese New Year using its public account on WeChat, a popular app in China similar to Facebook and WhatsApp. By using the WeChat features, Pepsi made it possible for people to send good wishes to friends and family creatively and digitally during the traditional holiday season.

The Chinese users could send their own voice recordings to the account and have them remixed into the customized "Bring Happiness Home" theme song, before being delivered to the smartphones of their friends and relatives across the nation. In addition, the audio features gave the users the option to include sound effects, such as the sound of horses galloping in celebration of the Year of the Horse. The brand message was incorporated in the theme song, and the Pepsi name was also cleverly embedded in the campaign title through the use of a pun on the word "Happiness", as the translation of Pepsi's name in Chinese is "Happiness in Everything".

In parallel to PepsiCo, Coca-Cola started a similar "Lyric Coke" campaign with contemporary Chinese pop songs. Each Lyric Coke bottle included a QR code that could be scanned using WeChat's built-in reader. By scanning the QR code, a short song clip was activated, featuring popular Chinese lyrics like "Baby, I'm sorry" as well as the FIFA World Cup lyrics from the same year. The song clip could then be shared on WeChat and other social media platforms.

By adding lyrics to Coke products, Coca-Cola turned the Coke cans and bottles into a medium of self-expression. The Chinese drinkers could signal how they were feeling by sharing the respective song clips. The popularity of the campaign also inspired fans to "collect" different Lyric Coke cans and bottles like stamps would have been collected in the past, generating further consumer attention. The Lyric Coke marketing campaign transformed the global Coca-Cola brand into a special, personal experience for the consumers.

Pepsi and Coke competing on the WeChat advertising platform is just one remarkable example of mobile technologies' profound implications for companies doing business in China. A mobile social network like WeChat not only provides users with a new messaging service or entertainment channel, it also reshapes the behavior of the consumer and the business stakeholders clustering around them. These trends are so important and powerful in shaping consumption decisions that even multinational corporations that have conducted business in China for many decades are rethinking their strategies in China comprehensively.

At a broader level, Chinese e-consumers, probably among the most mobile-advanced in the world, are still demanding more innovative online shopping experiences, while major retailers are rushing to offer ever more sophisticated online services. This also opens up new opportunities for non-indigenous companies who do not have, or need to have, a physical presence in China. As illustrated by the cases of brands and retailers in this chapter, for both multinational companies in China and any companies thinking of bringing products to China, mastering mobile internet strategy and developing social network advertising will separate the winners from the rest.

The New Digital Middle Class

The first wave of "open and reform" policies in the 1980s and 1990s created a large working class in China, the next wave of globalized growth in the 21st century has created an enormous middle class. This middle class in China is already the size of the US population and is expected to double within seven years. In addition to its extent and significant disposable income, this new middle class is also characterized by its quick adoption of mobile applications in their everyday activities.

According to China Internet Network Information Center's (CNNIC) most recent annual report, as of December 2015, China had the world's largest mobile internet user population of 620 million, and the percentage of those using mobile phones to go online reached 90.1%. They use the internet more for entertainment and consumption – text messaging, social network sharing, online game playing, movies and videos streaming and shopping – than for work, which is bringing seismic changes to China's customer markets.

Firstly, this new generation of consumers is extremely comfortable with mobile e-commerce. Because of the broad ownership of smartphones and the broadband infrastructure across the country, Chinese customers are online from the start, and they are turning into mobile shoppers at a fast pace. They are quick adopters of new technology and digital media, so they are extremely comfortable with the e-retailing ecosystem. For example, Western consumers prefer clean and streamlined website designs, while Chinese shoppers prefer a crowded and compact website, which seems to signal creates a high-energy shopping atmosphere.

CNNIC's 2014 annual report also found that Chinese internet users' attitude towards the internet is exemplified by "trust and sharing". As of December 2014, 54.5% of the internet users showed trust in online information, a remarkable increase from 35.1% in 2007. The general trust in the online information flows becomes an integral part of social trust, which lays the social foundation for the application and development of deep networks of e-commerce and internet finance. For example, brands lacking the funding for traditional advertising are now able to engage online consumers and, in many cases, in ways that the traditional media cannot.

Secondly, internet coverage has brought unprecedented exposure to foreign brands to Chinese customers. When they shop online, Chinese consumers have more choices among retail brands than in brick-and-mortar shops. For branded goods, e-commerce is an important channel to expand their distribution beyond first-tier cities into the hands of consumers who rely on online shopping in the lower-tier cities.

In addition, the explosive growth of online entertainment content presents the middle class with an even more widely expanding selection of brands. With brand images carefully built in the backdrop, movies, television shows, sports broadcasting and other content have reached a broad range of Chinese viewers, from coastal cities to rural areas, through the various video streaming websites.

For example, Champagne or even sparkling wine has been less commonly used to celebrate special occasions or ceremonies in China than red wine, but a recent Chinese blockbuster movie series *Tiny Times* – known as the *Sex and the City* of China – provoked new interest in French champagne among the young generation. The movie series, which depicted the lifestyle of high society girls in their 20s, appealed to a young audience, while simultaneously offering viewers a glimpse of numerous fashion brands. For instance, the latest episode of *Tiny Times* featured the flagship stores of numerous fashion brands in a scene filmed in Rome.

Thirdly, social networks have tremendous influence on customer purchasing decisions. According to A.T. Kearney's 2014 Connected Customer Study, Chinese consumers are ten times more reliant on social media in the making of purchasing decisions than are Americans. PWC's 2014 Total Global Retail Survey indicates that 86% of Chinese consumers purchase products through social media, compared to 48% consumers worldwide, and almost all customers use social media to discover, research and review brands.

This might be explained in part by a cultural difference: social engagement and purchasing behavior are so intertwined in China that Chinese customers tend to seek friends' input before they make shopping decisions. Consumption is an extension of social interaction, and purchasing decisions are made not only to satisfy personal needs or desires, but become an integral part of the relationships between individuals. Another cultural difference could be that Chinese consumers are more skeptical of formal communications, such as quality certificates, which tend to be widely distrusted; instead they put more value on peer-to-peer recommendations. As a result, with almost instantaneous feedback and easy-to-use interfaces, social media platforms are indispensable in the life of Chinese e-consumers.

By combining features from Twitter, Facebook, Instagram and other social media services, WeChat, the social network and messaging app developed by Tencent, is by far the most popular forum. It started as a messaging app, but has evolved into a major mobile commerce ecosystem. Its social network function shapes consumer behaviors in significant ways. Brands have also used it as an effective channel to keep customers engaged. Now it also offers a platform for companies to sell recommendation-driven products such as cosmetics, healthcare and insurance directly.

Like Facebook in the US, WeChat offer special value to targeted marketing because of its users' "circles of friends". For instance, one young professional may have one WeChat circle for her high school classmates, one for college classmates, one for graduate schoolmates, one for current colleagues, one for colleagues from her former position and so on. Each circle relates to certain common social activities: a circle of former colleagues may have dinner together frequently, whereas the circle of graduate schoolmates mostly share information about IT seminars and executive training opportunities. As a result, the WeChat circles can be used by marketers to target specific groups with customized product offerings.

The eager adoption of social media by Chinese consumers has created unique opportunities for companies that want to gain insights about, and to engage with, the enormous middle class. Therefore, global brands in China such as Burberry,

Estée Lauder, Mulberry, Starbucks – to name just a few – have actively engaged the social networks in China (such as WeChat) to develop new advertising strategies. Some of their creative WeChat campaigns will be analyzed in the next section.

Fourth, the younger generation of consumers are conspicuous consumers. The younger generation of consumers enjoy the status conferred by luxury brands, and they routinely trade up to the next tier of luxury brands. White collar professionals constantly look for the newest products and trends featured in Western movies and TV shows on the video streaming sites. Even young migrant workers, who are clearly in the lower income bucket, may spend a month's wages on high-end products like Apple iPhones. As depicted in shows such as *Tiny Times*, wine appreciation is another expression of the growing middle class in China making a thoroughly globally-aligned lifestyle choice.

Younger consumers like to share their unique experiences online. The CNNIC 2014 annual report statistics have shown that 60% of Chinese internet users are positive about sharing their experiences online, 13% of them show strong desire to do so and 47% show moderate desire. In particular, among users aged between 10 and 19, approximately 66% of them are strongly or moderately interested. In fact, showing off (or "shai") their lifestyle online is part of the social fabric for many young Chinese, as is the case globally. **(See the "Shai on Social Network" box.)**

As a result, this younger generation of middle class consumers has a strong demand for customized and personalized products and experiences. Western brands therefore cannot simply turn their global advertisement into Chinese language, as they did during their entries into the Chinese market in the 1980s or 1990s; instead they constantly have to create new aspirations and identities in their stories. Every brand has to generate unique sparks to keep the young conspicuous consumers engaged.

For example, British leather retailer Mulberry used WeChat as a platform for Chinese consumers to experience the brand in a personalized way, as the company considered Mulberry a brand with a rich heritage and a sophisticated, nuanced identity, and viewed the campaign as having entertainment value. The registered WeChat users could browse its collection of leather products and digital content, some of which were exclusive to the app, and they could also get a behind-the-scenes look at Mulberry's Autumn/Winter 2014 advertisement campaign that featured Cara Delevingne.

"Shai" on Social Network

Chinese consumers are both voracious e-shoppers and active social network users. The combination of both leads to a new social phenomenon called "shai" which is essential for digital marketing aimed at the younger generation born in the 1980s and 1990s.

"Shai" in Chinese means to put something under sunshine. In social media, it becomes a term to describe the young generation "showing off" their lifestyle, such as a luxury brand one just bought or a fancy restaurant one is sitting at. By definition, important status items are "shai-ed" by visual contents, with photos and videos as the most important part of communication. Social media platforms such as WeChat provide the perfect platform.

For brands, "shai" means the young netizens are not passive consumers; instead they actively find a voice in social media to express their appreciation of the brands (or they may similarly express dissatisfaction with brands on their social network). Major brands are paying close attention to "shai" in the social networks, as it is an important marketing channel to develop a better understanding of the young consumers.

Foreign cosmetics brands have been a popular category for Chinese consumers to "shai" when they enjoy "trading up" into luxury brands. As discussed later in this chapter, fresh foreign food is a new kind of "affordable luxury" that appeals to the young middle class. For example, their consumption of imported fruits such as Canadian blackberries or Chilean cherries is often "shai-ed" in their circles.

In summary, because of the new mobile connectedness, many Chinese consumers are experiencing global brands for the first time in their life. The brands need to rethink their Chinese advertising campaigns in this new context. As shown in the examples, localized marketing that integrates cultural references (such as PepsiCo theme song's linkage to the Chinese New Year's tradition) and appeals to the specific behavior of online Chinese users (such as the Lyric Coke bottles "collection") have proven to be the most effective at converting online participation into material sales.

WeChat: A New Platform for Foreign Brands

WeChat ("Weixin" or "micro-message" in Chinese) is a Chinese innovation story: Tencent initially built it based on the functions of proven overseas social media platforms, but it later designed features with Chinese characteristics, which attracted more than half a billion users in China and abroad.

WeChat is now the most popular social forum in China. It started off as an instant messaging service, but Tencent has since built an entire ecosystem of interrelated services and functions within WeChat. Alongside text, video and voice messaging, WeChat users can now shop online and make mobile payments, play games, book hotels and flight tickets, order a taxi and do many other things without ever leaving the app ecosystem.

One important reason for its popularity is that Chinese users can (or at least could) send text, links, videos and photos to friends more cheaply through WeChat (data package charges) than traditional texting services offered by wireless carriers (charging by the number of calls and texts). Also, WeChat is a more convenient platform to use. For instance, many people find typing Chinese characters on a smartphone screen time consuming, so WeChat has developed strong voice capabilities and offered the free voice messaging feature. In China it is commonplace to see WeChat users holding up their smartphones like walkie-talkies as they convey voice messages and listen to replies.

In addition, communication by WeChat is considered a more intimate, controlled and trusted environment. Chinese shoppers are increasingly resorting to friends' reviews and recommendation online when they make purchases, so WeChat becomes a platform of choice. Many users are almost addicted to WeChat: they tend to pick up their phones several times an hour to access WeChat and will often spend several hours a day using the platform. For all the above reasons, WeChat is an ideal place to introduce offerings that are heavily influenced by word-of-mouth recommendation and peer reviews, such as branded goods and experience consumption.

Using WeChat's messaging, image and audio features, brands can easily develop a multi-media marketing campaign supported by user-generated content on a mass scale. For example, similar to Coca-Cola and PepsiCo's marketing campaigns mentioned above, McDonald's has also used WeChat's voice capabilities in 2014 to run a "Big Mac Rap" contest to promote its signature Big Mac hamburger.

The "Big Mac Rap" contest featured famous TV host Hua Shao from the hit singing show *China's Good Voices*. At the beginning of each *China's Good Voices* show, Hua Shao always started by introducing the show and thanking sponsors in a fast-paced monologue. McDonald's asked customers to record a "Big Mac Rap" in the "Hua Shao Talk" style and then upload their videos or sound clips to McDonald's WeChat account. Numerous spoofs from the contest successfully attracted wide participation from the public. In particular, the main theme of this "Big Mac Rap" campaign was being casual, easygoing and fun, which aligned well with McDonald's brand identity.

Interestingly, the most dramatic example of such a "popularity marketing campaign" on WeChat came from the mobile payment service "WeChat Pay" that is directly linked to WeChat itself. To challenge Alibaba's monopoly in e-commerce, Tencent entered the mobile payment territory traditionally dominated by Alibaba-affiliated Alipay. WeChat Pay had a major breakthrough in user adoption after it launched a "digital red envelope" campaign during the 2014 Chinese New Year season. The digital red envelope service enabled people to give holiday gifts to relatives and friends conveniently through bank accounts instead of cash, and it incorporated additional features to make the process more fun and engaging, something that was more than a simple transfer of funds. The campaign was an incredible success: hundreds of millions of users were glued to their smartphones during the Spring Festival season, and they happily registered their banking information with WeChat to become WeChat Pay users.

Targeted marketing on WeChat, however, may provide even more value for brands in the future. Generally speaking, the information on WeChat users' age, gender, interests, educational background, social behavior and consumption habits can be used by retail vendors to target consumers more specifically than through mass email or micro blogging. Because it is also a messaging app, WeChat enables brands to have something akin to a one-to-one interaction with their followers. Numerous Western companies have embraced WeChat to connect intimately with their fan base in a way that is both cost effective and welcomed by the advertisement recipient: with no unwanted banners, no redirection clicks and quick responsiveness to followers' reviews or suggestions.

For example, Burberry ran a "parallel social event" on WeChat to promote the opening of its new flagship store in Shanghai in April 2014. By giving the participants a chance to watch its Autumn/Winter 2014 runway show in real time, Burberry strengthened its ties to the followers because they needed to add Burberry's public account to their WeChat network before watching the show.

Then the interactive button "My Burberry" led users to images of Burberry products and the details on how to order them.

Another evolving marketing strategy is to combine brand identity and certain social responsibility concepts into an integrated social media message on WeChat. In these cases, companies sometimes use both social network tools and traditional TV programs to maximize the marketing impact. One case in point was a family value-based marketing program by the food brand Oreo.

In a 2014 marketing campaign, Oreo targeted parents who worried about the lack of direct communication between themselves and their children due to the long working hours so common in China. Collaborating with WeChat, Oreo created a customized app around "Emojis", the icons of little smiley faces that were gaining increasing popularity in China at the time. WeChat users could take photos of themselves and their children and then paste the heads into Emojis before sharing them with friends. In parallel, the campaign also included a television advertisement in which a mother and her daughter played together and shared a bag of Oreos. Because the brand identity is played out with a cross-generation social responsibility message, the combination of a TV advertisement and social network was a great success in grabbing consumer attention in the Oreo Bonding Emoji campaign.

While the digital platforms like WeChat could work to foreign brands' advantage in China, there are also special considerations that may pose risks because WeChat was designed to facilitate intimate communications within closed social circles. For one thing, when a social media conversation about a brand turns negative within some closed circles, the company may not be able to identify it quickly and respond in time. For that reason, marketers must establish and maintain constant two-way engagement with customers. For another, because the engaged consumers expect companies to respond to their every post, they may be disappointed when their expectations of a direct relationship are not met.

In addition to partnering with brands for a marketing campaign on WeChat, Tencent is also testing sending regular advertisements to WeChat users directly. **(See the "Are you BMW worthy?" box.)** Since 2014 the market has also seen thousands of merchants bringing China's popular direct-sales model to WeChat. They formed semi-private WeChat groups of 50–100 people each, bringing in friends and friends of friends to sell everything from organic vegetables to the latest fashion brands. These are now referred to as little WeChat Stores. As China's social networks expand in features and users, new marketing models will continue emerging from WeChat and other similar platforms.

Are you BMW worthy? Or in the Coke camp?

In January 2015, Tencent started including advertisements on its WeChat platform for the first time. That initiative was intended to demonstrate the power of combining big data with social media. To everyone's surprise, while targeted advertisements on social networks such as Facebook were viewed as negative by most users, in China many WeChat users became anxious when they were selected not to be shown certain advertisements.

In WeChat's first direct advertisement trial, it sent out three targeted adverts to different groups: one group was shown the BMW car advertisement, the other was shown the mobile phone brand Vivo and the third was shown a Coca-Cola advert. Soon the Internet community saw the lucky ones receiving the BMW advertisement "shai-ing" screenshots of the advert as a status symbol. Meanwhile people from other groups protested on WeChat against "discrimination". In particular, the Coca-Cola crowds, who were apparently not "BMW worthy", began to refer to themselves jokingly as "Diaosi", the Internet term for losers.

The WeChat users paid close attention to the advertisement they received, because they considered it an indication of what Tencent's big data thought of their net worth and social status. For many, BMW was linked to wealth, Vivo possibly linked middle class, but Coke was undoubtedly viewed as low income. The social status anxiety created by those adverts was obvious: this was demonstrated by one person who didn't receive the BMW advertisement claiming he was rich and announcing he would buy a Mercedes right away.

Different theories soon emerged to explain the criteria used by WeChat for those three targeted advertisements. One theory was that Apple iPhone users received the most BMW adverts. Another suggested that Tencent looked into the users' historical records of mobile payments. Some domestic media reports, quoting unidentified insiders, suggested that the main factors considered were the users' age and location. Of course it could have all been a clever marketing ploy intended to create brand awareness for all three brands involved by sending adverts randomly.

Alibaba: Access for Foreign Products

Because the consumption boom in China is mostly a 21st century phenomenon, its retail consumer market remains fragmented. There is no extensive bricks-and-mortar retailer infrastructure similar to that in the US, let alone brands of national retail chains (such as Walmart in the US). Despite the recent boom of shopping malls, the overall coverage ratio is about two shopping malls per one million people (about one-tenth of the rate in the US).

The growth of internet coverage and e-retailing has filled the gap. Online marketplaces such as Alibaba have emerged, which not only connect buyers and sellers, but also provide related support services such as marketing, delivery and payments. This levels the playing field for the smaller merchants to participate in the market. According to Alibaba statistics, by 2015 there were about 10 million entrepreneurs running small businesses on Alibaba's e-commerce websites. Going forward, online retail is expected to grow at three times the rate of the overall retail market, with the main growth coming from the third- and fourth-tier cities, where the shoppers leap into e-commerce directly.

In a similar way, the e-commerce sector has also created a significant opportunity for cross-border trade. In 2014, Alibaba launched a dedicated Tmall Global site to host online shops for foreign products. Soon its main rival, JD.com, also started a new venture called JD Worldwide to compete head on. Smaller players such as Ymatou.com have also launched similar sites. They are especially useful for small Western businesses, because by way of this channel to market many products are now able to reach the world's fastest-growing consumer market without having to set up physical shops in China. Also, digital access may mean faster and broader reach to consumers across China than physical stores would ever be able to provide.

For example, in 2015 the UK's Royal Mail set up an online shop front at Alibaba's Tmall site, serving as a link between mid-size and small British companies and Chinese consumers. Royal Mail would handle the necessary documentation for the firms, as well as supporting services such as marketing, promotions and customer services; in return, Royal Mail would receive commissions on the sale of products as well as fees for shipping the products through its Parcelforce express unit. The arrangement aimed to provide the Chinese market with access to British retailers and exporters who

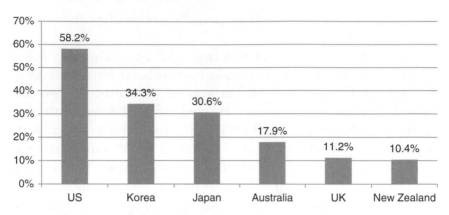

Figure 2.1   Which Country's Goods Do You Mostly Buy on Cross-Border e-commerce Sites?
(Data Source: CNNIC, December 2014)

could not afford to set up a physical presence in China on their own.

The cross-border e-commerce industry is booming in China. For the new digital middle class, the demand for high quality goods and services has never been higher. According to the CNNIC data, as of December 2014, the US market is the most visited by the users of cross-border e-commerce sites, as more than half of the Chinese customers (58.2%) placed orders for US goods (see Figure 2.1). The goods from Korea (34.3%) and Japan (30.6%) followed.

In particular, because domestic Chinese goods can no longer fulfill the demand of the Chinese consumers fully, they increasingly shop online to search for offerings from the overseas markets. The online food business is now one of China's fastest growing markets and therefore an important sector for Alibaba, JD.com and other e-commerce companies. While foreign luxury brands have led the trend, the latest cool products are fresh food and fruit from abroad, such as New Zealand lamb, Alaskan crab and Mexican avocados, this is not only the result of consumer aspirations, the Chinese public have strong concerns about food safety issues.

In recent years, Chinese customers' faith in local food was shaken by a slew of food safety scandals, which appear to have turned everyone into food safety experts. The discovery of tainted baby formula milk in 2008 was a high profile incident that raised the alert level for many Chinese customers. Later the wide use of cooking oil retrieved from city drainage also shocked the country. (See the "Di-gou-you (Gutter Oil)" box.) Foreign companies operating in China had their share of safety issues too, with McDonald's from the US and Fonterra from New Zealand among those forced to recall products due to quality concerns.

As a result, information technology companies have responded with some creative suggestions, but they are still far from being able to offer a complete solution. Some innovation uses data techniques to track the food transportation process to ensure the food has not been contaminated during the journey. For instance, Joyvio Group, a Legend Holdings' portfolio company, is the largest end-to-end fruit company of its kind in China. It has large-scale farming operations in China and abroad that produce high quality fruit, and it has also developed a "whole chain traceability" app to track the food from its plantation field to the end-user's dinner table. Using the smartphone app, shoppers can simply scan a code on the food item to find information on the fruit's journey as well as examine the soil and water tests from the farm.

"Di-gou-you" (Gutter Oil) and Smart Chopsticks

Cooking oil is traditionally used heavily in Chinese cuisine, but "di-gou-you" is a new phenomenon. To the shock of many Chinese customers, some cooking oil in the market is derived from, as the name suggests, gutters. Apparently, waste oil is collected from restaurant fryers, grease traps, or even sewer drains before being recycled into illicit cooking oil.

Gutter oil is frequently involved in urban legends on China's social networks. On April Fools' Day in 2014, China's search engine giant Baidu offered a video clip on smart chopsticks that could determine whether a dish contained gutter oil. According to Baidu, when the video was made, it had no serious intention to pursue it as a product. However, because the fake advertisement generated so much buzz on social media, Baidu decided it could be a timely innovation.

At the company's annual technology conference in September 2014, Baidu's Chief Executive Robin Li unveiled the "smart chopsticks" prototype that was called Baidu Kuaisou. They were equipped with sensors to collect data on pH levels, peroxide value and temperature, and they could be connected to a smartphone app to provide users with analyzed readings on the oil being tested.

So far, Baidu has only manufactured a small batch of smart chopsticks prototypes for testing. But some food experts have already warned that gutter oil producers could outsmart the smart chopsticks. Because the sensors only take a small number of variables into account for its analysis, the gutter oil producers could, according to the experts, easily add relevant chemicals to give its oil products a false safe reading.

However, because the widespread food scandals have shaken consumers' trust, Chinese consumers are also suspicious of the certificates generated by their smartphone apps. They worry that this verification can be fabricated as well. Even with smart devices designed by tech companies to detect chemicals, such as the smart chopsticks from Baidu, they are still concerned that unscrupulous food producers could easily outfox them. Therefore, the demand for imported food has grown rapidly. A recent study by the China Market Research Group showed that many consumers are willing to pay premiums of 30–40% for imported milk, meat, fruits and vegetables as a result of their perceived safety.

In 2013, Tmall.com, Alibaba's online marketplace, started allowing US food companies to ship directly to customers in China. The enthusiastic response from Chinese customers made this venture a huge success. For example, farmers in the Pacific Northwest sold 180 tons of cherries to China in 2013 through Alibaba's platform. It set off a cherry frenzy in China, and the sales in 2014 more than tripled to reach 600 tons.

Encouraged by the market growth, the e-commerce companies are now in a race to sign up foreign governments and producers for fresh food and fruit supplies. JD.com, Alibaba's main rival in e-commerce, has also made a major push into the imported food business with partnerships in the US,

Australia, France and more. In 2015, it led a $70 million investment round in FruitDay, which claimed to be China's largest online fresh produce firm and on course to hit 10 million customers the same year. SF Express, one of China's biggest logistics firms, also launched a portal in 2015 to sell food products it sourced from retailers.

The cross-border e-commerce field still involves significant challenges for foreign merchants however.

First, for cross-border e-commerce, logistics and delivery are natural challenges. Even for the largest e-commerce platforms in China, the whole value chain may take some time to function smoothly. What is promising is that the latest government policies on cross-border e-commerce have encouraged e-commerce sites to upgrade overseas shopping services, and the internet giants have already put some advanced supply chains in place. For example, through Alibaba's Tmall website, New Zealand kiwi orders could arrive in Shanghai customers' hands within two days. For JD.com, which operates as a direct sales channel and views its own logistics network as a main differentiator from Alibaba's online marketplaces, its commitment to cross-border e-commerce should lead to significant investments in its own distribution infrastructure for overseas products.

Second, the competition on pricing is fierce, as most daily necessities are available through domestic sources at much lower prices and, in many cases, offer same-day free delivery. Standard products that have higher base pricing before additional import duties and shipping costs will have a hard time being competitive in the over-crowded mid and lower ends of the market. It is critical for the foreign suppliers to distinguish their products from those of their domestic peers. Fresh food and fruit from overseas farms are a good example, as their popularity is a result of the Chinese consumers' safety concerns. Another example is Western fashion brands. These can charge a premium to cover taxes and transportation costs because Chinese customers in general still perceive foreign brands as more stylish and of a better quality than local brands.

In addition, while the foreign merchants do not have to set up shops in China, the e-platforms are certainly not free (as transaction commissions and other charges apply). Furthermore, some physical presence or partnership in China may still be needed for the merchant to be able to scale its operation and to understand the subtle details of a completely new market. The bottom line is that in an ultra-competitive market, a physical shop is still a proven way to stand out and grab the attention of consumers. For example, the US brand Gap has set up a presence at Alibaba's Tmall, has launched its own online shop and also has its physical stores in China.

Thirdly, and probably the most complex issue to deal with for an outside vendor, is that the foreign businesses need to team with the online marketplace to combat counterfeits. Counterfeits and gray market goods affect e-commerce platforms around the world, but the scale of the Chinese market makes this an especially important issue. Alibaba is well known as the powerhouse of e-tailing and the main channel for foreign brands' online sale in China. It is at the forefront of this complicated battle, which involves multiple stakeholders of customers, marketplaces, brand companies, vendors and regulators.

As mentioned earlier, Alibaba's Taobao site is a bazaar-like platform for smaller merchants, whereas the Tmall site is mainly intended for larger retailers and global brands. Both sites have faced complaints from foreign companies and industrial groups about counterfeit goods or unauthorized listings, such as fake cosmetics and knockoff handbags.

Some counterfeits are obvious: these goods may be labeled as "special factory direct sale" items, and typically their offering price is at a huge discount to the retail price. However, some consumers are more sensitive to price than quality, and some are just happy to own a branded product, whether it is authentic or not. So they may buy these questionable products without questioning whether they are authentic. Some non-authentic products are not outright fakes, however, so they are harder to categorize.

Some so-called "web products" are known as gray market goods, such as factory overruns that are authentic products by definition; yet they are sold cheaply without the authorization from the brands, and this may have an adverse impact on the brand's market positioning. Some products are imitations of foreign brands, but they also add in specific new features to cater to domestic consumers' needs, such as cell phones with an ultraviolet light setting that could detect fake bank notes. For those, it is debatable whether they are pirated products or alternative versions of existing products that fill a vacuum that major brands have either abandoned or not yet exploited. **(See the "Shanzhai" box.)**

Shanzhai ("Knock-off" or "Copycat")

"Shanzhai" is the Chinese term referring to fake or pirated products as well as the businesses based on these products. When smartphones were introduced to China a few years ago, cheap "shanzhai" phones flooded the market. The "shanzhai" phones are more affordable, which was an important factor for the fast adoption of smartphones in China.

The term "shanzhai" came from traditional Chinese literature. It means "mountain fortress", and refers to a stronghold of regional bandits who are free from government control. The most famous of these bandits was probably the gang in the Song dynasty depicted by the Chinese classic literature *Tale of the Marshes* (*Shui-hu-zhuan*, which is also translated as "Water Margin").

After gaining popularity with smartphones, "shanzhai" soon became a general social term for low-cost imitations of cars, mansions, movies or even events, where the once high-end and exclusive ones were made accessible for the consumer at a lower point of entry. For example, some rural areas organized Spring Festival variety shows involving performers who looked like famous movie stars so that the people who could not afford to engage with the real stars could enjoy a "shanzhai" show.

Many internet firms in China that were once viewed as "shanzhai" web firms themselves, have developed core competencies to differentiate themselves from the other firms. They have grown into innovators, creating products and services that are different from (or even superior to) those of their Western counterparts. When the State Internet Information Office Deputy Director Peng Bo commented at the recent 2014 China Copyright Annual Forum that "China is on a fast lane to become an innovative nation", his opening sentence was that "China is saying goodbye to shanzhai".

From time to time Alibaba has been criticized for not adequately policing fake and substandard goods. To some extent, the fake goods problem stems from Alibaba's own success, i.e. its dominant position (with close to two-thirds of the e-commerce market). Alibaba insists that it has a robust system in place to protect brand owners and consumers and will continue to improve it. In recent years, Alibaba made public filings to the US Trade Representative and the World Intellectual Property Organization, providing details on the measures it takes to reduce counterfeit goods on its marketplace sites.

To combat fakes, Alibaba employees and volunteers monitor the platforms by conducting random checks, employing big data to target their checking and also maintain an online complaint forum. If consumers discover counterfeits, they may be refunded five times the amount they paid for the products. In order to discourage fake merchants, Alibaba may shut down their online stores, seize their security deposits and impose penalties. In its 2014 report filed with the World Intellectual Property Organization, Alibaba stated that it spent more than $16 million a year fighting counterfeit goods.

The issue was highlighted in January 2015, when China's main business regulator, China's State Administration for Industry and Commerce (SAIC) sent a stern message to Alibaba. The SAIC publicly criticized e-commerce companies for not sufficiently cracking down on the sale of counterfeit goods as well as other harmful practices by online vendors, which included advertising with misleading messages and faking transactions to manipulate online sales volumes.

The SAIC's report in early 2015 was based on its inspection of online products between August and October 2014. The inspection process sampled 92 product categories across several e-commerce marketplaces. Among the three major B2C websites, JD.com's rate of authentic goods (90%) is slightly ahead of Alibaba's Tmall (85.71%) and another site Yihaodian (80%). But the eBay-like C2C (consumer to consumer) site Taobao only had a 37.25% rate of authentic goods. In other words, the inspection result suggested that two-thirds of the products on Alibaba's Taobao platform were not genuine products.

In its report, the SAIC also highlighted four areas of issues among e-commerce companies. The first was the lack of background checks on online vendors; second, the lack of review on products' information; third, the lack of supervision of sales activities; fourth, the flaws in the products' online rating system. The report also touched on bribery and other illegal activities in e-commerce marketplaces. Because Alibaba had "long failed to take effective measures to control the problem", the SAIC report concluded that Alibaba was "facing its biggest credibility crisis since it was founded".

In response, Alibaba emphasized that the company had complied with China's laws and regulations, while acknowledging that it had more to do to crack down on counterfeit sales. As would be expected in the mobile era, Alibaba challenged the SAIC inspection methodology and procedure through an open letter posted on Taobao's verified account on the social messaging service Weibo (known as the Twitter of China). The letter said that Alibaba "welcomes fair and just supervision", but that the regulator's approach was not objective. It went to considerable lengths to illustrate that the SAIC's inspection process had flaws (for example, the small number of samples).

As the confrontation escalated, the SAIC published a white paper summarizing its findings of the deficiencies on Alibaba's sites. The white paper was based on discussions between Alibaba and SAIC in July 2014, and it highlighted five main problem areas on Alibaba's sites. The white paper was completed in the summer of 2014. But according to SAIC's explanation, it decided not to publicize the white paper then to avoid causing disruption to Alibaba's IPO plan. (Alibaba had its US IPO in September 2014.)

Within days of the SAIC announcement, Alibaba's founder Jack Ma met with the chief of SAIC and pledged to work more closely with the regulator to combat counterfeits. Alibaba stated it would strengthen its internal systems and announced a plan to hire 300 people to form an anti-counterfeiting task force. The regulator maintained that the e-commerce companies like Alibaba needed to improve their self-policing, and SAIC would work with them to develop new supervisory mechanisms. With that, the SAIC removed the white paper from its website and categorized it as an "internal" document that did not have any legal implications. (Nevertheless, the white paper triggered interest from US securities lawyers, and class actions quickly showed up at the courts in New York, where Alibaba was listed.)

Alibaba has since tightened up on its internal rules on accepting merchants to the popular goods categories at the Tmall site. Some of those categories, such as women's bags and cosmetics, are known for gray market products. Under the new rules, only those merchants with quality products and services, as determined by Alibaba, will be invited directly to the Tmall platform. For others, vendors need to apply and prove the authenticity of their offerings. It has also shortened the time required to investigate vendors who are suspected of being involved in selling fake products and imposed more severe punishment on vendors selling counterfeit goods.

However, most major brands still believe that counterfeits on Alibaba's marketplaces – the C2C site Taobao, in particular, primarily because its standard of entry is low – remain a serious challenge to their businesses in China. In April 2015, the American Apparel and Footwear Association, in letters to the US SEC and Trade Representative, described Taobao as one of the biggest platforms for counterfeit goods world-wide. The letter to the US Trade Representative stated that Alibaba was either incapable of or not interested in addressing the problem. The letter to the SEC called the US capital markets' regulator to increase scrutiny of Alibaba's efforts to supervise Taobao for counterfeit products. Later in May, several luxury brands including Gucci and Yves Saint Laurent filed a lawsuit in New York alleging Alibaba had failed to combat counterfeit goods on its Tmall marketplace.

Of course, Alibaba is incentivized to build up its efforts to tackle fake and unauthorized goods listings further. With better control of the quality of the merchandise sold from its platforms, it will be able to defend against attacks from its competitors better and strengthen its market leading position as well. However, because of the sheer number of transactions and enormous number of vendors on Alibaba's marketplaces, it is hugely challenging to eliminate gray market products outright. To put the issue into a bigger context, the lack of trust and credibility is a prevailing problem in the consumer goods industry in China beyond e-commerce, as shown by the example of food safety scandals. On the other hand, there is the pressure on consumers to be "upwardly mobile" and to demonstrate their consumption to their peers, which is driving the trend of less expensive, but passable "counterfeits". These issues will only be fully resolved by the maturing of the market ecosystem, including regulation and the change of consumer spending habits.

Investors: Among the Biggest Winners

As China's mobile economy and e-commerce leap forward, foreign financial investors have emerged as some of the biggest winners. They invested in BAT (Baidu, Alibaba and Tencent) in the early years in exchange for sizable stakes in these companies, and by now they have had tens of billions of capital gains. For example, the Japanese investor Softbank started investing in Alibaba as early as 1999 and it held a 34% stake in the company's IPO. Naspers, a South African TMT company, bought a large stake in Tencent in 2001 and it had 38% ownership when Tencent went public.

Figures 2.2, 2.3 and 2.4 illustrate the foreign ownership of BAT's IPOs and their market capitalization as of December 31, 2015.

JD.com is a relative newcomer and is smaller in size, but its multi-billion market capitalizations have also brought hefty

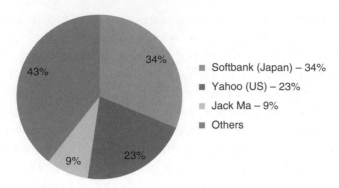

Figure 2.2   Alibaba ($200 billion)
(Data Source: Bloomberg)

returns to the foreign institutions and venture capitalists (see Figure 2.5).

The investment themes for these Chinese mobile e-commerce players are obvious: they are basically directional bets on the fast growth of China's consumption power as well as the irreversible trend of mobile e-commerce being a more important channel to market than traditional retail. Their high valuation not only reflects their dominance in the world's largest mobile commerce market, but also includes the investors' optimism in the special business models or product

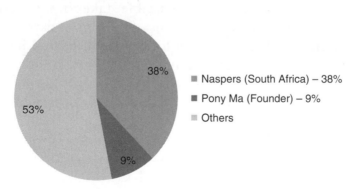

Figure 2.3   Tencent ($184.5 billion)
(Data Source: Bloomberg)

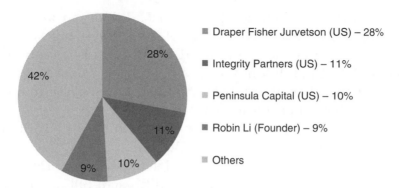

Draper Fisher Jurvetson (US) – 28%

Integrity Partners (US) – 11%

Peninsula Capital (US) – 10%

Robin Li (Founder) – 9%

Others

Figure 2.4   Baidu ($65 billion)
(Data Source: Bloomberg)

features that they are pioneering. Relating to the same theme, in the recent past there has been an unprecedentedly large flow of venture capital from both domestic and foreign entities into Chinese start-up companies.

Throughout this book there are many examples of capital investments in younger internet companies in China. If the first generation BAT were stories of "adapted to China", where the entrepreneurs adopted internet business models of Western markets into China, then the new generation start-ups are

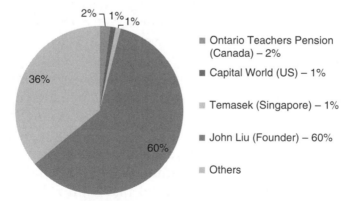

Ontario Teachers Pension (Canada) – 2%

Capital World (US) – 1%

Temasek (Singapore) – 1%

John Liu (Founder) – 60%

Others

Figure 2.5   JD.com ($45 billion)
(Data Source: Bloomberg)

mostly stories of "innovated in China". Taking advantage of the enormous size and fast growth of the Chinese market, new companies are creating advanced features and unique business models. In addition, they are steadily expanding in overseas markets to become global technology powers. For financial investors, this is a promising landscape.

For example, Xiaomi, the fast-rising Chinese smartphone maker, was valued at $45 billion in December 2014 when it completed the latest round of financing. Its investors include Singapore's sovereign wealth fund GIC and Russian billionaire Yuri Milner's DST Global fund. In 2015, US investment funds Tiger Global Management, Coatue Management, Farallon Capital Management and other institutions became investors in the Didi Dache-Kuaidi Dache taxi-hailing company, a Chinese version of Uber. The 2015 financing round pushed the company's valuation beyond $10 billion.

Disruption: All Are Not Winners

Of course, not every player is a winner in China's mobile commerce revolution. Some consumer goods companies failed to realize how deeply and rapidly the retail business is changing in China. According to a recent Nielsen Survey, about half of Chinese consumers are already buying groceries online (almost twice the ratio for global consumers). Yet even some of the largest multinationals in China have been slow to react to this important trend.

For example, competition from online grocers is one of the biggest threats to bricks-and-mortar sales at chains such as Walmart. Walmart was forced to focus more on its online strategy, as the number of its in-store customers had fallen steadily in recent years. Although Walmart was one of the first retailers to set up online shopping in China, only in 2015 did it create a mobile app enabling customers to place an order on their smartphones and then choose whether to pick it up or have it delivered. When compared to its rivals, as well as new online grocers, Walmart's mobile presence was lagging behind.

In fact, according to a 2015 report by OC&C strategy consultants, almost all the major grocers in China had experienced near-consistent negative growth since 2010. During that period, their sales growth had come almost entirely from new store openings. Consequently, the shrinking role of large traditional retailers hurt the major consumer-products companies that occupied their store shelves. For example, Unilever has been a dominant player in China for more than two decades when it comes to buying daily necessities. But in the last two quarters of 2014, the company surprised the market when it announced consecutive 20% drops in quarterly sales in China.

In short, the emergence of mobile e-commerce means the major consumer brands may have to rethink their strategy fundamentally. In the past, the major brands could easily dominate the store shelves of traditional retailers with their branded products. But in the mobile era, technology has massively disrupted the competition landscape.

Firstly, online marketplaces like Alibaba have aggregated all the brands and offerings, so customers have many more choices when they shop online. Furthermore, as in the case of fresh food and fruit, customers also have access directly to foreign offerings through cross-border e-commerce. Therefore, established makers of consumer products who want to take advantage of online sales may have to develop more complex brand and product portfolios for the online market.

Secondly, in the context of mobile e-commerce, every brand is competing for the users' attention on the smartphone screen, where the advantage of big players who can dominate physical store shelves is neutralized. At the same time, the tech-savvy young generation is watching fewer broadcast television programs and TV advertisements are not holding their attention, which means that the marketing on mobile devices is becoming increasingly important. In order to respond, major brands may have to refocus their attention on digital marketing plans.

Thirdly, and probably the most challenging aspect of this change, is the fact that the e-retailing market favors

early movers. For brands that are latecomers to the online marketplaces, the sales figures of their products will most likely start small, so their search ranking at sites like Alibaba tend to be lower (as sales figures are an important parameter for ranking). This makes it harder for those products to be picked up by online customers, resulting in steady small sales volumes that are difficult to increase irrespective of the size of the brand behind the product. In other words, for companies that are slow to adopt online strategies, their move to mobile is an uphill battle.

Adding complexity to this revolution is the overall trend for integrating online and offline consumer activities and blurring the line separating the two. For example, JD.com is a direct sale e-commerce site, but it has also partnered with convenience stores to distribute fresh and frozen products. The customers may choose to pick up the products at the shops or have them delivered to their homes. In the same way as the options for products online are hugely varied and have expanded, the options for delivery are another game changer as the real estate price for physical stores has rocketed in China, while the fulfillment centers for online retailers could locate in cheaper areas. For delivery, there are armies of economical delivery teams who cover the streets in China with every possible transportation tool, including bicycles and electric scooters.

As a result, the traditional multinational retailers are fighting back by expanding both online and offline to develop multi-channel capabilities. In this context, they are rethinking the role of malls, the types and sizes of stores, the product categories they select to show online and the inventories they keep. It would be a mistake for online entrants to ignore the major groups' scale advantage (the strongest buying scale in many categories) and their first mover's advantage (holding prime shopping locations that will continue to draw customers).

Therefore, the traditional players' game plan is to turn their stores into distribution hubs, to leverage their brand trust to attract online shoppers, and to use their existing store networks to deliver multi-channel shopping experiences such as click-and-collect. In 2015, Unilever opened a store on JD.com's cross-border e-commerce platform, JD Worldwide, to create an online channel. Walmart's 2015 activities included renovating existing shops, a plan to increase the number of physical stores, and a new shopping app for smartphones. It remains to be seen which side will become the ultimate winner of the retail consumer market.

In summary, the mobile transformation has had profound implications for all companies doing business in the Chinese market. In this, China's digital boom, foreign investors are richly awarded, more consumer goods companies see new avenues to reach the expanding middle class, multinationals who have had an early presence in China are rethinking their strategies in this fast changing market, and Silicon Valley tech giants are taking notice of new competition arising from the East. No doubt, the global tech industry's competitive landscape itself will, in the future, be significantly altered by the emergence of the internet and tech companies in China.

In the last decade, the US tech firms such as Amazon and eBay were attracted to the Chinese market primarily due to its enormous size and therefore potential opportunity, but their early entries did not really take off due to language, regulatory and cultural barriers. Their focus remained on the US and other developed markets. Similarly, with the size and growth pace of China's mobile economy second to none in the world, a generation of homegrown companies in China like BAT chose domestic dominance as a priority over overseas expansion. But now, there are some sizable Chinese players analogous to their counterparts in the US in each sector and product category. Going forward, interestingly for both sides, the other side's home market is the most important market for continuing growth.

BAT and other Chinese firms are now expanding globally. At the same time, the internet companies in Silicon Valley like

Uber and Linkedin are focusing on China as the single largest market for growth after the US.

Uber's explosive growth in China may be the best performance by a US tech company in years. Inevitably, Uber and its local rivals in China (backed by Alibaba and Tencent, as one would have expected) are on a collision course in the world's largest car-hiring market (detailed discussion of this can be found in Chapter 10). In a new twist to their rivalry, their merger discussions took place in mid-2016 with Uber offering to sell its China operation to its major local rival Didi in order to create a cross-holding alliance. Of course, such a merger would first need to pass the Chinese government's often strict antitrust scrutiny.

Whereas the last decade saw Chinese and US innovators establishing themselves in two isolated home markets respectively, the competition between them is set to heat up. In addition, in order to fight more directly in each other's territory, the Chinese and US tech players are also beginning to compete with each other in other global markets, especially in emerging markets in South-East Asia and Africa. Very likely because the intrinsic nature of a mobile economy is interconnectedness, the Silicon Valley giants and China's internet firms are developing a delicate relationship of both competition and collaboration in many of the market sectors to be examined by this book.

3

Xiaomi: The Most Valuable Start-up in China

A few days before the end of 2014, Lei Jun, the founder and CEO of Xiaomi, the fast-rising Chinese smartphone maker, announced the receipt of $1.1 billion in investment funds following its latest round of fund-raising. Just months before, in the Summer of 2014, Xiaomi took the No. 1 position in China's smartphone market – the world's largest. That investment round valued Xiaomi at $45 billion, making it the highest valued start-up in the world at that time (close to Yahoo's market value), even ahead of $41 billion achieved by the US car-sharing service Uber Technologies Inc. earlier in the same month. (Uber's valuation exceeded Xiaomi later after additional fund-raising rounds.)

Consistent with Xiaomi's signature online-first marketing for its smartphones, the founder announced the investment terms in a post on his verified account on Weibo, China's Twitter-like messaging service. The mobile world, both in China and the West, immediately erupted into heated debate about whether this rising star could justify a $45 billion valuation. Was Xiaomi just an Apple copycat? Could it maintain its leadership position in the fast-maturing market of China when competing with domestic technology conglomerates as well as foreign behemoths like Samsung and Apple? Most importantly, how likely was it that Xiaomi would be able to apply its successful model for low cost smartphones into other product areas to create a new global internet powerhouse?

The Black Horse in a Crowded Market

Xiaomi, whose name means "millet" or literally "little rice" in Chinese, was founded as recently as 2010, yet has become the biggest success story in China's smartphone market. With about $40 million in initial financing, Mr. Lei teamed up with a former Microsoft and Google engineer, Lin Bin, and five other engineers to set up Xiaomi in a small office on the outskirts of Beijing. The company was originally a lean start-up looking to sell phones at cheap prices over the internet, and it also started a software platform named MIUI adapted from Google's Android system to power these phones.

In August 2011, Xiaomi introduced its first smartphone, the Mi-1, which meant that Xiaomi was decidedly late to the hardware game. (As a point of reference, Apple was releasing the iPhone 4S at the same time.) But Xiaomi never positioned itself as a premium device manufacturer. Instead, it insisted that it was an internet company; or if one had to associate the company with smartphones, it was a smartphone company with internet DNA. As discussed in detail later in this chapter, that positioning was reflected in its user base on social media as well as its online marketing strategy. Xiaomi's initial target demographic was young users, and the online buzz around its products attracted frenzied attention from young and trendy Chinese consumers.

In less than 5 years (by 2014), Xiaomi became the leading smartphone brand in China (although various market research firms in China occasionally publish conflicting ranking). From time to time Xiaomi was referred to as "the Apple of China" owing to the excitement it generated among Chinese consumers. Xiaomi's high growth and leadership position are not unchallenged. The iPhone6 release at the end of 2014 put Apple Inc. back into the top vendor position in China. More importantly, with help from its premium brand positioning,

Apple took the lion's share of the profits of the smartphone market in China.

In 2015, the battle among the smartphone brands became ultra-competitive as the domestic market started to show signs of maturity and slowing growth. During the second quarter of 2015, according to reports from two analyst firms, Xiaomi regained its crown as the top smartphone firm in China. Shortly after that, in the third quarter of 2015, Chinese technology giant Huawei Technologies Co seized the top place in smartphone sales, while Xiaomi's year-on-year shipments declined for the first time since 2010. As one would expect, doubts arose about whether the most valuable start-up was able to sustain its high growth in an increasingly cut-throat and maturing Chinese smartphone market.

Before the discussion on the current competition and challenges that Xiaomi is facing, it is helpful to first examine several factors that have made it the dark horse in the world's largest smartphone market:

First, the young Mi-fan base before its smartphone release. Before Xiaomi launched its first smartphone in August 2011, it had worked on its Android-based MIUI software platform for more than a year. The MIUI system had gathered more than 300,000 fans (who called themselves Mi-fans), who became the initial core consumers for Xiaomi smartphones. The phones suited young, college-educated consumers who wanted a smartphone but could not afford a premium brand. Despite their limited purchasing power, these young users were internet savvy and active in social networking, and their online interactions with the company and among themselves at the internet forums further strengthened the Mi-fan base.

Because of its existing fan base, Xiaomi's first smartphone, the Mi-1 sold out in two days, and its Mi-2 and subsequent products sold out in a similarly quick fashion. Each new model would initially be sold in a limited quantity (perhaps 50,000 units) through a flash sale on its website. The lucky ones who managed to get the phones would "shai" them at the Mi-fan forums, creating a pent-up demand for the product. One may argue that Xiaomi simply created artificial shortages to generate buzz through "hunger marketing", but in reality the loyalty of the fan base was more critical. Xiaomi's "hunger marketing" does not seem to be as effective as it has been in the past, which could be attributable to the fact that the offering is no longer novel or, possibly, to a permanent erosion of the fan base due to comparable offerings from the company's competitors.

Second, using low price strategy to grab market share quickly during the Chinese market's explosive growth. Smartphones are like personal computers (PCs) in China ten years ago. For many people in China, smartphones are a status symbol. People pay close attention to what kind of phone their circle of contacts is using, and even the people in the lower income buckets are eager to have a "presentable" a functional smartphone. Focusing on a niche passed up on by premium brands like Apple and Samsung, Xiaomi's low price, high performance devices have played well into the wider Chinese population's desire to own a smartphone and to access the internet for the first time.

Both Xiaomi's Mi (flagship) series products and Redmi series (budget) products are price-competitive devices. Its 2014 flagship model the Mi-4, whose hardware specifications were only slightly inferior to those of the iPhone 6, was sold at about $330 per unit, less than half of the latter's price, and the Redmi phone was sold at about a quarter of that of the iPhone's price. It is important to note that the telecom carrier environment in China has been a favorable factor for Xiaomi. The decline in the telecom carrier subsidy has pushed the majority of Chinese consumers to buy devices that are not associated with a carrier, creating room for entry for a new low-cost brand.

At the same time, Xiaomi has been generous in offering top-notch metal material, screen resolution, chip processor, camera and other features, in order to ensure that its low price is associated with a quality brand instead of a "cheap" product. The similarity of the design to that of the iPhone almost makes it an easy alternative to the Apple brand for many Chinese consumers. Furthermore, its online marketing strategy and the buzz in social media continue to create an attractive image linked to the young and chic lifestyle. With all that, Xiaomi has successfully created an inspirational brand for the consumers at the lower end of the spending power spectrum. As the domestic market begins to saturate and the incremental demand is generated from consumers looking for upgrades instead of their first ever smartphone, Xiaomi's products are moving towards consumers with higher spending power, and it is adjusting its brand identity accordingly.

It is worth noting that Xiaomi willingly accepts a lower profit margin on smartphone sales as part of the internet business model envisioned by the founder Mr. Lei Jun. In recent public interviews, Mr. Lei commented that on the Internet "the best products" – the products that the netizens use and enjoy the most, such as emails and most entertainment content – are all free. He believed that the quickest way for an internet company to attract users was through a flagship product that is offered free of charge, and this is the reason Xiaomi has been attracting and accumulating its users by selling its products as close to cost as is possible.

Of course, not all Xiaomi products and services will be provided at cost. Xiaomi's game plan is to use its high quality smartphone to build a loyal following at a large scale quickly (again, like Apple). Subsequently, a major revenue source will come from charging for services and accessories that accompany the phones. It also plans to generate revenue by providing proprietary software solutions for users' other needs on the internet, which is similar to the way Amazon released low-price Kindle tablets to motivate customers into buying more e-books and entertainment content. This is the reason Xiaomi's founder likes to call Xiaomi an "internet company" instead of a smartphone company. The smartphone is simply the platform grabbing market share, the profit is connected to it, but lies elsewhere.

Third, a low cost structure based on the internet. Unlike other domestic smartphone players such as Lenovo, Huawei and ZTE that sell a large volume of smartphones through telecom carriers, Xiaomi sells almost all of its phones by way of the e-commerce channel. From the very beginning, Xiaomi's logistic system resembled the "just in time" model from Dell PC computers. Because the phones are ordered and distributed online, Xiaomi has shortened the circulation period of consumer data significantly and thus developed a speedy and very efficient supply chain.

This online model ensures that Xiaomi does not have to worry about the costs for middlemen and distributors, because the e-commerce sales only involve fulfillment and shipping costs, which is also consistent with Xiaomi's vision to be an "internet company". It is worth noting that because online sales are less transparent, the industry ranking data compiled by the independent research firms are sometimes in conflict, and the corresponding ranking of the brands becomes uncertain and controversial as a result.

Following the same rationale, Xiaomi does not invest in traditional marketing. Instead it focuses on word-of-mouth advertising and social media channels, which are a lot less expensive than traditional advertising. Xiaomi management is also good at using creative strategies to generate buzz on social media to gain free publicity and potentially attract new customers. For example, after an executive meeting in late 2014, the company's co-founder and President Mr. Lin Bin proposed a push-up competition to his executive team. With a Xiaomi tablet on his back, Mr. Lin and other executives did push-ups until they all eventually collapsed from exhaustion. A photo of the competition was released and was broadly shared by the Mi-fans on the social media. This type of internet-based publicity is essentially free promotion for Xiaomi, and it also highlights Xiaomi's brand identity as a young, fun start-up. There is an important lesson here for innovators and entrepreneurs out there – the public face of the company can be a potential asset and a key part of a marketing strategy. Whether it is Steve Jobs or Lin Bin, consumers respond more strongly to a brand represented by a persona with whom they can connect on a personal level.

Fourth, the ongoing deep engagement with the fan base. Xiaomi intentionally and carefully develops, invests in and nurtures a fan community that drives purchases through lifestyle affinity. Thanks to social media, Xiaomi has more than 10 million fans that extend well beyond China's most developed coastal cities to lower-tier cities. These communities are well organized and share a common passion (even to the point of idolatry) for Xiaomi and its products. The company's online forum has hundreds of thousands of posts a day and many Mi-fans make new friends that way. Those who spend a massive number of hours on the Xiaomi forum may eventually become a "VIP" in the community and be invited to parties that are specifically set up for select fans. This has the effect of making membership and online activism all the more desirable.

One particularly important way in which Xiaomi has been able to strengthen user loyalty is by involving its fans and users in software updates. Xiaomi releases a new version of the operating system every Friday and it listens to the online suggestions on design and features from its Mi-fans. This "updates based on user feedback" approach is also applied to hardware testing. The suggestions from the fans once they are adopted are quickly reflected in the new versions, and the fans enjoy a long-lasting sense of participation, achievement and ownership.

Essentially, the core value of the brand lies in its customers' engagement. In a way Xiaomi is not selling a product, but the invitation to be a part of a virtual community. This is best illustrated by the many Mi-fan events and Mi Fan Festival organized by Xiaomi each year. At the fifth anniversary of its founding in April 2014, many new products were launched to celebrate the company's major milestone. What was remarkable was that in addition to more than 1 million handsets being bought by the fans on that single day, Xiaomi also sold hundreds of thousands of Mi Rabbits – Xiaomi's mascot, a stuffed toy bunny that wears a Chinese army hat. Nothing else demonstrated more strongly that the consumers in this instance went beyond simply buying a chic smartphone with a high performance-to-price ratio and were actually buying into the brand itself.

Changing Landscape, Fierce Competition

Although Xiaomi was the leading domestic smartphone brand in China in 2014 according to some research firms' statistics, currently its sales volume are neck and neck with Lenovo and Huawei, the two most important domestic competitors of Xiaomi. Since Apple and Samsung are the two undisputed market leaders, Lenovo, Huawei and Xiaomi are now competing directly for the No. 3 position in the global market. (The two domestic rivals and Apple's Chinese business will be discussed in detail later in this chapter.)

It's worth noting that just like Xiaomi (and many other smartphone producers in China), Lenovo and Huawei have also adopted the Android operating system for their smartphones. So, from an operating system perspective, Google's Android system wins by a landslide (over Apple's iOS system) in China and globally, boosted by faster growing Android-based handsets from the Chinese manufacturers. (Of course, as discussed later in this book, the profit share of the global smartphone market is a totally different story. In recent years, Apple's iPhones have steadily been the most profitable phone business in the world by a huge margin.)

As China's smartphone market continued to mature, it started to show early signs of saturation in 2015, according to a recent study by the industry research firm IDC. The IDC report put the smartphone shipments during the first quarter of 2015 at 98.8 million, down 4.3% from a year earlier, which was the first decrease in new orders in the past six years. Of course, China's smartphone market is still the largest in the world, with Chinese brands still comprising roughly 50% of smartphone shipments globally in 2015 (and a similar share expected for 2016), but its pace of expansion is slowing down.

Amid ever higher smartphone penetration, the Chinese consumers' tastes are shifting away from low end smartphones. Consequently, the domestic brands need to focus more on existing smartphone owners' potential device upgrade than on the first-time buyers, and the battle for winning market share from competitors or, preferably, retaining buyers who have a tendency to gravitate to the major brands when upgrading has never been more intense.

In response to this change in market conditions, Xiaomi has developed a full product line that covers low, middle and high end price categories, with the middle and high ends as its new focus. Despite its attempts to be nimble it is clear that Xiaomi is facing fierce competition from both domestic and foreign rivals in every category. In the low price category, brands like Meizu and LeTV that people outside of China may never have heard of are using the same strategies as Xiaomi, selling their price competitive phones online throughout the country. Because their phones are even more competitively priced than Xiaomi's phones, these lower-tier manufacturers, if successful in attracting market share, may take a significant part of the lower end market share away from Xiaomi.

In the high end category, there is no easy way for Xiaomi to win the battle with the formidable Apple brand and its ultra-desirable premium products. As a result, Xiaomi has had to focus on the mid-price products category, which is crowded with domestic players like Lenovo and Huawei as well as the strong foreign rival Samsung. (The case of Samsung's early success and current struggle in the Chinese market is discussed in a different context in this book.) All are competing, at the cost of lower profit margins, to attract Chinese consumers who want to upgrade to phones with premium features. Apple, Xiaomi and Huawei were respectively at the top of the market share ranking in the first, second and third quarters of 2015, according to the statistics by the research firm Canalys.

Lenovo

Lenovo Group Ltd, formerly known as Legend, was founded in 1984 in Beijing. After more than 30 years, it has grown into a tech manufacturing conglomerate producing PCs, tablets, notebooks, servers and a wide range of devices. Lenovo now has three major business lines in traditional PC manufacturing, enterprise solutions and smartphones. Since 2013, Lenovo has surpassed Hewlett-Packard and Dell to become the world's largest personal computer (PC) maker by volume, but it has also made significant investments in the smartphone sector to balance the decline in global PC sales.

Compared to Xiaomi whose business is centered on smartphones, Lenovo's multiple major business lines are likely to be an advantage in the low margin competition in China's smartphone market. However, when Xiaomi reached the $45 billion valuation at the end of 2014, that number was roughly three times the market capitalization of Lenovo. That was an interesting phenomenon, as the net profit of Xiaomi in 2014 was most likely only a fraction of Lenovo's (due to the low price margin in Xiaomi's core business in smartphones), even though accurate numbers were not readily available as Xiaomi has remained a private company.

Part of Xiaomi's high valuation definitely came from the market's optimistic expectation of the growth of smartphone penetration and the potential high profitability from the add-on products and services that it offered. Lenovo's leadership, however, have expressed their view publicly that the smartphone market will soon become saturated, just like the personal computer (PC) market had been previously. Using the PC market as a reference, Lenovo expects the Chinese smartphone market to become less crowded in the near future as some weaker players have to drop out as a result of the cut-throat competition. With its experience in the earlier price wars for personal computers, and its multiple product streams, Lenovo is set to be a formidable rival of Xiaomi in the price war of smartphones.

Lenovo also provides "trendy" smartphone offerings to compete with rivals like Xiaomi. While Lenovo traditionally sells its phones through carriers, it has also expanded into the non-carrier retail market, as well as online sales through social media. For example, in 2015 it launched a sub-brand ShenQi ("Magic" in English) that was offered exclusively online to attract the young netizens. Also, after its acquisition of Motorola Mobility in 2014 from Google for \$2.9 billion, Lenovo relaunched Motorola in China with a festival event modelled on Xiaomi events. Fans of Motorola were flown in from different parts of the country to appear on the center stage, with interactive social media feeds on the big screen.

The Motorola acquisition adds a new dimension to Lenovo's smartphone strategy in China. Motorola was a pioneer in mobile phones and a household brand in China many years ago, and it dominated the Chinese market before any real Chinese domestic brand ever surfaced. But it collapsed under the pressure of disruptive technologies and changing consumer behavior. After the merger, Lenovo decided to market both brands in the Chinese market, apparently hoping that its foreign-flavored brand could gain some advantage in the competition for the middle to high end market. Unfortunately, most young Chinese consumers do not remember the earlier glory days of the Motorola brand in China. (Motorola having departed from the Chinese market years ago.) As discussed in later chapters, the Motorola brand may end up helping Lenovo in its attempts at overseas market expansion rather than in the domestic market.

Huawei

Huawei was established 1987 in Shenzhen, the tech innovation and manufacturing hub in Southern China. During the last decade or so, Huawei has grown out of the domestic market to become one of the most competitive and dominant players in the global telecommunications markets. It is best known as the leading telecommunications equipment company in the world. It is also a major multinational networking services provider globally, with footprints in most of the world. Just like Lenovo, the profit from Huawei's smartphone business represents only a fraction of its networking business.

There are two possible reasons for Huawei joining the highly competitive smartphone field. One reason is that the telecom equipment market, just like the PC market for Lenovo, is growing increasingly saturated and is expecting slow growth, so the smartphone market is a potential high growth area for the company. The other reason is probably more important: Huawei has long predicted the convergence of the telecoms and IT businesses, and its leadership seems to believe that this convergence is happening with the emergence of smartphones, wearable devices and the internet of things.

Although in the middle of a pricing war, all the middle-market Chinese brands (which includes almost everyone, since Apple is the unquestionable top premium brand) are aiming to move into the premium brand category. Instead of seeking bigger sales volumes, Huawei's strategy has focused on heavy investment in R&D to offer superior technological features permitting them to charge a premium price. Huawei is justifiably proud of its extensive investment in R&D as well as its mobile network equipment background is also an advantage. Huawei is also a global leader in fixed broadband and mobile broadband technology, which translates into expertise in making phones that could work best with the latest network technology.

Recognizing the advantages of Xiaomi's online marketing approach, Huawei succeeded in increasing the ratio of sales through retailers and e-commerce sites to 80% and reduced sales through telecom operators to 20% by 2014. Interestingly, although Richard Yu, the head of its consumer business group and a Huawei group Executive VP, publicly acknowledged that Huawei's marketing model transformation came from Xiaomi's business practice, he nevertheless publicly insisted that "Xiaomi was never a competitor of Huawei".

Indeed, Huawei has seen encouraging success in the mid to high-end category, and its Mate7 phone has been one of only a few domestic brands whose price tag has reached $650. The premium comes primarily from unique technological features (for example, Mate7 phones could work with removable hard disks). Meanwhile, Huawei's low-price brand Honor has also proved popular, creating a real challenge to Xiaomi in that lower end market. Richard Yu of Huawei said in a recent public interview that "at most, Xiaomi is a competitor to Huawei's Honor brand (the budget phone model)".

During the 2015 Chinese New Year season, Richard Yu posted a public comment on Weibo (the Chinese version of Twitter), sending a "friendly reminder" to a "Diao-si brand" that its plan to move up to become a "Gao-Da-Shang" brand may not work out easily without unique core capabilities. Richard Yu's post didn't specifically mention the name of the target of his comments, but people naturally concluded that Xiaomi was the "Diao-si brand" he was addressing, because his comment highlighted the brand's fan base and good price-to-performance ratio. **(See the "Diao-si" box.)** In addition, Mr. Yu warned that Xiaomi might lose its original "diao-si" consumer base when it tried to move into a premium brand.

That Weibo post was deleted after only seven minutes online, but still stirred up angry remarks from the Mi-fans. Irrespective of the intended meaning of his post, Richard Yu made his point: Xiaomi could have a difficult time in repositioning its brand in the changing market. It needs to either seek high sales volumes at a low profit margin (like the PC market that Lenovo has dominated), or find a way to transform itself into a premium brand which either offers distinctive features (as with Huawei's success in its Mate series), or is an aspirational product that once again unites its fans.

"Diao-si" (grassroots) vs "Gao-Da-Shang" (high society)

The term "diao-si" involves a vulgar reference to the male genitalia, and it became a popular term in the Internet era as a synonym for "loser". It was originally a term for the young men who lived on the margins of an otherwise booming economy. They were in the workforce after a basic school education, but were paid so poorly that they could not even afford to contemplate a relationship. Nowadays the term is broadly applied, sometimes self-mockingly, to any people who work in entry-level positions, have not purchased a home, or have little in terms of personal assets.

Overall, the term is no longer derogatory; instead it is more of a reference to the purchasing power of a specific demographic. In 2014, Peking University's Market and Media Research Center released a national report on the "Living Conditions of Diao-si." Using a collection of over 200,000 questionnaire responses from people in 50 large, medium and small cities, the study calculated the average monthly salary to be about RMB2919.7 (approximately $480). To put this in context, this average one month salary of a diao-si youth in China is less than the price of a premium brand smartphone. Consequently, a diao-si brand smartphone has to be offered at a low price to be attractive to its target market.

In contrast with diao-si, "gao-da-shang" is an internet buzz word linked to the high society and the luxury lifestyle. The term is a combination of three words, including "gao duan" (high end), "da qi" (elegant or regal) and "shang dangci" (high grade). It is often used to flatter, with a touch of humor and sometimes sarcasm, and to describe a luxury product or upscale lifestyle. Chinese smartphone brands have to offer a wide range of products to cater to the different purchasing powers of "diao-si" and "gao-da-shang" consumers.

Because Xiaomi's brand identity was previously linked with high quality and low price, the risk it faces is that some Xiaomi users may use Xiaomi phones as a transition product before they can upgrade to a luxury brand smartphone. When those customers have a greater surplus of purchasing power, they may not remain loyal to Xiaomi. Xiaomi's branding must therefore evolve with its consumer base's growing purchasing power, because deep in the hearts of many diao-si, they aspire to join the gao-da-shang class someday.

Apple

Examining the Xiaomi phone's overall design, one will quickly notice that its device contours and display style show a remarkable degree of similarity to Apple's iPhones. From time to time the company has been criticized for borrowing so extensively from Apple and other rivals (such as Samsung). It is unclear whether it would have been possible for a company such as Xiaomi to offer a product such as this if intellectual property protection was more robust in China, but this is an issue for Xiaomi (and its rivals) and the courts. This book is simply noting the existing situation. Some critics suggest that Xiaomi has simply taken advantage of Apple's high-end brand identity in China: many Chinese consumers have idolized the Apple brand, and Xiaomi provides a similar product at a much lower price point so that customers are effectively buying a product that is viewed as an "affordable iPhone". Given the opportunity and greater earnings, those same consumers will happily leave Xiaomi behind.

Traces of imitation of Apple can also be found in Xiaomi's management team, who do not hide their attempts to emulate closely Apple and its late founder Steve Jobs. When Xiaomi releases new products, founder Lei Jun typically comes to the stage in a black T-shirt and Converse shoes, similar to Mr. Jobs's signature outfit. In recent Xiaomi events, founder Lei Jun has also started to use the line "One more thing…" at the end of the presentation, which was the line that Jobs famously used for a surprise announcement of new innovations at Apple's product introduction events.

There is one notable difference however. Xiaomi phones are more "accessible" than the iPhones. Xiaomi takes a more open and dynamic approach to its software updates than Apple's iOS. Xiaomi invites "fans" on its forum to suggest new features, and it sends updates to users every Friday. Soon after each new version's release, thousands of Mi-fans on the internet forums quickly provide feedback to the company on functions, designs, bugs and potential solutions.

In contrast, Apple handles system development internally – Steve Jobs once famously said "customers do not know what they want", and the customers receive iOS upgrades much less frequently in bundled form. Apple's system design is opaquely controlled by the company itself; therefore no matter who the customer is, there is only one set of standard solutions. Whereas Xiaomi develops a strong fan group based on engagement and community engagement, Apple accumulates its fan group based on exclusivity and a community centered on the cult of design and usability.

Apple opened its first store in China in 2008 and began selling the iPhone in the country in 2009. From the very beginning, Apple made the decision to maintain the iPhones' high prices, making Apple a luxury brand in China. When the iPhone 5 series was introduced to China in 2013, its golden version quickly became a status symbol in China's high society. **(See the "Tu-hao-jin iPhone 5s" box.)** In 2015, Apple ranked as China's most coveted luxury brand, according to the Hurun Research Institute's annual survey of 376 ultra-wealthy individuals (whose average net worth exceeded $6.8 million). The survey found that Apple overtook traditional luxury brands including Hermes (2014 top ranking), Louis Vuitton, Cartier, as well as its immediate competitor Samsung as the "best" gifting brand of choice for China's wealthiest individuals.

Tu-hao-jin iPhone 5s: Gatsby's golden phone?

In China, the golden color symbolizes wealth. When Apple introduced the iPhone 5s in China in 2013, they were offered in three colors – gold, silver and black. Among them, the gold-colored version was the runaway winner for Apple. It was sold out almost instantly online, and the gold-colored phone quickly became a status symbol in China. Soon a new term was created on the Internet known as "tu-hao-jin", meaning the gold ("jin") of "Tu-hao".

Tu-hao is not a new term. The word is the combination of the character "tu" (meaning dirt in English) and the character "hao" (meaning despot), and in traditional Chinese it was understood to mean "local tyrant". In the modern society setting, the "tu" character is more of a synonym for unrefined or uneducated, and "hao" picks up a new tone from the Chinese phrase "fu-hao", which means rich and powerful. Thus, Tu-hao is analogous to the phrase "nouveau riche" that still has some currency in the West. It tends to denote an individual who has recently acquired wealth and who is perceived to be ostentatious and/or vulgar.

Tu-hao-jin is one of many words repurposed by Chinese internet users to mock the nouveau riche in China, who tend to spend newfound wealth lavishly on tasteless goods. To some extent, the term (and a few similar ones) also offers a way for ordinary people to vent their anger about the widening wealth gap. The term "tu-hao-jin" quickly went beyond the reference to Apple's iPhones, and it was used to describe all luxury goods and settings with the similar color, including gold-plated sports cars, extravagant decoration of apartments and the golden exterior of office towers.

After the Hollywood movie *The Great Gatsby* hit the movie theaters in China at the end of August 2013, Chinese filmgoers readily attached the "tu-hao" label to Leonardo DiCaprio's Jay Gatsby role. The Gatsby story reflected the American dream in the 1920s, and the lavish poolside parties and excesses of the period. Many commentators on social media commented that if Gatsby was to live in China today, most likely he would have picked up a tu-hao-jin iPhone for himself as well. It is the author's view that the term would better be applied to another of Di Caprio's characters connected to Wall Street.

However, in all the years before the iPhone 6 release at the end of 2014, Apple's highest ranking in China's smartphone market was fourth place in the first quarter of 2014, according to data from research firm Canalys. At the end of 2014, the strong demand for the iPhone 6 and iPhone 6 Plus helped Apple to win the No. 1 market share spot in China for the first time, and this sales momentum carried on into the first quarter of 2015.

There were several reasons for this iPhone 6-led jump in market share for Apple. The most obvious one is the increase in purchasing power of the middle class during the past several years. As the average monthly salary and disposable income continue to increase in China's major cities, Apple's target market keeps expanding. Second, and perhaps more important given the sudden nature of this shift, in December 2013, Apple was able to strike a partnership deal with China Mobile, the largest telecom network operator in China, to sell the new series of iPhone.

The third key factor, however, was Apple's response to its customers' requests to increase the screen size on the iPhones. For the young demographic, and other active Chinese users, the smartphone is the device used most frequently for entertainment and e-commerce (instead of, and not in addition to, laptops or PC computers). The screen of the earlier versions of iPhones was too small for comfortable video viewing or efficient mobile payment transactions. Also, the small screen made inputting text more difficult because current Chinese character input methods still require users' paying very close attention to the character keyboard displayed on the screen. The iPhone 6 series gained from the pent-up demand for such a product in 2014, particularly from the middle income group who liked the iPhone as a status symbol, but had picked up an Android phone earlier because of the latter's bigger screen.

As opposed to typical Western companies that would team up with a local partner to offer localized products, Apple played to its global core strengths and advantages, betting on the same premium brand strategy in China. So far, the successful sales of the iPhone 6 series have proved the strategy to be a success. By focusing on the mid- to high-end consumer demographic as the exclusive target for Apple apps and services, Apple has been able to maintain the high price of the iPhone and protect the integrity, as well as premium value, of its brand. This case offers an interesting reference point for other brands in China: in this booming market, should a brand go with a low price and mass distribution, or keep a premium brand and specifically target the purchasing power of the rapidly expanding upper middle class? The Apple case in China illustrates that the latter strategy could also lead to enviable market positioning and strong profits.

Of course, it remains to be seen whether Apple will be able to hold on to its top position after the wave of pent-up demand for the larger-screened iPhones. Using the gray market during the release of the iPhone 6 series as a reference point, the Apple phones' scarcity premium seems to be on the decline. During the last few years, scalpers in Hong Kong rushed to purchase the new devices at almost every new Apple phone release and quickly flipped them to smugglers to generate a profit. The scalpers mobilized Hong Kong residents with local identity cards to pre-order phones before they collected them to transport across the border. But in the case of the iPhone 6 and the iPhone Plus, the gray market had mostly dried up.

The reason for this was not difficult to discern: the iPhone today is just one option among many for Chinese customers. Local players like Xiaomi, Huawei and Lenovo are offering high quality phones at lower prices, while also competing with

Apple's "coolness" factor. The local brands are also more sensitive to the local users' needs, offering Chinese-oriented features such as large screen sizes, optimized connectivity for Chinese networks and dual SIM cards. In fact, Xiaomi and Huawei took the No. 1 market share position from Apple in the second and third quarters of 2015. And their ability to compete will likely improve going forward. As Xiaomi and other Chinese brands expand rapidly into the global markets, the battle is very likely to extend into the global marketplace.

Beyond Smartphones: The Future of Xiaomi

Because it is a private company, Xiaomi does not disclose its net income and profitability, but the news media have nevertheless reported on its estimated financial position. Just like Alibaba and other US-listed Chinese internet companies, Xiaomi's corporate structure includes a mix of domestic and offshore entities. At the top of the group structure is Xiaomi Corp., a Cayman Islands incorporated entity. Xiaomi H.K. Ltd., an offshore entity that is wholly owned by Xiaomi Corp., is believed to be the unit of Xiaomi that directly or indirectly controls the company's domestic units. When Xiaomi closed its latest fundraising round that valued the company at \$45 billion, some media entities that had gained access to some of Xiaomi's internal documents reported that that Xiaomi H.K. Ltd. had a profit margin of 13% and net profit of \$566 million in 2014.

Those margin and profit numbers appear to be consistent with Xiaomi's "selling close to the manufacturing cost" strategy. On the one hand, Xiaomi chooses to sell cheaply priced phones to capture a large number of users for Xiaomi's mobile e-commerce businesses quickly before monetizing this community of users at the next stage. On the other hand, the fierce competition in the Chinese market has led to a price war among the smartphone brands based on the Android system, forcing everyone to use a low price as a key differentiating factor. Xiaomi has had to accept a thin profit margin for its smartphone business, as have its competitors.

According to a research report by the investment bank Merrill Lynch Securities on the state of the global smartphone industry in 2014, Xiaomi, Huawei and Lenovo were barely profitable, and the gross margin for each smartphone business was estimated to be at a single digit percentage level. Now that the Chinese market is showing signs of saturation, their profit margins will most likely be squeezed further going forward. Thus some people argue that Xiaomi is in a weaker position than Huawei and Lenovo in this war of attrition, because the latter two have additional business lines that are well established and profitable, whereas Xiaomi's revenue is mostly tied to its smartphones.

Insisting that it is an "internet company" instead of a smartphone company, Xiaomi explains that it focuses more on the internet software and services it sells to its loyal user base. Whereas most mobile phone brands see a sale as the end of the relationship, the company sees it as the beginning. Xiaomi's software and services are supported by its proprietary MIUI system, and Xiaomi is confident that the higher profit margin on them will more than compensate for the low profit margins on the phones.

However, one need only look at Apple – which Xiaomi strives to emulate – to find that this strategy, while effective, may need some time to generate profits. Unlike other smartphone manufacturers who use the open platform Android operating system, Apple uses its proprietary operating system and keeps this entirely under its own control. There is no question that Apple has developed an enormous user base for its product family of iPhone, iMac, iPad and iWatch. But when it comes to Apple's operating income and net profit, it is the iPhone sales that have consistently contributed the lion's share, while the income from software and services is only a small fraction of the total. According to some news reports in late 2014 that quoted Xiaomi's management, Xiaomi's hardware division contributed 94% to its total income.

Connected to the "user" strategy, an even bigger issue is the bifurcation between the smartphone hardware and mobile apps. Xiaomi does not fully "own" its phone users for internet services and transactions, because the Xiaomi device may simply be a medium for the users to access the mobile commerce platforms of other internet entities.

For example, using their Xiaomi phones, Chinese netizens may find the latest online gaming recommendations from their virtual network of friends through Tencent's WeChat, or make online purchases through Alibaba's mobile marketplace Taobao, or search for nearby restaurants' locations and booking information using Baidu's search engine. Furthermore, each of these mobile platforms includes almost all e-commerce services, and the user could accomplish much without ever leaving the app ecosystem. Since the apps, as well as users, are "phone agnostic" for online activities, they may choose to ignore Xiaomi's own ecosystem of internet services as they continue to engage with the virtual world through their favorite apps. In other words, the activities (or "contexts") supported by the dominant e-commerce players may be a more important gateway for users' activities than those offered by the smartphone manufacturer itself, irrespective of how well entrenched its hardware is with its end users.

Xiaomi has fought back by creating an interface called Xiaomi Yellow Page which links the providers of local services to end users and vice versa (see Figure 3.1). The users of Yellow Page do not have to pre-install apps that they do not use frequently, such as those for express delivery tracking and train ticket ordering. To some extent, the Yellow Page helps Xiaomi to keep users of internet services at its own platform. However,

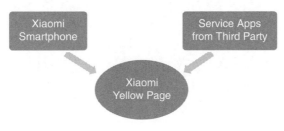

Figure 3.1   Xiaomi Yellow Page

the Xiaomi Yellow Page is more of an app consolidation than an innovative platform in its own right. So its "stickiness" – the ability to attract users, capture their attention and keep them coming back – remains questionable. As in the case of the killer apps from BAT, the users will surely install their favorite apps directly if they visit them frequently.

At the end of the day, the high valuation of Xiaomi by the market is a forward bet and is mostly linked to Xiaomi's future, which in founder Lei Jun's own words is "software + hardware + internet". He considers the mobile phone to be a converged system of software, internet services and hardware, instead of a simple device for communication; he also believes Xiaomi could apply the same "internet thinking" to many other smart devices. The future of Xiaomi is to become an important player in the "internet of things", and the "smart home" is among the company's top development and growth priorities.

Essentially, Xiaomi has evolved into a company of three layers of product offerings (see Figure 3.2). At Xiaomi's core are its well-established products of smartphones, TV set-top boxes and routers. The immediate next level is the internet services

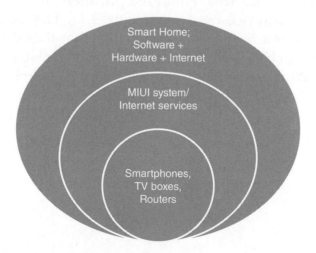

Figure 3.2   The Future – Three Layers of Xiaomi

based on Xiaomi's MIUI system that supports the hardware products. According to the company's data, the MIUI system supported 27 languages and had 85 million users at the end of 2014. (In comparison, the main apps from the internet giants BAT already had hundreds of millions of active users.)

A third level aims to develop a family of smart home devices that are seamlessly cross-linked under the Xiaomi "ecosystem". For a start, the company has jumped into consumer electronics like cameras and even home appliances like air purifiers. In 2015 alone, Xiaomi spent nearly $1 billion on acquisitions and investments in 39 companies offering a wide variety of products. In a recent public announcement, Xiaomi indicated that it plans to invest $5 billion into 100 smart device companies to further augment its system.

This "software + hardware + internet" strategy, however, is not without its own challenges:

First, many internet firms are also working on integrating software and hardware businesses. While Xiaomi builds an internet company from smartphone hardware origins, other major internet companies are expanding into the hardware business from their existing core strength in mobile e-commerce. Just as the MIUI system and its app store are pre-installed on Xiaomi's own phones, the e-commerce players are investing in smart hardware so that they can fully shape their own users' mobile experience, starting with the mobile terminal or access point. The best example is the e-commerce giant Alibaba, which has not shied away from investing directly in smartphone manufacturing.

In January 2016, in a move that surprised the market, Alibaba bought a minority stake in Chinese handset maker Meizu Technology Co., whose earlier version of the MX4 smartphone runs the YunOS system from Alibaba. The cloud-based mobile operating system YunOS ("yun" is the Chinese character for "cloud") was developed by Alibaba in 2011, but only had limited success in attracting users. (Right before the investment into Meizu, according to some news reports it had just collected 10 million users, a tiny proportion of the gigantic Chinese

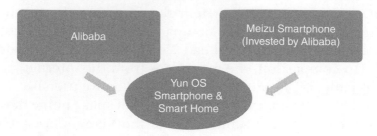

Figure 3.3   YunOS Smart Home

market.) Compared to Xiaomi, Lenovo and Huawei Technologies, Meizu has a tiny market share in China. At the time of the Alibaba investment, Meizu's 2015 smartphone shipment target was about 20 million units, whereas the three top players were targeting 100 million units of annual sales. It remains to be seen whether the backing of Alibaba, and access to its funding, will provide a strong boost to the market share of Meizu phones in China.

The more interesting consequence of the deal, however, is that the two companies are collaborating to further develop Alibaba's existing YunOS system in the context of a "smart home" (see Figure 3.3). When this is considered, Alibaba's investment in smartphone hardware is not that surprising: since the major smartphone brands are not likely to give up their autonomy in terms of design and marketing, Meizu was probably the only available smart hardware partner for Alibaba. Just like Xiaomi, Alibaba is working on various smart hardware products, and the YunOS system opens the way to partnering with manufacturers.

For example, in mid-2015, Alibaba teamed up with the Chinese film company DMG Entertainment and the Hunan Satellite TV station to offer smart set-top boxes and bundled content to cable TV subscribers. For the first time, subscription-based internet, cable and mobile entertainment content was all offered as part of a bundle, similar to those offered in the US. The service reportedly began with six million cable TV subscribers in Hunan province, and it was expected to expand

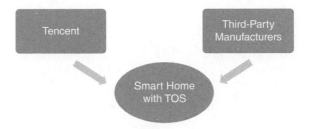

Figure 3.4   TOS Smart Home

across China. The bundled content service and set-top box have included Alibaba's YunOS operating system, which may gain wider adoption as Alibaba continues to link smart devices with its strength in entertainment content and e-commerce.

Tencent has a customized version of the Android operating system called Tencent OS, which has also expanded into the fields of internet-connected smart hardware such as TVs and fitness bands. In a model similar to Google's Android OS, Tencent seems content to be a pure software player that offers its system as an open platform for device manufacturers (see Figure 3.4). It is worth noting that as the phone market profit margin has been driven to a minimum on the hardware side, some phone makers may choose to form an alliance with Tencent, akin to Meizu teaming up with Alibaba.

Second, Xiaomi is a late entrant to the internet content competition. In particular, entertainment content is being viewed by all internet firms as strategically important to attracting internet users to the mobile world, because the main theme of China's internet is entertainment. On the one hand, the entertainment business can be an important line of revenue growth by itself. On the other hand, when the e-commerce sector for consumer goods becomes increasingly saturated, unique content can effectively serve as a distinguishing factor to draw users to a particular e-commerce ecosystem, keep them hooked, and potentially lead them to related mobile transactions. (In later chapters, the explosive growth of the entertainment businesses on mobile platforms will be discussed in detail. All the

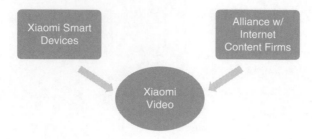

Figure 3.5   Xiaomi's Content Alliance

major internet firms have invested aggressively to build an expansive content set, as well as platforms, that integrate online and offline entertainment businesses.)

The content business is drastically different from Xiaomi's origins in hardware manufacture and distribution, and Xiaomi has responded by providing a unique set of offerings. In parallel with Xiaomi Yellow Page that integrates service apps, Xiaomi has set up a loose alliance with almost all the major video streaming companies to share their content within its own aggregating system (see Figure 3.5). In this new platform called Xiaomi Video, the users can easily access content from its alliance partners without having to install their respective interface content from Youku Tudou, Tencent Video and iQIYI as it is all available via a single interface. As Xiaomi's founder Lei Jun stated, Xiaomi "offers twice as much content as its competitors without charging customers their annual fees". Of course, the content offered is also freely available on those platforms, which retain control of their unique content, hidden behind subscription walls. The benefit to them is the ability to market directly to Xiaomi users.

The the only major internet content company that is not part of the Xiaomi alliance, LeTV, is Xiaomi's most direct competitor because it offers its own "smartphone + content" ecosystem. Originally a video streaming company that has been compared to Netflix, LeTV has expanded its hardware business into smart TV-boxes, and then smart TVs, and more recently smartphones. Its new product, Superphone, is being promoted as a new kind of smartphone that gives access to a collection of exclusive content. If the customer also uses a smart TV from LeTV's product family, the user can use the phone as a remote control.

LeTV's offering is content-centric, and delivers premium content across different devices within its own software ecosystem. From LeTV's perspective, a content alliance is unlikely to provide users with high quality content, because no alliance member will contribute their unique content for free in this loose partnership with Xiaomi. On offer on Xiaomi Video is content that is freely available and could be watched without a subscription to their platform.

LeTV employs a subscription fee model based on exclusive content (and it is worth noting that this annual fee could be applied to offset the LeTV phone cost). Because it has substantial lead time in the content area, LeTV has developed a rich content library and has its own production team. By offering internally-produced content as part of its subscription package LeTV believes that it can offer users a much better "experience" than would be available as part of Xiaomi's alliance. For example, in 2015 LeTV announced a new partnership with NASDAQ-listed Immersion Corp. to provide viewers with four-dimensional (4D) videos on their smartphones. When watching 4D videos on smartphones, viewers could experience special effects like bomb explosions, car races and the wind blowing by interacting physically with their mobile phone.

These two different approaches to internet content led to a war of words between Xiaomi and LeTV in mid-2015. In practice, however, Xiaomi has quietly stepped up its efforts in acquiring and controlling unique content, as have the internet giants Alibaba, Tencent and Baidu. (As will be seen in the later chapters on the mobile entertainment business, the production of unique content has proven to be extremely costly for the internet firms, but the fee-paying model is gaining momentum in China where viewers have been used to free content.) Xiaomi has not only invested significant capital into several major online video sites, but also plans to set up its own content production capabilities.

One of the biggest investments ever made by Xiaomi, was ploughing $300 million into the Baidu-backed online video portal iQIYI. iQIYI is one of the largest online video sites in China, and it also has a division called iQIYI Motion Pictures, which, among other things, co-produces movies in collaboration with foreign partners. This investment should give Xiaomi important access to high quality content to further supplement its video streaming capabilities. At the beginning of 2016, Xiaomi also announced that it is building up a new unit to be named Xiaomi Movies for the film business. Because the content business is drastically different from Xiaomi's core competence, it remains to be seen whether its efforts in this direction will be successful and whether it can catch up with the competition.

Finally, when Xiaomi expands into overseas markets and much broader products offerings, it will be increasingly difficult for the company to maintain its existing business model. The $45 billion question is whether Xiaomi can replicate its smartphone success in other smart devices and integrate them seamlessly into its mobile ecosystem.

To a large extent, Xiaomi's success in China's smartphone market has much to do with Chinese users' particular preferences and unique market dynamics. There is no guarantee that the model can be replicated elsewhere. For the Xiaomi model to work, the target market may need to have a large population, a developed e-commerce culture and weak telecom service providers. All these factors are important for Xiaomi's low-cost business model. For example, in a developed market like the US, the subsidies from telecom carriers could easily neutralize Xiaomi phones' price advantage. In another example (to be discussed in detail later in this book), Xiaomi's internet distribution model could not work well in some parts of the Indian market due to the lack of internet infrastructure.

As a young start-up company, Xiaomi is also constrained by the relative absence of existing resources when expanding abroad. For example, Xiaomi does not have much in the way of a patent portfolio, so when it expands to the US or Europe, it may not have access to a sufficient number of patents to strike cross-licensing deals with other smartphone manufacturers, making the company vulnerable to lawsuits from competitors as it tries to innovate to match the features their products offer. Will that make access to overseas markets prohibitive, or simply mean Xiaomi's advantage will be a little less pronounced (because it has to pay for the use of others' patents for example)? The answer will only become clear as Xiaomi engages with markets outside of China.

Xiaomi spreads itself thin as it expands into such a large variety of "smart home" devices. The value proposition represented by Xiaomi's smartphone, means that the brand is linked to high quality in the minds of consumers. As Xiaomi launches a variety of new product categories, however, quality control could become an issue. Also, as the variety of devices expands it becomes increasingly difficult for Xiaomi to maintain its close contact with its users, something that it depends on for both innovation in terms of features, as well as ability to maintain an engaged community of users around the device. The Mi-fan culture has been instrumental to the success of the Xiaomi smartphone – in fact, Xiaomi had developed its Mi-fan base from its MIUI system before its very first smartphone release. With three layers of Xiaomi businesses, the company now has a much larger consumer base than before. But as a result, customers who are further away from the core business may have difficulty thinking of the company in a manner similar to the loyal fans that launched it on the path to success. It could be argued that it is these challenges that go to the heart of Xiaomi's brand identity, core culture and business model that may be the most critical to the company's future.

Despite all these challenges, Xiaomi's grounding in hardware and its successful smartphone business may prove invaluable in the smart device competition. Because its core business in smartphones has focused on competitive pricing, Xiaomi has developed extensive knowhow in supply chain management. As a result, it is likely that it can also do better in controlling costs of other smart devices than its content and platform focused competitors. Because internet firms like Alibaba and Tencent do not have hardware DNA, they will have to work out the complex supply chain issues or acquire hardware know-how by acquiring or partnering with device manufacturers.

In summary, the $45 billion start-up story of Xiaomi has yielded both resounding adulation by fans as well as harsh criticism by sceptics. Founder Lei Jun used to say that Xiaomi looks a bit like Apple, but it is really more like Amazon with some elements of Google. So far, Xiaomi has succeeded beyond even its wildest expectations, but citing a lack of core technological innovations and patents, some people are questioning the sustainability of its projected future growth. One thing is clear, in order for Xiaomi to become the "internet company" that its founders envision, a considerable amount of work needs to be done.

4

The Omni-Channel Age of e-Retailing

"JD.com will become a tragedy. I have warned everyone of JD.com's model from the very first day."

This statement was apparently part of a private conversation between Jack Ma, the founder and chairman of Alibaba, and his personal friend. In the private conversation Jack Ma criticized the business model of its e-commerce archrival JD.com, but without his knowledge, his friend incorporated it into a new book. Thus, Mr. Ma's colorful commentary became public knowledge in early 2015, creating a drama for billions of Chinese people during the New Year's holiday season.

At the core of Mr. Ma's comment was the sustainability of JD.com's business model. "It's not that we are better," he said, "It's an issue of direction." Similar to Amazon, JD.com holds inventories at its own warehouses and arranges deliveries from its own distribution network. Jack Ma reasoned that such a model would eventually become prohibitively expensive, because JD.com "may need to hire 1 million people" when "daily e-retailing packages reach 300 million in 10 years". Hence his advice: "Never ever touch JD.com."

Alibaba's Jack Ma did apologize for calling JD.com a tragedy shortly after the post went viral on China's social media, saying that it would be both ignorant and a real tragedy if there could only be one right e-commerce model for China's internet market. JD.com accepted the apology, but in its reply it highlighted its own model's core value by stating: "we continue to focus on providing China's best online retail experience".

Because JD.com's mascot is a dog, while Alibaba's marketplace, Tmall, has a cat symbol, their direct competition has been called a cat-and-dog war. They are the top two leading e-commerce players in China, both listed on the US market and both achieved remarkable valuations in 2014, yet they represent two different business models.

Alibaba operates the largest marketplaces for e-commerce, while JD.com is the largest online retailer in China. Alibaba is more like a combination of eBay and PayPal, and its marketplace serves as a platform to connect buyers and sellers, and provides services like online payments. JD.com, however, is more like Amazon which deals with inventory, sales and distribution directly. Alibaba dominates transaction volume in the market with high profitability, while JD.com reaps growing benefits from its control of its own distribution network. Putting aside the war of words, the competition between Alibaba and JD.com is really about the future direction of e-retailing in China.

Alibaba's Dominant Position

The Alibaba Group was established in 1999 by 18 people led by Jack Ma, a former English teacher from Hangzhou, China. To understand Alibaba and the e-commerce sector's explosive growth in China over the last decade, it is helpful to first take a look at a small village in Zhejiang Province, Qing-yan-liu (where Alibaba is based). Qing-yan-liu became well known as "China's No. 1 online village" after Premier Li Keqiang's visit in November 2014, when he talked to online shop owners, suppliers and couriers, praising e-commerce for creating equal business opportunities for both rural and urban residents and narrowing the gap in living standards between them.

Until 15 years ago, Qing-yan-liu was a pure farming village. It is part of Yiwu city in Zhejiang Province, a small city known worldwide for its small appliances. The Yiwu International Trade Center is the largest small commodity wholesale market in the world. When the internet boom reached the village in recent years, some farmers with entrepreneurial spirit decided that the village was the perfect place for online store operators, because it was a few kilometers from the city center, next to a large freight market (the Yiwu International Trade Center), and filled with empty houses (due to the migration of farmers to city jobs).

Qing-yan-liu village has become the headquarters for many vendors on Alibaba's e-commerce website. There are now 10 times as many shops associated with e-commerce as there are households in Qing-yan-liu. Filled with warehouses, logistics companies, advertising agencies, packing companies and all kinds of service providers, it is more like a large, busy, open-air transfer center. Moving from mostly farmland to an e-commerce hub, Qing-yan-liu is a microcosm of rapid urbanization and internet adoption in China.

Numerous shops in Qing-yan-liu and similar places have formed the backbone of Alibaba's e-commerce empire, which is China's undisputed market leader in both C2C (consumer to consumer) and B2C (business-to-consumer) e-commerce. It is a platform that no one can ignore when any merchant enters China. Among other things, Alibaba operates two distinct and powerful marketplaces: Taobao (C2C) is a frenetic and eclectic online bazaar that offers a huge range of consumer goods. Tmall (B2C), in contrast, is a more refined platform for established brands (see comparison in Table 4.1).

The first thing that sets Alibaba apart from its competitors is its enormous trading size. The most important business metric for Alibaba for many years has been the gross merchandise volume (GMV). GMV is generally defined as the value of transactions through a specific e-commerce site, so it is directly linked to Alibaba's revenue. But it also provides additional information on the company's growth and market position, because it helps the market to evaluate the pace of a firm's expansion and market reach relative to those of its competitors.

After more than 10 years of fast growth, Alibaba's e-commerce business in consumer goods is by a considerable margin the leading player in China. In 2012, the total GMV of

Table 4.1   Comparison of the Taobao and Tmall marketplaces

	Taobao	Tmall
Year of start	2003	2008
Concept	C2C Bazaar (comparable to eBay)	B2C Mall
Setting	Sellers post new and used goods for sale or resale	Each brand can set up its own virtual store in the mall
Users	Individuals, small merchants	Popular brands from home and abroad such as Apple, BMW and Tesla
Cost to Users	No commission fee; main revenue from online marketing services for vendors	Sellers pay a deposit to list on the site and Tmall earns commission on transactions

Taobao and Tmall already exceeded the combined transaction volume of Amazon and eBay. China has become the largest e-commerce economy globally, and much of this is attributable to Alibaba's expansion. According to Alibaba's data, Taobao and Tmall account for more than half of all parcel deliveries in China.

Among the main B2C shopping websites, based on GMV, Alibaba's transaction volume exceeded JD.com's volume by a wide margin, and only two other players reached more than 2% market share in 2014 (see Figure 4.1). In fact, after Alibaba's 2015 merger with Suning, which was formerly among the top B2C e-tailers in China, only one company – Vipshop, the largest flash sale website – has a meaningful market share outside of Alibaba and JD.com's domain.

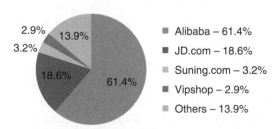

Figure 4.1   e-Commerce Market Share by GMV in 2014
(Data Source: iResearch 2015)

In the well-publicized 2016 New Year's speech by Alibaba's CEO Daniel Zhang, however, he emphasized that Alibaba's business model going forward would no longer be centered on GMV growth. He compared GMV to the GDP of a country – China used to emphasize its GDP growth rate, but its new focus is on the sustainability of the national economy as a whole. Since the founder Jack Ma once famously said that Alibaba would last at least 102 years (for a company that was founded in 1999, that means the company will span a minimum of three centuries), it is important for Alibaba to focus more on sustainability than GMV to ensure that its culture, business models and systems are built to last.

It is also worth noting that GMV is not as accurate a parameter as the revenue concept under generally accepted accounting principles. In general, the GMV of e-commerce sites includes all transactions on those sites regardless of whether they were paid for and completed. That means the GMV data may include the value of transactions that were later returned or cancelled. According to news reports, the return rate for 2014 Singles' Day was a single digit percentage of total GMV.

In addition, the GMV data is also impacted by the market practice of "brushing the sales volume" – including fake transactions on the e-commerce site – by unscrupulous vendors. **(See the "Shua-Xiao-Liang" box.)** As described in the risk factors in Alibaba's 2014 prospectus filing for IPO, the sellers on the site may "engage in fictitious or phantom transactions with themselves or collaborators in order to artificially inflate their own ratings on our marketplaces, reputation and search results rankings". In addition to sales volume, customer reviews and other transaction-related parameters apparently could be "brushed" as well.

The main reason for fake orders and reviews is marketing advantage. Because online customers have endless choices in the marketplaces, competition among vendors for online visibility is cut-throat. One way to climb to the number one spot in search results on Alibaba's sites, for example, is to place the highest bid for a prime advertisement spot on the two websites. But some vendors consider online advertisements to be too expensive and too complicated for gaining popularity on the websites. Hence, one shortcut for those vendors is to create artificially high volumes of past transactions to potentially trick Alibaba's internal systems into putting them in more prominent slots. Tmall, for example, ranks sellers based on their sales volume (among other factors), and those with the highest sales numbers are mostly likely to appear on the main promotion page to get the most customer attention.

These "brushing" practices are detrimental to customers, and it is also important for the internet firms to reduce fake orders to improve the e-commerce ecosystem. Alibaba has taken various counter measures to clean up its platforms. The company uses big data techniques to identify fake transactions. If a vendor is found to falsify its trade volume and rating, Alibaba may delete the fake goods reviews, remove the vendor from search results, impose a fine, or delist the vendor from the online marketplace.

However, because vendors with more sales volume and good reviews often gain higher standings, merchants have a strong motivation to "brush" online sales, and they have also invested in advanced techniques to make "brushing" less detectable. Therefore, even though e-commerce players are putting more resources into policing their sites, this cat-and-mouse game may continue for some time before it is eliminated.

Shua-Xiao-Liang ("Brush the Sales Volume")

The Chinese character "Shua" can literally be translated as "brushing", which is why some English media used this translation to suggest people artificially "painting" a fake number for transactions. However, when "shua" is related to sales volume, it may derive from the term "screen refreshing" (shua-ping), just as a screen is refreshed and the sales volume number (xiao-liang) is updated when a new transaction is booked.

"Brushing the sales volume" can take many forms. The common practice is to arrange fake orders by hired part-time staff, vendor employees or professional service providers. (For the reason mentioned above, some media call these people "brushers".) After the fake order is placed, the vendor still needs to arrange for delivery because sites such as Alibaba require a unique delivery code to be entered with each order.

Initially vendors simply sent an empty package to their contacts for a fake order. Today, because Alibaba and others have increased the scrutiny of empty boxes, the vendor may send a box containing clutter or junk, such as empty bottles, piles of paper and small rocks. Sometimes vendors may even send these boxes to strangers – those online customers whose personal information was obtained from earlier online shopping.

As the operators of online retailing platforms use improved techniques to monitor their websites, the vendor community also works hard to keep them in the game. Discussions on latest best practice in brushing can be found in social media. Software that can "brush" the transaction numbers without actual purchase processing has also emerged and is readily available. With a quick search on the internet, one can easily find links that offer to help with "brushing the sales volume", "brushing the reputation", and "brushing the satisfaction review".

The software for brushing is also getting more sophisticated. The new versions support many set-ups to make the fake orders look like human activities, such as setting up different times on the web page for different orders, different time gaps for each step of an order, and providing random reviews for transactions. No wonder the punch line of one of those advertisements was: "Brush as many as you want!"

Another huge advantage of Alibaba is its marketplace model and the corresponding high profit margin. The enormous scale of Alibaba's trade volume and the importance of GMV does not imply that Alibaba is running a low profit margin business. On the contrary, Alibaba also enjoys a high profit margin in simply providing a transaction platform for buyers and sellers, without having to house inventories or operate distribution.

Because Alibaba is a facilitator of online sales instead of being an online retailer itself, the company's profit margin more closely resembles that of a software company than a retailer. This helps to explain why it earns a higher profit margin than the "direct online retailers" like JD.com, as well as the premium multiple it enjoys in the capital markets. In 2014, Alibaba reported operating profitability above 40%, an amazing number for any consumer goods company with such a large transaction size.

Generally speaking, however, disproportionate profit margins are often related to an immature market and early mover advantage. So skeptics of Alibaba have been expecting that as e-commerce markets mature, this advantage will gradually recede until the whole industry reaches a more normal and uniform profit margin. But Alibaba's fans argue that the "network effect" of the marketplaces is self-reinforcing, making it extremely difficult for competitors to steal its customers. The argument goes that the large number of existing sellers and buyers makes it too costly for any buyer or seller to move to a new online venue; instead, more buyers will attract more sellers, and more sellers will attract more buyers.

This debate is ongoing and Alibaba's profitability remains high. However, the usual rule is that a generalist operation may not keep all high profit margins to itself forever. For one thing, Alibaba's Tmall, and in particular Taobao, has developed on such a huge scale that it's almost overwhelming for potential buyers. Because Alibaba simply provides a platform for the sellers, it does not completely "own" the information of sellers and goods. As a result, some sites have emerged to guide consumers through the crowded traffic on Alibaba's marketplaces and subsequently created their own offerings.

Interestingly, one such example is the website **Mogujie.com** ("Mushroom Street" in English) founded by a former Alibaba employee. The site started out as a social shopping service platform where users could exchange photos and information about women's fashion items. According to news reports, the two founders were part of the Alibaba team that had designed the interface of Alibaba's shopping site Taobao. The social aspect is Mogujie's distinguishing feature: when young female customers shop for women's clothing, accessories and other fashion merchandise, they are usually eager to check out the items tried and commented on by fashion opinion leaders or people they are familiar with. Mogujie.com enjoyed fast growth by directing buyers to good deals on Taobao before becoming a specialized fashion e-commerce platform that attracts merchants directly.

Another example is that as online customers become more experienced and sophisticated, they look beyond a bazaar or a mall for more specialized offerings and a different shopping experience. Specialists are emerging to provide services that are different from routine e-commerce in standardized goods, and **Vipshop.com** stands out as a significant niche player right behind the two e-commerce superpowers Alibaba and JD.com. As the largest "online discount retail" platform in China, this "niche player" is listed on the New York Stock Exchange and had a market capitalization of close to $10 billion at the end of 2015, reflecting the enormous size of China's e-commerce business in another context.

As its name suggests, Vipshop provides special offers to its customers. But these special offers are not expensive VIP services. Instead, it conducts "flash sales", where it partners with popular and well-known brands to sell their excess inventory at substantial discounts; however these deals may only last for a limited time window and for limited numbers. The site started out with luxury brands, but soon incorporated more mass market brands of clothing, cosmetics and accessories, etc. and promises a steep discount to what the products are sold for at brick and mortar stores.

With about 3% of the total e-commerce market share, Vipshop is the largest player in the flash market. The large volume of overstocked goods that Vipshop deals with, gives it priority in the selection of excess inventory when working with vendors. Its buyer team has several hundred staff, including former fashion magazine editors and regional brand managers who are experienced in selecting a good "brand mixture" of goods for its site. As Vipshop has expanded into broader categories of consumer goods, it is now a hybrid of time-limited in-season discount and off-season overstock clearance, and the price range is getting wider with a combination of both luxury and mass market brands.

For merchants, flash sales provide a way to clear their inventories. Since it was founded in 2008, Vipshop has rapidly built a base of brand partners, thanks partly to cut-throat competition in the fragmented retail sector and the growing impact of e-commerce. During China's recent economic boom, many retailers have expanded substantially. They have reached into additional product categories and built up inventory and warehousing. But price competition has also intensified, leaving many firms with extra inventory that they cannot sell. With more shopping moved to online channels these days, it is even more difficult for smaller vendors to manage their inventories.

For retail consumers, the old-fashioned thrill of fighting for limited bargain offers is a fun shopping experience which is different from the static B2C site purchase. There are a limited number of offline discount stores in China, the majority of which are located in top-tier cities. As such, Vipshop and other flash sale online platforms meet a demand in the market, especially for the segment of the middle class that seeks the "affordable luxury" experience.

Because of the powerful combination of substantial discount, time pressure and limited supply, consumers are likely to make more impulsive purchase decisions than in a typical online shopping context, where they rationally search for goods from their pre-planned shopping list. Nowadays the instant accessibility of mobile platforms brings internet connection to the lower-tier cities, leading even more customers into this new shopping experience.

Alibaba has undoubtedly noticed "flash sales" becoming a particularly successful sales model in the China market. According to news reports from mid-2015, Alibaba has acquired more than 50% of Mei.com, for about $100 million. Similar to Vipshop, Mei.com is a flash sales platform for luxury and fashion goods and offers discounted products to consumers. Following the deal, Alibaba formed a specialized service team to help Mei.com grow its user base and logistical services, while Mei.com seeks synergy with Tmall in providing more premium luxury goods to consumers.

The third advantageous feature of the Alibaba model is to be "light" in assets, since there is no need for it to invest in its own distribution infrastructure (and the related employee hiring). This is at the core of the debate between the Alibaba model and the JD.com model and will be discussed in detail in the next section. Similar to eBay, Alibaba merely matches buyers and sellers; instead of having its own distribution network, it invested in a joint venture with delivery companies to establish a logistics network. JD.com on the other hand invests heavily in its own infrastructure, considering it a key factor for superior consumer experiences. Going forward, will JD.com see its infrastructure build-up as too costly to be sustainable (as Jack Ma predicted)? Or will Alibaba be forced to develop its own distribution network so as to serve its customers better?

JD.com vs. Alibaba

By many measures, JD.com is not nearly as big as Alibaba, especially when it comes to gross merchandise volume (GMV), i.e. the total value of all online transactions. For the 2013 fiscal year, JD.com's GMV stood at around $20 billion, making it China's second-largest retail e-commerce company after Alibaba, whose GMV was close to $250 billion.

JD's GMV is still much smaller than that of Alibaba's e-commerce business, but that difference has a lot to do with their models. As mentioned earlier, Alibaba is mostly a platform provider for buyers and sellers (similar to eBay in this respect), while JD.com buys inventories and sells them to consumers as a direct online retailer (more like Amazon.com). In recent years, the competition between them is much more direct and fierce than the gap in GMV size suggests.

First, they have different approaches to the logistics of e-retailing. In recent years during JD.com's anniversary celebrations, the young billionaire founder Richard Liu used to put on the JD.com red uniform and a big motorcycle helmet before hopping on a three-wheeled electric bike to make some package deliveries himself. One could see this as a smart publicity campaign, but by doing so, Mr. Liu highlights that superior delivery and service are at the center of JD.com's corporate strategy – so important that even the founder and CEO needs to experience the logistical difficulties that JD and ordinary customers are dealing with directly.

Delivery by the CEO is not all that dramatic when one considers the company's development path. JD.com, whose former English name was 360Buy.com, was set up to be an online retailer in 2004. China still lacked inland infrastructure in the market then, and there were no high quality delivery services in China such as UPS or Fedex in the US. With its low prices and fast delivery, JD.com stood out from the competition.

Today these features remain at the core of JD.com's DNA, while the retail shipment and service areas in China still need significant improvement (although many new roads and bridges have managed to connect most parts of the country smoothly after many years of urbanization). For example, damage during delivery is a common issue in the market as a whole. Customers in the interior of the country, especially in the mountainous regions, find that their orders are much slower to arrive.

Since 2007, JD.com has been the first and probably the only Chinese e-retailing company to invest substantially in its own logistics network (see Table 4.2). At times JD.com's business model is viewed as a combination of Amazon and UPS, because JD.com promises quality goods and on-time deliveries to its e-commerce customers. It has spent billions of dollars on the warehouses and distribution centers for inventories, as well as on its own team of couriers, equipped with trucks, motorbikes and any other possible means of transportation in some of the busiest cities in the world.

JD.com's rationale is to handle the whole process itself, from online orders to physical drop-off, to better control the delivery service and product quality. Accordingly, JD.com's IT

Table 4.2   Summary of JD.com's logistics system in 2014

Category	Scale
Warehouses	86 (1.5 million square meters in 36 cities)
Distribution Stations	1,620 (in 495 cities)
Self Pick-up Stations	214
Courier Staff	24,412
Storage Staff	11,145
Customer Service	5,832

(Data Source: JD.com's IPO Prospectus, as of April 1, 2014)

system supports and supervises the whole process, and the data from this system are shared with merchants. Although it has proved costly to build its own infrastructure system, JD.com is able to process orders more quickly than its rivals. Also, JD.com's supporters believe this model sets JD.com apart from its competitors by having fewer counterfeits and a lower chance of damage during deliveries (of particular importance in the case of healthcare products or fresh fruit, for example).

Unlike JD.com, which operates its own logistics services, Alibaba relies on third-party providers. But that is not to say that Alibaba considers the delivery process as unimportant to consumers' shopping experience. It works with its delivery partners to accelerate delivery services in more and more Chinese cities amid rising customer expectations, and it has even made direct investments into the logistics system. In 2013, Alibaba announced its vision of achieving 24-hour delivery throughout China within 10 years.

For example, in 2013 Alibaba invested nearly $400 million in a 48% stake in China Smart Logistics (CSL), a joint venture for a modern logistics system in China. This arrangement gave Alibaba many delivery partners without directly owning any of the physical logistics infrastructures in the venture. In return, Alibaba provided the big data and IT capability to help build a logistic information system on delivery route planning, real-time tracking, customer satisfaction rating, order volume forecasts and so on. This information system should allow Alibaba's logistics partners to optimize their warehousing, transportation and human resources for better delivery services.

JD.com and its founder, Richard Liu, believe that as more Chinese join the middle class, they will put a premium on superior services for shopping. For this reason, JD.com considers its advanced delivery system and strong customer service as a decisive advantage in the e-commerce competition. For example, during a recent "Singles' Day" sales season, JD.com used the advertisement slogan "Same price, buy genuine". There was also an advertisement in which a young professional became embarrassed during a job interview when her new red dress, which she had bought online, left marks on the interviewer's couch. No name was mentioned in those adverts, but it seemed everyone knew which online firm was being referred to.

Alibaba's founder Jack Ma, however, argued that JD.com's model would be difficult to scale up in the long term to deal with the explosive growth of China's e-commerce market. According to a recent KPMG report, the Chinese e-commerce market is already bigger than that of the United States, and by 2020 is projected to be the size of the markets of the United States, Britain, Germany, Japan and France combined. In fact, even with over 40,000 employees in its inventory and distribution system, JD.com's logistics network was reportedly still drastically insufficient during peak times like Singles' Days, and was forced to hire temporary workers from around the country to provide extra help. One senior executive at JD.com once famously depicted the current e-commerce logistics challenges in China as "having 30 NBA basketball teams, but only a few high school gyms to play in".

Using specific figures, Mr. Ma argued that the capital investment needed by JD.com's infrastructure-heavy model would increase exponentially as the market expands. **(See "The Metaphor of Horse and Oxen" box.)** "How many people does JD.com hire right now?" he asked and then answered the question himself. "50,000 people! Alibaba has expanded slowly [implying that they've been in business for longer], and by now we only have 23,000 employees. Why do I choose not to do the delivery myself at Alibaba? Right now, JD has 50,000 employees, adding on between 30,000 to 40,000 people for inventory, but they only handle 2 million parcels a day. But Alibaba deals with 27 million packages a day. How would you deal with that?

"In ten years, China's e-commerce markets may have to deal with 300 million packages a day. You may need to hire 1 million people, how can you manage that?" By suggesting that a self-run delivery system was impractical given the market size, Mr. Ma concluded that the JD.com business model was a "tragedy", he commented further, "It's not that I am better than him (JD.com's founder). It's a question of direction."

The Metaphor of Horse and Oxen

During the 2015 Chinese New Year, Alibaba's founder Jack Ma and JD.com's founder Richard Liu's colorful exchange on their business models via social media brought festival laughter to Chinese netizens. In response to Mr. Ma's direct challenge to its business model, JD.com chose to deliver its elaborate response in a Chinese poem, titled "We will do our best and time will prove it". The JD.com poem sarcastically praised Mr. Ma as a lonely wise man, on whose "sagacity" JD.com would meditate.

Then the poem went on to make a comparison of the two companies, suggesting JD.com was focusing on improving customer services while Alibaba was short on quality control when managing a large marketplace. As the poem put it, Alibaba had "a grand posture at podiums", while JD.com bowed down to "serve at store counters"; Alibaba was good at "glamorous talking", while JD.com "built on infrastructure in hard labor"; Alibaba as a marketplace "earns money easily", but JD.com chooses to internalize inventory and delivery to "have better quality control", in the hope of "winning over customers". In summary, even though "we (the two companies) look at each other often, we are on different paths. You are minding our business so much that we are moved to tears."

In a show of confidence in its own model, JD.com in conclusion suggested that time would be the perfect judge and a "fair mediator". The poem's punch line was a subtle double pun on Jack Ma's last name, as the Chinese character "Ma" means "horse", as well as Alibaba's vision to last at least 102 years, because there is an old saying by Chinese ancient philosopher Zhuang Zi describing the quick passing of time as "a white horse jumping through a narrow gap". The line read: "A horse disappeared in a flip, I am still bending and plowing [suggesting diligent farming oxen]. Keep a pure and empty mind, and there is no need to get overly sentimental."

In the middle of animated online chatter, Jack Ma issued a clarification and apologized to JD in his verified post on the social media platform Sina Weibo. He conceded that no business model was perfect, but insisted that his comment was a private conversation taken out of context. "You were chatting to friends? Didn't you expect your friends could tape it and put it into a book?" (According to Mr. Ma, his head of public relations teased him.) "Not much that you can do about it", was his answer to his PR chief.

But Mr. Ma made a resolution to his PR chief that he would be more careful in future – by mimicking the practice of inside traders according to urban legend. Securities traders supposedly sometimes have their discussions at places where people do not wear much – so that the participants cannot bring along a microphone or recording device. "Next time I have a conversation, I will go to a public bath house."

The war of words between the two internet giants created quite a bit of drama, and the strong personalities of the two founders added more color to the exchange. However, the e-commerce industry viewed it as a serious debate about which model represented the winning e-commerce model in the long term. On Mr. Ma's challenge to JD.com's sustainable growth, JD.com's response did not provide economic analysis directly justifying its own model. To some extent, in JD.com's own poem, it indirectly admitted that its model involves high cost and input ("hard labor") but does not necessarily generate returns as high as Alibaba does (the latter "earns money easily").

But JD.com has continued on its own path to build up its logistics network. On its official website, JD.com claims proudly to have the largest warehousing facilities in China's e-commerce industry. By June 30, 2015, JD.com owned seven major logistics centers in China, running 166 warehouses in 44 cities, 4,142 distribution centers and pick-up stations, covering 2,043 districts and counties throughout the country. The more important question than the "light asset vs. heavy asset" model debate is whether JD.com can find a path to sustainable profit while expanding its logistics infrastructure, which requires the investment of large sums.

JD.com is usually compared to Amazon, the leading internet retailer in the US. They have had similar development paths and share similarities in their models. Both are online retailers with "heavy" assets on their balance sheets. Both spend significant capital on a self-constructed inventory system. In the same way as JD.com believes that fast and reliable delivery is the distinguishing factor for consumer experience, Amazon also places much emphasis on ever-faster deliveries. However, there is a gap between JD.com and Amazon in terms of operational efficiency and revenue sources.

For example, Amazon's sophisticated systems and data processing power provide an additional revenue source besides direct retailing. When it opens its inventory and logistics system to its partner retailers, Amazon retains a portion of the sales price as commission. JD.com on the other hand still has to play catch up on cloud technology and big data capabilities. Amazon could also benefit from the synergy of its internet ecosystem. For instance, Amazon consumers may use Amazon devices (the e-reader Kindle, for example) to watch Amazon-produced content that is surrounded by adverts for Amazon products. JD.com, however, has a narrower focus on retailing, and a significant portion of its losses is attributable to pricing wars with other retailers.

As such, although JD.com is often viewed as Amazon China, at this moment JD.com is mostly "a retail company that has fully incorporated the internet into its business model". In recent years, JD.com has worked on expanding sources of revenue, such as logistics services, financing services and its own marketplace to create its own ecosystem. The case of the US retailer Walmart shows that the profit from retailing is limited, but the retail business offers trade volume and cash flow that the company could play with, and JD.com is also going in that direction.

During JD.com's annual Web sales event in June 2015, the company disclosed that about 8% of its internet shoppers borrowed from the company to pay for online goods. This had increased multiple times from the year before. Apart from the growing number of people who borrow money from JD Finance to shop on the company's e-commerce platform, the financial services firm has also offered small loans, as JD.com has set up its own credit rating system, given that the company has a large pool of online shopping data readily available after being in e-commerce for more than 10 years.

The consumer finance business is likely to be an important new source of revenue for JD.com going forward. In that context, it will not only be a retailer but also an online supply chain and finance company like Walmart. In many other areas JD.com is rapidly innovating and transforming itself into a true internet company becoming more and more like Amazon, which itself operates e-commerce in many business lines besides retailing and is an internet company in everything they do.

Second, China's rural areas have become the largest new battlefield. Almost half of China's population is still in rural areas, so the market potential for e-commerce is huge. As the city markets become more saturated, the rural areas provide the most growth potential for e-commerce companies. On the one hand, hundreds of millions of villagers are being linked to e-retailing websites and becoming active customers. On the other hand, when new channels are created to transport farm produce to the cities, every farmer can be an online merchant as the demand for fresh, safe agricultural products grows rapidly in the cities. Not only are China's villagers becoming increasingly big online spenders, but they also quickly embracing e-commerce as retailers.

According to CNNIC's 2014 data, however, the internet penetration rate in China's rural areas has shown signs of slowing down lately (see Figure 4.2). Future growth in the rural internet population, which requires substantial investment in the network infrastructure in remote areas, may need further central government policy support. Also, changing shopping habits from brick-and-mortar stores to online platforms may take time for many rural residents. They have to build up their

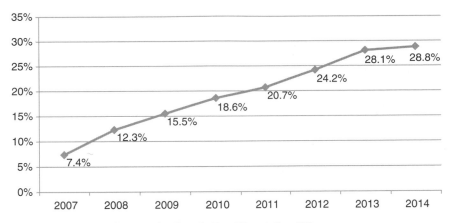

Figure 4.2   Internet Penetration Rate in Rural Population (%)
(Data Source: CNNIC, December 2014)

trust in purchasing goods from virtual shops, develop brand awareness and learn how to place orders online.

In recent years, both Alibaba and JD.com have launched large-scale campaigns to stimulate e-commerce interest in rural areas. In May and June 2014, JD.com cooperated with the Ministry of Agriculture to launch a campaign inviting villagers to shop on its website. It also sent a team of employees on a six-month, nationwide tour to host marketing events in more than 100 towns. The locals were invited to learn how to shop online for books, groceries and other daily necessities, which was already second nature to urban residents. For one week in July 2014, Alibaba offered to deliver all home appliances bought through its shopping websites without extra charge to rural buyers nationwide.

So far, the trend of farmers becoming online customers and vendors has been promising. A 2015 report by the consulting firm McKinsey showed that despite lower internet penetration, more than 60% of rural digital users shop online, making them just as active as their urban netizen counterparts. More interestingly, the survey reported that 25% more rural shoppers, compared with those living in the first- and second-tier cities, feel "empowered" by the online channel and see themselves as "online gurus" eager to be the first to try out new products and services.

That helps to explain why "Taobao Villages" – like Qing-yan-liu village mentioned at the beginning of this chapter – are rapidly emerging across the country (**see the "Taobao Village" Box**). According to a report by AliResearch, Alibaba Group's research arm, the number of "Taobao Villages" had increased more than tenfold from 20 in 2013 to 211 by the end of 2014. As the experience from first-generation vendors at Qing-yan-liu showed, it was very easy for a villager to participate in the Taobao marketplace: one rural entrepreneur only needed to have a 20-square-meter space, buy a second-hand computer and find a basic internet connection to embrace e-commerce as a retail start-up.

Taobao Village

A "Taobao Village" is defined by Alibaba as "a village in which over 10% of households run online stores and village e-commerce revenues exceed RMB10 million (roughly $1.6 million) per year". These Taobao Villages are the best illustration that the internet has transformed the way of life of China's rural communities.

According to Alibaba's data, in 2014 there were 211 Taobao Villages where more than 70,000 online marketers were selling their products across China. The Taobao Villages were in 10 different provinces, but were concentrated mostly in the coastal provinces of Zhejiang, Guangdong, Fujian, Hebei and Jiangsu, which collectively accounted for more than 90% of the total number. Their customers were typically from nearby provinces and picked up some products from these villages due to quicker delivery time and cheaper shipping fees. Therefore, more Taobao Villages should emerge as e-retailing hubs as e-commerce reaches more remote regions.

Alibaba has committed to providing financing, marketing support and e-commerce training to encourage rural entrepreneurs to extend their business across the Taobao platform. For example, the Alibaba group will offer financial solutions and launch special promotions on products sold by Taobao Village merchants. In addition, Alibaba has a Taobao University (a major training division within the group) that offers seminars in rural areas so that the villagers have the opportunity to learn how to sell online. In some villages, long banners with large characters can be seen on the walls promoting e-commerce, such as "Want a better life? Get on Taobao now!"

Compared to getting rural areas excited about e-commerce, the delivery system is an even bigger challenge. In the largest and most affluent cities on the country's eastern coast, almost anything can be delivered within a day. But the state of logistics in rural areas lags far behind. Many of the delivery companies do not provide services in rural areas below county level, because the villages are spread out, addresses are difficult to find, and the narrow roadways in the villages often make it difficult for delivery trucks to move about. The key areas in need of improvement are better door-to-door delivery (so that rural customers can enjoy the same express service) and better after-sales service (things their urban counterparts take for granted).

JD.com has announced that the company plan to open hundreds of brick-and-mortar service centers in underdeveloped counties in the coming years. Apart from being the "last kilometer" delivery infrastructure in the rural areas, the centers are going to recruit and train tens of thousands of staff to "showroom" the e-commerce business, help rural customers order products online and support after-sales services. It remains to be seen whether Alibaba's more mature ecosystem with the Taobao Villages or JD.com's infrastructure network will win more users in the rural regions. The competition in the rural areas may very likely determine the ultimate market share winner in China, because with about 600 million people in rural China, this is nearly double the population of the US.

Thirdly, the battle in the mobile e-retailing field has just started. With the largest population of smartphone users in the world, Chinese customers are making their e-purchases while moving around during daily life. This aligns with the Chinese consumer's desire for speed and the convenience of "any time" shopping. For example, according to CNNIC's 2014 data, 13.9% and 10.6% of customers, respectively, purchase goods on smartphones while using public transportation and waiting in line. For both Alibaba and JD.com, one major priority is to adapt the business setting for the next phase of mobile e-retailing.

Before its alliance with Tencent, JD.com had a limited mobile channel. Just before JD.com's 2014 IPO, Tencent bought 15% of JD.com for $215 million. Following the partnership, JD.com's services gained prominent positions on the WeChat platform, which is by far the most popular social network platform in China. Tencent's mobile payment tools also filled a vacuum for JD.com's e-commerce setting, as Alibaba's e-commerce empire is supported by its affiliated Alipay system, which is the dominant online payment system in China. (As will be discussed in the next chapter, relying on its unique strength in social networking, Tencent is also building its own mobile e-commerce and other online-to-offline businesses.)

For JD.com supporters, the addition of Tencent and WeChat can bring a multitude of changes to JD by injecting so-called "mobile internet DNA" into the direct sales retailer. Tencent's mobile social network could potentially bring new users to JD.com, especially young and tech-savvy Chinese consumers, to help JD.com achieve better economies of scale. JD.com has tested different marketing methods to leverage the purchasing habits of WeChat users. For example, in 2014 it pre-sold Microsoft's Xbox One in China to users that connected to its retail outlet through Tencent's QQ and WeChat social media networks.

Of course, Alibaba has not been complacent in either the social or mobile realm. To compete with the popular WeChat, Alibaba put in the effort to build an Alibaba version of the messaging app named "LaiWang" (in Chinese this means "Interactions"). But LaiWang failed to take off due to the network effect of WeChat, which probably further incentivized Alibaba to build up its social and mobile capabilities aggressively. In recent years, Alibaba has made significant investments in, among others, Sina Weibo, China's version of Twitter, and UCWeb, one of the biggest web browser companies in China.

Both sides have their strengths in mobile e-retailing, and the battle has just started. So far, Alibaba's e-commerce prowess has carried the momentum into the mobile world. As Figure 4.3 shows, in 2014 Alibaba owned an even bigger share of mobile shopping than in the overall online retail market. Only JD.com and Vipshop managed to achieve more than a 2% market share each.

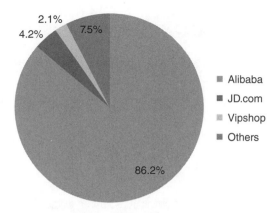

Figure 4.3   Market Share of China's Mobile Shopping Market in 2014
(Data Source: iResearch 2015)

Of course, the JD.com/WeChat alliance has a lot of potential for mobile e-retailing. JD.com's founder Richard Liu disclosed in an October 2015 interview that in the second quarter of 2015, more than 20% of new JD.com e-commerce users came from the WeChat and QQ social networks. But the challenge is to effectively convert social chatting intent on WeChat into purchasing intent and then into purchasing activity. (Alibaba's visitors, by definition, are buyers with plans to purchase.) In the same interview, Mr. Liu conceded that JD.com had only been able to use less than 10% of the user traffic from Tencent.

Nevertheless, Richard Liu was optimistic that with JD.com's integration with WeChat, the social recommendation side would have a bigger impact in the future when consumers went for more branded goods than standardized offerings. According to CNNIC's report on the 2014 online shopping market, Chinese customers in general still considered price to be the more important factor than brand in purchase decisions (see Figure 4.4). For necessities, there was less room for word-of-mouth marketing. Mr. Liu and JD.com are betting that when the post-1990 and post-2000 generations become the mainstream customers, they will look for quality brands and actively share with their peers on the social network, potentially leading to a jump in the businesses at the JD.com/WeChat platform. The two companies in October 2015 announced another joint

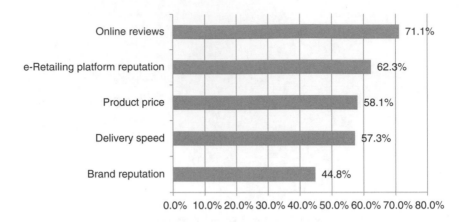

Figure 4.4 Key Factors for Online Shopping Decisions
(Data Source: CNNIC's report on the online shopping market, December 2014)

venture called "Brand-Commerce" to put their best resources into products with strong brands.

Alibaba's Jack Ma also gave a verdict on the JD.com/ Tencent alliance. The book that included Ma's comment on the JD.com model apparently also included a quote by him criticizing Tencent's partnership with JD.com. He believed that Tencent (along with many other companies) had profound difficulties shaping a coherent corporate strategy. He viewed the move by JD.com and Tencent as primarily a tactical play rather than a strategic transformation and did not, therefore, consider it "a real threat to Alibaba".

"In China today, strategy helps you win and we are much better than Tencent in that regard", Mr. Ma said, according to the book. "Today WeChat is working with JD.com, and that is even more stupid." The mobile battle has just begun, so the market probably looks at this discussion of models with even more interest than the e-retailing model clash. Once again, time will be the judge and mediator in this debate.

Convergence: The Omni-Channel Model

The debate on the future e-commerce model in China is still ongoing, and Table 4.3 summarizes the top two players' differences in strategy.

Table 4.3   Main differences between Alibaba and JD.com

	Alibaba	JD.com
Business model	Online platform for retailers	Online direct sales
Business lines	e-Commerce marketplace Broad, various services; integrated online ecosystem	Mostly direct retailing and logistics services; Into open platform (WeChat) and finance
Transaction volume	Huge	Relatively smaller
Logistics	Partnership with third-party companies to provide logistic services	Own nation-wide warehouses, dispatch centers and delivery networks
Source of profits	Marketing and services income; commissions	Difference between retail price and cost
Profit margin	High	Low
Asset heavy/light	Light	Heavy
Development direction	Into "heavy" (for example, banking, healthcare)	Into "light" (for example, internet finance, smart electronics)

Despite the difference in operating models, both companies rely on economies of scale to keep their costs down, and Alibaba currently leads in this important area. So far, Alibaba's marketplace/third-party deliveries model has proven to be more scalable than that of JD.com. Because Alibaba's model only needs internet access, customer orders and a shipping address to reach new customers in new regions, overall it has expanded faster in China. In contrast, JD.com's model is capital intensive and has resulted in slower growth and smaller market share.

However, although Alibaba currently enjoys light investment in assets and a high profit margin, it does not necessarily mean that the "heavy" model of JD.com's platform has no competitive advantage. JD.com owns its goods, inventories and logistics system, which not only gives JD.com more control of its shipping process and product care, but also, on a comparative basis, provides the company with more risk-bearing capabilities in a fast-changing mobile internet market.

In practice, it seems that both Alibaba and JD.com are moving into a more balanced model for their future development. For example, Alibaba is going into asset-heavy businesses like banking and healthcare, while JD.com moves into "lighter" areas like internet financing and smart electronics to improve its profitability. Oddly enough, their convergence is perhaps best illustrated by the fact that both are increasing their cooperation with traditional retail conglomerates.

With the rise of online shopping in recent years, the traditional retailers have steadily lost customers to shopping sites such as Alibaba's Taobao and JD.com. The first wave of disruption naturally affected standardized goods – the so-called "shopping-basket goods" – such as stationery items, kitchen utensils, accessories and so on, because e-retailing proved both convenient and price-competitive. Soon afterwards even items like brand-name clothing, which customers prefer to handle before making actual purchases, were affected by e-commerce. The retail shops found themselves taking on the role of "showrooms" or "fitting rooms", where customers came to browse in stores first, but bought the items online later. In short, the ecosystem supporting traditional retail in China has been fundamentally challenged.

In this context, Alibaba has surprised the market lately by making significant investments in traditional retailers, at a time when customers are shifting to online shopping and going mobile is accelerating. In March 2014, Alibaba acquired a 10% stake in the department store operator Yintai (Intime) with a $692 million investment. At the time of acquisition, Intime was operating 28 department stores and eight shopping malls, and had more than 1.5 million regular customers throughout China. In their announcements, the two companies planned on an "omni-channel" strategy by combining Intime's retail store infrastructure across China with Alibaba's e-commerce platform and big data on consumers.

After the investment, Intime planned to put its entire inventory online and link its frequent customer information with

Alibaba's Alipay payment system. One part of this is smart inventory, whereby Intime could develop an advanced system for the pricing information, updated quantity and physical locations of various goods. For example, if a customer could not find the right size or color for a shirt in a store, the database could find an inventory item near the customer's home and then place an order directly for home delivery from that physical location. In the past, the store would first request a delivery from another store, or a warehouse to send the item to the store, but it could take a few days before the customer was able to call in to the store to pick up the item in person.

Alibaba's recent acquisition, which happened to be its biggest investment deal ever, brought more shock waves to the e-commerce industry. In August 2015, Alibaba invested $4.6 billion in Suning Commerce Group to become Suning's second largest shareholder, while Suning spent approximately $2.3 billion to acquire a stake in the Alibaba Group. (The transaction was effectively also a stock-swap deal between the two companies.) Suning was one of the largest retailers in China and its main strength was a network of more than 1,600 stores spread across 289 cities in China, selling electronics, appliances and other products. (Notably, the electronics sales business was at the root of JD.com too.)

Not to be outdone, in the same month that Alibaba and Suning formed their strategic alliance, JD.com bought a 10% stake in Yonghui Superstores, another major domestic supermarket, for $700 million. Founded in 1998, Yonghui Superstores at the time of the JD.com investment ran 364 supermarkets in China, with plans to add hundreds more in the coming years. Similar to Alibaba's investment into Intime, JD.com also aims to leverage Yonghui's existing networks of bricks-and-mortar stores to boost its supply chain and diversify its offline offerings. The e-commerce competition is now an all-out war in "omni-channels".

Among the three investments, the alliance of Alibaba and Suning was particularly interesting when one considers the fact that Suning had developed substantial e-tailing capability itself before the partnership. As a traditional electronics retailer,

Suning entered the e-commerce domain relatively early, and it had also invested in technology to provide smooth cross-channel fulfillment between their online stores and physical stores. As mentioned at the beginning of this chapter, Suning itself was rated amongst the top three B2C e-retailers in China before its 2015 partnership with Alibaba.

The alliance between Alibaba and Suning is the best example that in the omni-channel age of retailing, no single retail company can easily claim full coverage of consumers in both online and offline settings. In today's hyper connected world, a consumer's buying journey spans offline and online platforms. The merchants must ensure that they serve the consumers using all possible channels, because consumers are getting smarter every day with the increasing penetration of smart devices and can easily handle all channels.

To provide customers with a seamless experience, the internet firms and the traditional retailers have to use both online and offline touch-points to cover the full decision and purchase journey of the consumers. This includes searching and comparing online, trying products at offline shops, paying online or at offline outlets, arranging delivery online or pick-up at physical shops. In the omni-channel context, the storefronts at convenient locations will continue to attract foot traffic, but they are also adding an online persona when using the internet, managing marketing, logistics, post-sale services and customer engagement. As a result, the difference between online commerce and offline commerce is blurring and tend to disappear.

The omni-channel model promises unprecedented choice, convenience and simplicity to consumers. All companies in the value chain, however, need to deal with a changing cost structure to maintain profitability. On one hand, when foot traffic slows in stores, supply chain costs will most likely increase. In an omni-channel world, the supply chain has more dealings with the purchasing process away from the stores. This requires more resources and pushes down profitability. On the other hand, manufacturers are also facing exploding complexity in an omni-channel context. They now have to plan on multiple delivery points for multiple channels, and demand patterns are very likely to become more dynamic and random.

This also means that the companies have to make significant investments in big data technology. The omni-channel consumer prefers to use all channels simultaneously, and retailers will accordingly track customers across all channels. This means substantial collection of commercial data, not only on consumers' retailing patterns, but also on their overall spending habits, as well as their social networks and behavior. To win over repeat customers, the merchants have to deliver a distinguishable and personalized shopping experience to customers, by understanding not just what customers want and need, but also where they want it and how they want to experience it.

For example, in the face of e-commerce challenges, the shopping malls are forced to differentiate by innovation in the building design, offering services in addition to goods and creating a relaxing environment. Some high-end malls mix "experience consumption" offerings like cultural shows with retail shops in the same location. The goal is to offer additional experiences to the mall visitors so that they have to be physically at the mall in order to enjoy the overall shopping experience instead of staying at home and clicking on their computers to make purchases. (The widespread integration

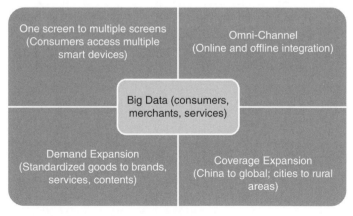

Figure 4.5   The Future Directions of e-Commerce

of consumers' online e-commerce and offline activities is the theme of the next chapter.)

The "omni-channel" trend explains why in his 2016 New Year's speech, Alibaba's CEO Daniel Zhang emphasized more "data" than "GMV" with respect to the company's future growth strategy. He went so far as to define Alibaba as a "data company", which uses the data from users, merchants and service systems to serve the overall Alibaba "ecosystem". In this context, data is at the core of the four future directions of e-commerce highlighted by CEO Mr. Daniel Zhang (see Figure 4.5).

To conclude this chapter, we will take another look at the debate around Alibaba's and JD.com's business models. As our analysis has revealed, the business models do not look as drastically different as the fierce debate between their founders would lead a casual observer to believe. Their continuing expansion and convergence in the "omni-channel" age probably means that they will likely resemble each other even more closely in the future.

5

Mobile e-Commerce and Online-to-Offline (O2O)

During the Spring Festival (the lunar New Year), it is a centuries-old custom for Chinese families to hand out red envelopes (called "hongbao") stuffed with crisp money bills to relatives and friends to wish them good fortune. The traditional "hongbao" scene used to be children in red holiday dress kneeling down and kowtowing to their elders to receive the gift, but now in the digital era it has become a fun game on mobile devices. On the eve of the Year of the Ram (early 2015), internet giants Tencent and Alibaba sent out numerous online "hongbao" collectively worth hundreds of millions of dollars to the public, using the traditional custom as a marketing competition for the control of the digital wallets of Chinese customers.

This marketing strategy was first introduced by Tencent during the Spring Festival season for the Year of the Horse (early 2014) on its popular messaging and social network platform WeChat. Individuals sending greetings to family and friends, and corporations showing appreciation to their employees, could conveniently do so by sending digital red envelopes via WeChat. The "hongbao" giver only needed to link the digital "hongbao" function with their payment channel (a bank account, for example). The giver could then directly transfer "hongbao" money from the bank account to the receiver

Red Envelope Giver

- Link their banking accounts to WeChat online payment systems
- Transfer money
- Post envelopes via WeChat Social Network

Mobile Payment System

- WeChat Social Network Tencent Payment System (WeChat Pay)

Red Envelope Receiver

- Install App
- Access envelope online
- Link bank account to retrieve money

Figure 5.1   The Parties in a Red Envelope – Fun and Value

through Tencent's payment system on WeChat (WeChat Pay). On the receiving end, the receivers also had to link their bank accounts to get their "hongbao" in cash or use the digital cash to pay for e-commerce services and products, such as mobile taxi-hailing (see Figure 5.1).

In addition to the digital red envelopes sent by WeChat users, Tencent itself also sent out a large number of "hongbaos" free to the public. Of course, Tencent was not just playing the "Santa Claus" role for the Chinese netizens' festival celebration. The animated digital envelopes were incentives for users to experience its mobile payment system. Because both the givers and receivers had to install the app linked to the WeChat Pay system, as well as registering their bank accounts or debit cards, Tencent was hoping that netizens would happily become WeChat Pay users while playing a fun game.

To the surprise of many internet firms (including Tencent itself), the concept of digital red envelopes "falling from the internet" received widespread acceptance from Chinese customers almost overnight. Many found gifting through electronic services more convenient and safer (versus traveling with cash). Young people in particular liked the "fun" aspect. Because the number of free red envelopes given out was limited, people had to rush to the links to secure a "hongbao", and this sensational process was referred to as "grab (or fight for) red envelopes!" in Chinese. The "grab" feature turned a passive custom into a participative activity and added an element of suspense, making the process more entertaining for the users.

In addition, a user could figuratively "throw" money into her WeChat groups of friends, letting the algorithm in the app divide the money randomly among them. No one knew the amount in their virtual red envelope before opening it. This "suspense" feature not only created more fun for the players, but also added "stickiness" to the process: it engaged the attention of the players before the actual results were known, and they would continue talking about the process in terms of joy, pride, jealousy, or disappointment, depending on how much they received from the overall pot of money. At the same time, WeChat designed the process to be very simple so that users at both ends were only a few clicks away from playing the game, and this also helped enhance its popularity.

The fun, stickiness and simplicity features of WeChat red envelopes created an extremely successful marketing campaign for WeChat Pay. With limited cash input, Tencent had multiplied its active users, acquired important data (banking information), and familiarized users with its WeChat payment service. During the 2014 Lunar New Year season, hundreds of millions of users were glued to their smartphones rather than the usual holiday activities, trying to "grab" as much as possible of the virtual red envelopes of money being doled out by their relatives, friends and Tencent itself. As a result, people opened the WeChat Pay app more often than they opened the Alipay app, even though WeChat had only launched the payment service some 10 years after Alibaba started Alipay. (As illustrated by further examples in this chapter, fun, stickiness and simplicity are the three key factors for the success of mobile e-commerce.)

No one was more shocked by the massive popularity of Tencent's new tactic than Alibaba's founder Jack Ma. He knew clearly that the jolly red envelope campaign would soon lead to the ultimate showdown in the battle for Chinese consumers' digital wallets. In his memo to Alibaba staff, Jack Ma called the red envelope campaign by Tencent "The Pearl

Harbor Attack", warning his staff that Alibaba's current dominance in online payments could be severely challenged by Tencent's WeChat Pay and its related mobile services. So in the 2015 Lunar New Year season, Jack Ma himself introduced red envelopes with his own twist to rival Tencent's popularity. On the eve of the Year of the Ram, Jack Ma posted a customized red envelope and a photo of himself with the question: "Who looks like an alien?" on the Twitter-like social network Sina Weibo. Those who gave the correct answer ("I do") received red envelopes directly from the Alibaba founder himself.

According to Chinese media reports, his 99,999 (a lucky number in Chinese tradition) red envelopes with a total amount exceeding $150,000 were "grabbed" within the first three minutes. At company level, the electronic payments unit Alipay handed out 430 million red envelopes with a total value close to $100 million, in addition to several hundred million dollars' worth of digital cash coupons. Meanwhile, Tencent worked hard to maintain its momentum from the previous year. Thanks to its partnership with CCTV during the popular New Year's Eve live TV broadcast that drew around 700 million Chinese viewers globally, WeChat sent out 120 million red envelopes during a segment when the audience "fought" for the cash gifts.

Then the drama turned into something else entirely. Soon the competition escalated to such a level that Tencent blocked Alipay's red envelopes on WeChat in early February to fend off its "invasion". When Alibaba's red envelopes were launched, they included one-click sharing of gifts via Tencent's WeChat and QQ mobile messaging apps, but within a day Tencent blocked the Alipay red envelopes, saying that they might result in a "security threat." In addition to Alipay red envelopes, Tencent cleansed several of its rivals' other entertainment services from its WeChat platform.

Alibaba put up a fight. While Tencent could block the sending of Alibaba red envelopes by users on WeChat, it could not prevent them from sharing pictures of the envelopes. The programmers at Alibaba turned the envelope into a picture that came with a digital password, together with a function enabling the Alipay user to open WeChat directly and send out the picture to circles of friends. Once friends had seen the picture and memorized the password, they could go to Alipay to retrieve the corresponding red envelope. To the credit of the hardworking Alibaba staff, it was an extraordinarily quick solution to bypass the WeChat block with a minimum of fuss (although the popularity of the Alipay red envelope was impacted to some extent by the disrupted user experience).

Looking beyond the New Year's fun and drama, the battle for red envelopes was a serious engagement between the two internet giants in the war for the future of the mobile internet. With e-commerce in China increasingly turning mobile, competition in the third-party mobile payment market had escalated. For Alibaba, this was a stronghold that it could not afford to lose. Compared to Tencent's WeChat Pay, Alibaba's Alipay had a longer history and a head start with hundreds of millions of active users from its affiliation with Taobao, TMall and Alibaba's other e-commerce sites.

However, building on the explosive penetration of the WeChat app, WeChat Pay has shown strong growth momentum in recent years. In addition, the innovative red envelope campaigns instantly attracted millions of WeChat users to sign up for its payment service for the first time, on the basis of which Tencent doubled its Tenpay market share from 5% to 10% within just a year. That shocked Alibaba's Jack Ma, and in an email to his employees, he wrote in alarm: "I'm worried about us getting lost in the competition and forgetting to do the things we are good at."

When e-commerce goes mobile, it is critical for internet firms to hook the users on their online platforms to their mobile payment systems. But that is only the start of a much broader landscape shift for online transactions. As more examples in this chapter will show, the mobile payment system has become an important link between the mobile internet population and their offline spending activities (known as "online to offline" businesses), such as restaurant bookings, grocery deliveries, in-home manicures and booking movie tickets, to name but a few. Internet users' familiarity with mobile payment services can facilitate the development in many more new areas of mobile e-commerce than digital retailing.

Compared to the hefty sums they had paid out, Tencent and Alibaba had gained far more value from cultivating a larger number of potential customers through the red envelope game. For the same reason, Jack Ma's concern was more about its competitive edge in the "online to offline" market rather than purely about Alipay's market share in mobile payment. After the "red envelope war": between China's largest e-commerce company (Alibaba) and its most popular mobile social network (Tencent), the question remained as to who would win control of the emerging and promising "online to offline" market?

Online-to-Offline (O2O) Market Potential

With rapid development in mobile internet infrastructure and smartphone usage, China is playing a leading role globally in the development of the online-to-offline (O2O) e-commerce model. O2O can be broadly defined as the integration of offline business opportunities with activities on the internet. O2O growth in China is closely correlated with its increasing urbanization, which has created more middle class spenders for consumer goods and offline activities in the cities year on year. At the same time, Chinese smartphone manufacturers have enabled the wider public to own a mobile device with high specifications, creating the largest smartphone user population in the world.

Empowered by smartphones and social media, Chinese consumers are increasingly using mobile channels to spend. Thanks to the rise of popular internet applications to book tickets, play games, watch videos, etc., China's mobile business has seen explosive growth in recent years. People of all ages and from diverse backgrounds have become accustomed to the internet lifestyle through mobile services. A few short years ago O2O was a mere concept in China, but it is now seen as the

Table 5.1   The Three Lines of O2O Businesses

O2O Parties	Line 1	Line 2	Line 3
Consumers (Goal)	To experience new services or non-standardized goods	Ad hoc purchases out of convenience or offline adverts	To receive promotions and benefits; More convenient delivery and services
Merchants (Goal)	To attract new customers	Online sales of goods	Loyal customers' repeat purchases
Mobile Platforms (Service)	Online "discovery" mechanism (discount coupon, customer review, social network, mobile payment and more)	Mobile payment system to close ad hoc transactions	Customer relationship management (CRM)

most fundamental disruptive force for the e-commerce model going forward.

The O2O market involves three main parties: consumers, offline merchants and online platforms. Their objectives are intertwined to form three main lines of O2O (see Table 5.1), which can be summarized as follows:

1. Merchants inform potential customers of specialized goods and services that customers are not aware of and guide the customers to their shop locations to experience these;
2. Customers make online purchases when they move around in the physical world (mobile e-retailing); and
3. Merchants provide targeted promotions to consumers to encourage repeat spending.

The first scenario covers all services sectors and has the greatest business potential; it is the focus of this chapter.

Line 3 – Online information to the offline world

The basic form of O2O relates to providing customers with consistent promotions and sales online and instore, which has already been covered in previous chapters. For example, in the omni-channel retailing context, e-commerce sites have been discussing with retailers how to send discount information, tailored to suit a customer's shopping habits, to their mobile phone as they enter the store. At a national level, some leading online businesses plan to team with partner stores to link customers in all cities with their distribution networks, allowing customers to collect their online orders from cities anywhere in the country.

Also, social networks like WeChat allow retailers to set up public accounts that could help them both to attract new customers and enhance customer loyalty (potential repeat purchases). They can use WeChat to distribute articles to subscribers, manage memberships, interact with frequent or potential customers and send targeted promotions. Any viable restaurant, flower delivery shop, beauty salon or language school in China has a QR code both on its signage and on WeChat for passers by on the street and the online population to link the offline store information. As mentioned earlier, numerous Western companies have embraced WeChat for direct communications marketing.

Line 2 – Mobile e-retailing

This O2O case can be referred to as "mobile e-retailing", and relates to customers making online purchases from a mobile terminal while they are moving around in the physical world. While Line 3 O2O simply uses customers' smartphones and other mobile devices as a new channel to send product promotion and company information during their everyday offline life, mobile e-retailing enables customers to place online orders anytime and anywhere, which requires many more software settings to provide a complete purchase process than in the traditional e-commerce sphere.

Mobile payment service is by definition a critical component of mobile e-retailing, which aligns with the Chinese consumer's desire for the speed and convenience of "any time" shopping. Many of these purchases are spur of the moment decisions arising from offline world advertisements, social conversations or simply random thoughts. As a result, a large percentage of purchase decisions may not eventually turn into actual transactions, if the e-retailing platform does not have a ready and convenient mobile payment function attached to it.

Launched by the Alibaba Group in 2004, Alipay has the longest history in China's third-party payment market. After the restructuring around its 2014 IPO, Alipay is not owned by Alibaba, nor is it part of the Alibaba IPO, but it is controlled by Alibaba's top executives. Alipay runs a PayPal-like internet-payment service and it is already the world's No. 1 processor of mobile payments. Alipay not only processes payments on Alibaba's Taobao and Tmall online marketplaces, but also handles many other types of online and offline payments, including utility bills, ticket booking, restaurant meals and taxi rides.

Mobile payment is much more widely used in China than in developed markets like the US or Europe. A large part of the Chinese population have never even used credit cards are now using the internet to manage their payments, savings and investments, just as in many parts of China people are skipping landline phones in favor of a smartphone to access the internet for the first time in their lives. This phenomenon is best illustrated by the mobile payment usage difference between more urbanized eastern coastal cities and the less developed western regions in China itself.

According to findings published by Alipay in early 2016, mobile payment is more popular – to the surprise of many – in China's underdeveloped western regions. With 83.3% of online transactions paid by consumers with mobile devices in 2015, the Tibet autonomous region led the country in mobile payment adoption. Tibet was followed by four provinces in Western China – Guizhou, Gansu, Shaanxi and Qinghai, where on average consumers processed nearly 80% of online payment transactions via mobile devices. The reason may well be very straightforward: there is a lack of bricks-and-mortar retail infrastructure in those regions, so the people there turn to online shopping more frequently for the products they are looking for, and they make more ad hoc purchases at random offline convenience stores while they travel in less populated areas.

In contrast to traditional e-retailing from PC terminals, mobile e-retailing can take place from online platforms other than e-commerce apps. Tencent lacks a platform similar to that of Taobao or Tmall, but social engagement and shopping behavior are so intertwined in China that WeChat is an ideal place to introduce offerings that are heavily influenced by word-of-mouth recommendation and peer reviews. Tencent has used WeChat to create a different e-commerce platform based on a social context, and its development process shows the importance of mobile payment systems for internet firms' mobile businesses.

In September 2013, Tencent started its "Wei Sheng-huo" system ("WeLife" or Micro Life in English), a merchant service package for O2O business on WeChat. But WeLife only gained limited attention, the major issue being the lack of an integrated payment system. As background, the WeChat development team had taken careful measures to limit excessive marketing and advertising on its platform. Even within Tencent management, there was concern that commercial activities on the WeChat platform could damage the user experience. At the same time, Tencent's own payment system was not yet widely adopted by internet users. Therefore, without the online payment function linkage, WeLife could hardly form a complete business circle for both e-commerce players and offline businesses, and the feedback was highlighted as "good advertisement, but few closings".

As mentioned at the beginning of this chapter, through the innovative digital red envelope campaign during the 2014

Chinese New Year, WeChat Pay successfully made its major push into the online payment business territory long held by Alipay. Shortly thereafter, Tencent permitted merchants to set up "little WeChat stores" ("Weixin Xiaodian" in Chinese) via verified public accounts linked to the app's own payment system. A WeChat store can use WeChat to advertise and offer discounts. Meanwhile the app users could pay for these goods directly by using WeChat Pay. The built-in payment feature further enabled the businesses to track transactions and analyze customers' shopping habits and preferences.

In addition, with the WeChat Stores Tencent officially permitted individual WeChat users to establish in-app stores to sell goods to their friends and followers. Based on the circles of friends, WeChat users could develop a "social distribution platform" to form franchising and pyramid sales. For example, one franchise manager of a branded face mask product in Shanghai was reported to be a beneficiary of this new "social sale" channel. This franchise manager used to rely on beauty parlors as his main sales channel, but with the WeChat store function, an increasing number of his goods were sold through WeChat users. The key was the multiplying factor of the "circles": the manager recruited no more than 100 top-active-level WeChat users, who then recruited other users to help them conduct further sales.

Seen from the perspective of small vendors, the little WeChat stores are an interesting alternative to selling on Taobao. The profit margin is potentially higher, not only because Tencent charges no fees, but also because it is becoming harder and more expensive for vendors to get noticed on Taobao. Alibaba has built up a network effect on the Taobao marketplace (it is costly for a buyer to leave an existing network of sellers, and vice versa for a seller), but once Alibaba monetizes the traffic, vendors have begun to explore other traffic channels to lower the cost. Overall, Tencent having major brands opening stores inside WeChat is a threat to Alibaba's Tmall, and its inclusion of smaller merchants is a challenge to Alibaba's Taobao.

As mentioned in the previous chapter, Alibaba's main e-retailing rival JD.com has set up an alliance with WeChat since 2014, but is still testing ways to convert WeChat user traffic into buyer traffic on JD.com's e-retailing platform. The WeChat stores, however, create a natural closed loop on the WeChat platform itself, covering the whole process of information gathering from the social network, initiating purchasing intent and placing orders, making payments using WeChat Pay, and sharing feedback with social circles. It will be interesting to see whether the WeChat shops become a direct challenge to Alibaba's e-retailing dominance in a significant way.

Line 1 – The biggest O2O market potential

The Line 1 of O2O business fits with the popular definition of O2O, which basically means attracting retail customers online, and then directing them to physical stores for the purchase of actual goods or real-life experiences such as movie going, dining out, shopping, taxi hailing and so on. It broadly covers almost every part of the economy, which is the focus of this chapter.

What makes this O2O model different from traditional e-commerce? The latter only covers standard goods, such as packages delivered in the mail, and cannot offer personalized social experiences like going to restaurants, bars and museums, or signing up for a yoga class or tennis lesson. The growth in "experience" consumption is at the core of the O2O trends in China, because the market sees the second or third generation of young consumers in the cities looking beyond necessities, and seeking out and being willing to pay for specialized leisure and entertainment consumption.

As reflected in CNNIC's December 2014 report, 39.2% of consumers in the country's biggest cities, including Beijing, Shanghai, Guangzhou and Shenzhen, used O2O services in that year, and the number in second- and third-tier cities was also gradually increasing. Along the same lines, the CNNIC report also found that restaurants, food catering and leisure O2O business started early and their market mode had become increasingly mature and the services more refined. For instance, mobile apps for travel reservation beat other mobile apps with an annual user growth rate of 194.6% in 2014.

And the O2O potential does not end with youth and leisure. More and more O2O models are emerging in many economic sectors. For instance, the O2O business for medical and domestic services started to take off in response to the strong demand from an ageing population. Healthcare providers are implementing remote patient monitoring to stretch their footprints to under-served patient populations while substantially saving costs for patients with chronic disease. Overall the O2O market is growing rapidly in both size and quality.

As previously outlined, since 2014 more Chinese people are users of mobile devices as the main entry point to the internet. Urban residents mostly turn to their smartphones to navigate their daily lives as they commute in the cities. In smaller cities and rural towns, those who do not own PCs at home are using mobile devices to experience their first internet connection, and they have also quickly adapted to mobile online transactions. Because China is more densely populated than many developed countries – for example, Chinese cities with a population of over 1 million significantly outnumber US cities of the same size – the O2O market potential for all kinds of services is huge in China. (**See the "O2O Services for Sperm Donation and Egg Freezing" Box.**)

O2O Services for Sperm Donation and Egg Freezing

Few would have expected that O2O would find its way into people's sex lives and reproductive plans. But it seems that O2O is going into every possible niche market offline.

In 2015, Alibaba's e-commerce platform Taobao and KingMed Diagnostics, China's biggest third-party medical laboratory group, jointly offered great deals online for paternity tests and sperm donation.

During the three-day campaign, sperm donors were able to register their personal information online, avoiding an embarrassing first visit to the sperm collection centers. Volunteers only needed to provide their name, the last six digits of their ID card and email address to complete the online registration. After their sperm donation, each volunteer would receive a subsidy somewhere between around $475 and $800. Within 72 hours, more than 22,000 men reportedly signed up for sperm donations at one of seven sperm banks nationwide.

The Taobao campaign also offered paternity testing services without customers having to make visits to hospitals, costing just over $100, a huge discount compared to the average cost of about $650. A testing kit was sent to the customer after he or she placed an online order. The consumer only needed to collect and send a saliva sample to a test center, which would provide the test result after 10 working days. During the same period, Taobao attracted 137 applications for paternity tests and 4,060 for sperm fertility testing.

Following the success of Taobao's online sperm-donation program, Southern California Reproductive Center, a Los Angeles reproductive clinic, started discussions with Alibaba's group-buying website Juhuasuan to promote its egg-freezing treatment. Its prospective customers included white collar women in their 30s who work in big cities, and who had chosen to delay motherhood due to career considerations. This was another example where O2O business continues to integrate with more niche demands and expand into overseas technology and services.

In short, O2O is simultaneously "creating a bigger pie" and "dividing a pie in new ways" among customers, offline business and internet firms. For businesses whose products or services, such as movie cinemas and stylish restaurants, cannot be packed up and shipped in bulk to customers, O2O helps win more business through the internet; for internet firms, they come to share the profits that used to be exclusively owned by offline merchants or service providers. Because the O2O market covers all services and non-standardized consumer goods, it potentially has a much larger market size than mobile e-retailing. As such, all of the major internet firms as well as numerous start-ups are competing for their positions in this promising market.

O2O Market: Still an Open Battlefield

It should be highlighted that O2O business aims to capture the users' "mind share" when they are in between the online and offline worlds. In other words, O2O happens at the fragmented time "in between" the two worlds, such as waiting in line for a bus, taking a taxi ride or sitting in the subway on the way home. This time could be used to go online and arrange offline activities at a later time (see Figure 5.2). As such, whoever can provide a fun, sticky and convenient link among consumers, online platforms and offline service providers is the ultimate winner.

The most direct link for new customers is for internet firms to send out discount coupons online that can be redeemed at stores on the street. This "subsidies for initial customer traffic" approach featured in almost every O2O start-up. Those ventures often started in a single niche, whether for car washes or massages, and many would use venture capital cash for subsidies to pull in customers and suppliers. (Another similar important sponge or trap for netizens' fragmented time is free entertainment content on mobile devices, which will be discussed in detail in the next few chapters.)

To use an example, unlike clothing and shoes, seafood is not a standardized product. It is difficult for consumers to gauge the quality of the product purely from the information

Figure 5.2   O2O – The "In-Between" World

provided online. Besides, most ordinary Chinese consumers are unfamiliar with imported seafood. In the O2O context, after the customer receives an online coupon, they have to turn up to redeem it, and this process enables them to interact with representatives from traditional outlets to get to know the products better.

Middle-aged shoppers in particular have more trust in the traditional stores where they can check out seafood directly. They prefer the situation where they can first buy imported seafood at stores before ordering the same products online in the future. In addition, if they are not satisfied with the products ordered online, they also have the option to return the food to the traditional stores, which is important in the context of non-standardized products that have a high probability of return or post-sale service requirements.

Investors, and the market itself, are beginning to have concerns about the subsidies model as there is too much competition and there are too many copycat products (i.e. a question of the "stickiness" of customers). The case of the group purchase sector later in this chapter will illustrate the ongoing price war and accelerating consolidation in the O2O market. At the same time, the internet giants BAT – Baidu, Alibaba and Tencent – are working on using their unique capabilities in the mobile world to link their online user traffic effectively with offline businesses. Because the whole O2O spending process includes many different linkage points, it is a test of an internet firm's overall strength, not its leadership position in one or two areas.

The main search engine in China, Baidu, has Google-like predominance in China's search and maps services, and it naturally centered its O2O initiatives around those capabilities. The best showcase of Baidu's expertise in location-based services is an interactive heat map on its website that visualizes the movement of people during the country's one-month spring festival travel rush, when millions of Chinese travel across the country for the Spring Festival holiday family gatherings. On top of that, Baidu also releases the "Spring Festival Homecoming Tool

Kit" on Baidu Maps. During the chaotic holiday travel season, the tool kit provides users with information about each city's weather conditions, traffic conditions, railway timetables, flight schedules and the location of holiday train tickets sales agents.

According to Baidu's data, searches on smartphones exceeded those on PCs for the first time in the second half of 2014, and the company continues R&D efforts to improve search services in the mobile context. In 2015, Baidu launched Siri-like O2O personal assistant "Duer" within the Baidu Mobile Search app. Users could verbally ask Duer various questions and the AI (artificial intelligence)-based Duer would respond with appropriate recommendations. For example, a user could ask Duer to find a pet service store near the movie theater she was going to, and Duer would search online to find a suitable one for her.

Baidu's Mobile Maps app has also been hugely popular. Baidu reported that the Maps app reached 300 million monthly active users in late 2015. According to Baidu's data, its Maps app covered "the largest number of points of interest (POI) of any map in the industry," with over 20 million POIs related to service providers. Over 70% of the search queries from Baidu Maps were about services, such as dining, transportation, education and pet-related services.

However, in the mobile world, customers' searches are more fragmented. Instead of being glued to a PC screen and using a search engine like Baidu, people tend to use multiple channels to seek information when they move around with their mobile devices. For example, they may use Alibaba's Taobao to check out imported seafood, or Tencent's WeChat to ask friends for new movie information, or customer review apps for promotion deals from nearby restaurants.

In addition, Baidu has not yet found a way to consolidate information in various apps. In the service market, the third-party service providers have their information in respective apps. For users to find specific service information, they have to install and open up those specific apps. Baidu and global search engines are all working on a solution to provide a search that could go "deep" into individual apps. So far, this kind of technology is still at an early stage even in the global markets, and no single solution stands out as the most effective to this "search on top of a search" question. The main reason is that most of the apps on the mobile internet have been developed independently and therefore are not interconnected. For these reasons, Baidu's leading position in search may not be as dominant in the mobile world as in the desktop PC world.

Tencent's WeChat, on the other hand, has as its special strength in attracting users' attention during fragmented time intervals. It can be difficult for anyone outside of China to fathom how deeply WeChat has become woven into daily life in the short period since its creation. Many WeChat users are addicted to checking it throughout the day, whenever they have a few seconds of free time. This is invaluable for Tencent's O2O businesses (as mentioned before, O2O transactions happen during users' "in-between" moments). Furthermore, the most active users on WeChat – dubbed "WeChat Bees" – have created a free distribution system of service information for Tencent.

According to a recent market survey by the Advertisement School at China Media University, a remarkable 55% of internet users in China may be categorized as "high frequency information receivers and distributors" on social networks like WeChat. This term was defined by the Advertisement School report as someone who received and re-distributed information on new products or new services more than twice a week. The survey covered overseas cities such as Tokyo, Osaka, New York and Los Angeles, and the results showed that the figure of 55% in China was much higher than in Japan (10%) and the US (40%).

Apparently these "high frequency information receivers and distributors" seek three things when busy collecting and distributing online information: to strengthen individual relationships within the circle, to demonstrate superior information-access capability, and to bring new life experiences to their circles after their initial testing. Like honey bees, these people not only share information with their circles of friends but also actively search for new product and service information, hence they are referred to by the Advertisement School report as "WeChat Bees." Overall, the social network channel is the most important link in Tencent's O2O businesses.

For Alibaba, Alipay's dominant position in the mobile payment field is a significant advantage that no competitor can ignore. Alibaba Group disclosed at the end of 2014 that Alipay had more than 300 million registered users and processed more than 80 million transactions each day. More importantly, the company also announced that Alipay is increasingly processing transactions through mobile devices. According to the company's data, 54 out of every 100 payments made with Alipay came from mobile devices, as the popularity of mobile devices has encouraged more than half of Alipay users to use their handsets and mobile apps as payment tools. (By contrast, only 22 out of every 100 Alipay payments were mobile payments in 2013.)

There is no better illustration of Alipay's competitive advantage than the war of red envelopes itself. Although WeChat Pay gained a lot of popularity through the campaign, there was a bottom line question about the digital gifts: how would people spend the money in the WeChat Pay account? The answer to the question highlighted one critical hurdle that the WeChat ecosystem still had to overcome: namely the limited usage of WeChat payments in the business context (the O2O play), especially in lower-tier cities and rural areas. In some areas, people could only think of applying "hongbao" money in WeChat to taxi-hailing and mobile phone service charges, which greatly reduced the broader public interest in using WeChat Pay, even though the people in these areas – typically the older generations – joined the New Year "hongbao" fun with the younger generations who were living in first- and second-tier cities.

By contrast, over a period of years, Alipay has become firmly established in numerous business settings. These include offline settings like restaurants, shops, supermarkets, convenience stores, taxi-hailing, hospitals and more. It also includes online settings like credit card payment, money transfers, lottery tickets, membership cards and more, in addition to the retail marketplaces of Taobao and T-mall e-commerce. (To develop its O2O business, Tencent has expended great effort in building partnerships with offline stores and service providers.)

Naturally, the more physical stores and offline settings that set up the linkage to Alibaba's Alipay system, the more customers will use Alipay for their daily purchases. The more familiar and comfortable those customers become with mobile payment, the more likely they are to use digital subsidies to check out offline service offerings. Over the years Alibaba's two main shopping sites – Taobao and Tmall – have also accumulated enormous customer data, which should generate synergy when it partners with traditional businesses in the O2O markets.

In addition, Alibaba has invested aggressively in social networks, mobile apps and mobile search areas, which are at the root of Tencent and Baidu. In April 2013, Alibaba acquired an 18% stake in Sina Weibo, China's version of Twitter, for \$586m, with the option to raise that stake to 30%. This investment provided an important social link to Alibaba's e-commerce. After the investment, Alibaba made the effort to merge the accounts between Weibo and Taobao so that users could access each other's platforms with Sina Weibo or Taobao ID.

For one thing, Weibo provides a new reason for users to get onto Alibaba's platforms. Alibaba's e-commerce sites are already widely known in China; but they are not really fun places to "hang out" – in fact, people go to Taobao only when they want to buy something quickly. Weibo, however, is a social place for users to post their views, check out opinion leaders and so on. Through the tie-up with Weibo, Alibaba may not significantly increase the user base of its e-commerce sites, but it may keep the Alibaba platforms visible for a little longer. The Weibo connection also speeds up Alibaba's effort to establish its own social-based e-commerce platform to compete with WeChat shops. For example, when Weibo users post emotional comments about polluted air in Beijing, an air filter advertisement on Taobao could appear nearby.

Furthermore, Alibaba invested its way into the messaging app business directly after its effort to build an Alibaba version of WeChat, named "LaiWang", failed to take off. In March 2014, Alibaba invested $215 million in return for a minority stake in the messaging and free-calling app Tango in the US. Having started as a video-calling application to rival Skype and FaceTime, Tango's service stood out, with an early focus on video messaging. Just like WeChat, Tango was broadening into a social platform for users to play games, stream music and share photos.

Soon after that, in June 2014, Alibaba bought the whole of UCWeb, a popular mobile browser company in China, after it had acquired two-thirds of the company in 2009 and 2013. UCWeb is one of the biggest web browser companies in China, with more than 50% market share. With full control, Alibaba turned UCWeb into a division of its own, overseeing the browser, mobile search, gaming, apps store and mobile reader operations, as well as working with Alibaba's mapping unit to provide location-based services. In addition, Alibaba also bought a 28% stake in Chinese mobile-mapping firm AutoNavi Holdings to gain a secure foothold in the mobile map service.

Apart from the three internet giants, another important player in the O2O market is the commercial real estate giant the Dalian Wanda Group. In contrast to internet firms, Dalian Wanda enters into the competition from offline roots. Dalian Wanda is China's biggest private property developer and runs more than 100 shopping malls and the largest movie theater chain across the country. For quite a while, the founder Jianling Wang and Alibaba's Jack Ma have been alternating as holder of the title "the country's richest man". As will be discussed in later chapters, Wanda's holding of movie theaters makes it a particularly strong player in the O2O movie market.

In summary, the O2O market has so much potential that all the internet giants and commercial real estate conglomerates are pouring resources and efforts into related areas. With O2O, the online and offline shopping experience is increasingly merged and unified. To be successful in O2O markets, important as it is for brick-and-mortar retailers to have an online presence, it is equally important for e-commerce companies to associate with physical stores. So it remains to be seen whether the companies with internet roots (BAT) or with offline strongholds (Wanda) will emerge as the ultimate winners.

Even within the internet firms, no single firm dominates in every area of the mobile linkages relating to the O2O market. If Baidu is understood to be the best link between people and information (search), Alibaba between people and goods (e-commerce), Tencent between people and people (social network), then O2O is the link between people and service, which requires the support of all three of the above links. To conclude this section, Table 5.2 provides a summary of the major players' relative O2O strengths. There is still no obvious single dominating winner in the O2O market. The case outlined in

Table 5.2   Comparison of the Major O2O Players

Connections	Mobile Technology and Resources	Leading Companies
People and smart devices	Smartphone	Xiaomi, LeTV
People and information	Search engine, mobile map	Baidu
People and goods	e-Retailing marketplaces, vendor network, mobile payment system	Alibaba, JD
People and people	Social network	Tencent
People and in-person shopping environment	Shopping malls	Dalian Wanda
People and services (O2O)	**All of the above**	**BAT is leading the competition, but still an open battlefield for all players**

the next section on the O2O dining market will illustrate that O2O competition is far more complicated than the red envelope war.

The Case of O2O Meal Services

Within the broad O2O markets in China, restaurants and food catering businesses were early movers, and their market mode is more mature than other fields. The reasons are simple. First the sheer numbers of the population: feeding nearly 1.4 billion people is a massive market by itself. Eating is also probably the most important and frequent social activity for the Chinese, who have a proverb that states "people regard food as their prime want" (or, as the Chinese character describes it, "heaven"). On top of that, the number of young professionals and workers in the cities is steadily increasing along with the trend towards urbanization, and they tend to eat out frequently due to their busy lifestyle.

Steep discounts in the form of group purchases have been a significant driver for growth in this sector. Group-discount apps generally sell batches of vouchers from merchants at a discount if a minimum number of buyers sign up, and they earn a commission on each voucher sold. A large number of Chinese companies entered the group-discount business in 2010 and 2011, often as clones of Groupon Inc. in the US, but many once high-flyers quickly burned through their investment dollars without ever reaching profitability. In this ultracompetitive field, Dianping, Meituan and Nuomi, each backed by one of China's top three internet companies, were the main survivors (before the 2015 Meituan/Dianping merger), while numerous other similar apps have emerged and failed (see Figure 5.3).

The biggest player, Meituan, had Alibaba as an important shareholder. Founded in 2010, Meituan had around a 50% share of the group-buying market, and it was the largest platform in China for services such as restaurant bookings, hotel reservations and movie-ticket purchases. After its fundraising round in January 2015, the company was valued at $7 billion, whereas its closest equivalent in the US, Groupon, was valued

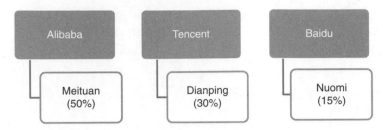

Figure 5.3   Main Players and Their Market Shares in O2O Meal Services
(Data Sources: Wall Street Journal, Economist, 2015)

at only \$5.4 billion at that time. The company claimed to have 20 million daily mobile users and to operate in more than 1,000 Chinese cities, representing a substantially larger user base than Groupon.

Dianping was a major competitor to Meituan, and its key shareholder included Tencent. The company had established itself as the go-to platform in China for customer reviews since it was founded in 2003. Yelp was often viewed as its closest equivalent in the US. It also had a major fundraising round in early 2015, which gave the company a valuation of around \$4 billion (also above that of Yelp). Strictly speaking, Dianping is part Yelp and part Groupon, because the Dianping app is for both restaurant reviews and group buying. Before the merger with Meituan, Dianping had about 30% of the market share, and the third player Nuomi, which was fully owned by Baidu, about 15%.

The important driving force behind the faster growth for the Chinese firms compared to their US counterparts was the generous subsidies that these companies paid out to win users. (This could be compared to the internet firms doling out red envelopes to gain mobile payment user sign-ups, or providing cash rebates to taxi drivers and passengers for using taxi hailing apps.) The group-discount companies were at war, offering freebies and deep discounts to gain the attention of both consumers buying and merchants selling. As such, some parts of the market were skeptical about the valuation of these firms, as the valuations were largely based on user numbers (which is not very different from the "eyeballs" metrics from the earlier tech boom). From their perspective, the existing players were mere survivors who were still trying to figure out a consistent revenue model (and then hopefully a profit model).

The biggest concern on valuation was the "stickiness" of the customers, meaning the customer might have their purchase choices based predominantly on the size of subsidies instead of the services. They would then likely move to a different service provider once the subsidies were reduced. The offline merchants also worried that the internet companies would eventually reduce or even stop subsidizing the O2O businesses once they became the dominant channels for service booking, leaving merchants to deal with customers who were used to artificially low prices. But the optimists believed that once customers were accustomed to O2O businesses, they would continue using the services out of convenience, even without the subsidies.

When Meituan and Dianping announced in October 2015 that the two companies would merge, the market had high hopes that the price war in group buying would soon come to an end. At the time of the merger, the combined company was estimated to be worth $15 billion. Shortly after that, the combined Meituan-Dianping raised $3.3 billion in January 2016, constituting the largest private fundraising round globally for a venture capital-backed start-up. Tencent led the latest round of funding, and it subsequently became the key investor in the new Meituan-Dianping.

As a result of the Meituan-Dianping merger, Alibaba decided to sell its stake, which represented about 7% of the company. The stake was reportedly sold in January 2016 to a group of investors that included some existing shareholders. For its future strategy in the O2O dining service market, Alibaba has signaled that it would refocus on its own online food coupon site Koubei and the Alipay payment system, which is commonly used in restaurants across the country. In response, Baidu has set up Baidu Waimai, a

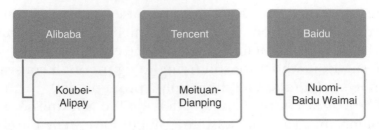

Figure 5.4   The Competitive Landscape Post-Meituan/Dianping Merger

food-ordering and delivery platform on which Baidu plans to build up its own catering logistical team to have better quality control. Its fully-owned Nuomi subsidiary announced that it would invest $3.2 billion in the business over the next three years. The competitive landscape has changed significantly since the Meituan-Dianping merger (see Figure 5.4).

Tencent's continuous involvement in the merged Meituan/Dianping is consistent with its strategy in many other internet areas. Because its messaging and social networking app has hundreds of millions of active users, rather than running its own operations, Tencent's strategy has been to take minority stakes in other technology companies and use the alliances to offer a wider range of services. In particular, the restaurant review aspect of Dianping is a perfect fit for Tencent's WeChat platform, given the social nature of meals and the customers' preference for peer opinion in China.

Dining at a restaurant involves interpersonal relationships, in much the same way as buying a car does. The basic principle for merchants is to treat customers well, so that they will sing the praises of the service to friends, family and so on. In this context, adding online reviews to social networks is not dramatically different from the old days. For merchants and shops, having a "social page" or "public account" on the WeChat social network is similar to having a Yellow Page listing in the past. Most of the companies are in the Yellow Pages, but this listing alone does not drive a merchant's business automatically. Personal recommendations are much more critical in instigating purchase-related activities such as signing up group deals.

The WeChat bees discussed earlier in this chapter provide the link between restaurant reviews and their circle of friends on the social network. In fact, a large part of the discussions among WeChat users is about where to book tables at restaurants for group get-togethers and where to find deals. In addition, although there is no question that WeChat is the most popular mobile social network in China (the consumer–consumer side), without a mobile map service its business connections with the merchants' side (the business–business side) are still catching up. Therefore the alliance with Meituan-Dianping provides a lot more relevant content to WeChat users, including merchant locations, special offers and catering services

For Baidu, its existing and unique competitive advantage is its location-based searches and services, as many daily deals are offered on the Nuomi site based on geography. By integrating group-buying business and map information into its searches, Baidu could turn a simple Sichuan restaurant search into a real-life dinner trip. This means that in one search, the Baidu system could figure out where the user's current location is, where the nearby locations for dining are, which restaurants have special deals available and then provide a map guiding the customer from the mobile screen to the chosen physical store. Furthermore, Baidu as mentioned earlier has developed a voice assistant – similar to Apple's Siri or Google Now – to improve users' search experience. But compared to Alipay and WeChat Pay, Baidu's mobile payment system is a relatively weak link in its O2O business.

Alibaba, on the other hand, seems to put Alipay at the center of its future O2O businesses. In a direct competition with the group-buying apps, Alipay has also sent out coupons to consumers. The trick was that consumers could download coupons directly and the discounts could only be realized when users paid for their meals with Alipay. Because Alipay has already been widely used by many merchants and shops, it is fairly easy for users to become accustomed to completing a meal purchase exclusively with Alipay.

In addition, Alibaba has made important investments in "deep mobile search" technology to potentially provide users with a fast and convenient search tool for the information scattered across various apps. For example, if one user wants to find a Sichuan cuisine restaurant with open seating in Shanghai's financial district, the user has to download Dianping or a similar app and then check the booking information embedded in the app. Ideally, users would like a program to first search for all relevant apps and then consolidate the information within each app before presenting it in the same way as a keyword search on the web. In the case of the Sichuan restaurant example above, the user likes to see the program search through Dianping, Meituan and Nuomi directly (without having to launch them on the handset) and list all the nearby places on one single screen.

In October 2014, Alibaba formed a partnership with the US "app search" company Quixey (for which Alibaba was also an early stage investor) in China, which will bring Quixey's search capabilities to Alibaba's mobile operating system YunOS. Quixey's core business is to help app developers modify or build their apps to have "deep linking" which facilitates "deep mobile search". Since Alibaba has controlled many internet businesses through acquisitions, those related apps could potentially add in deep links among them so that Alibaba's mobile search can easily find the information within them and consolidate it accordingly (see Figure 5.5). In the ultra-competitive O2O market, this feature could be highly attractive to users and a differentiator among peers.

Will the price war end soon in the new landscape post-Meituan-Dianping merger? The market's hope for a ceasefire was short-lived. Baidu's Nuomi has reiterated its commitment to putting more capital investment into the business, Alipay has actually become a new channel of coupons for consumers, and the new Meituan-Dianping has just received new investment for expansion. In addition, once known as group-discount sites, they are all broadening their services into other "life services" such as wedding ceremonies. Therefore, the price war among

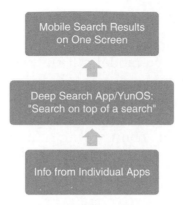

Figure 5.5   Quixey/Alibaba Partnership: Deep Mobile Search

them and their backers is likely to get increasingly intensive in more areas.

It is worth noting that although the new Meituan-Dianping financing was the single largest funding round on record for a closely held start-up with venture capital investors, there were also signs of investors' growing concern about the subsidy model and the company valuation. In 2015, Meituan sounded out investors on a fundraising at valuations as high as $20 billion, but investors pushed the company to lower its asking price and encouraged the merger with rival Dianping to cut spending on subsidies. The new Meituan-Dianping financing in January 2016 reportedly gave the combined company about $18 billion.

Today many O2O start-ups have burned out in the battle to attract users with heavy discounts and subsidies, but the internet giants like BAT have much bigger balance sheets and more related business, giving them an edge over other competitors. User growth remains strong as O2O spreads into more third- and fourth-tier cities in China, so internet firms are content to delay the use of revenue and profit metrics for valuation. But a shakeout is surely beginning, particularly among the apps offering generic services, and entrepreneurs will have to tighten spending and consider merging with rivals if they cannot provide distinguishable offerings.

The Biggest Cake: O2O + Omni-Channel

As we reach the end of this chapter, it becomes clear that the future e-commerce model – if the term e-commerce still applies – is a seamless platform that links customers across multiple screens of mobile devices, providing standardized products as well as specialized goods and experience offerings, and connecting online content with offline activities. In other words, future e-commerce will become O2O, integrating with omni-channel (as discussed in the previous chapter) for each and every consumer.

This concept is being tested by an ambitious venture between the commercial property conglomerate Wanda and the two e-commerce giants Tencent and Baidu. In August 2014, the three firms collectively invested about $800 million in a joint venture, upon which Wanda's chairman Wang Jianlin commented that the online-to-offline opportunity was the biggest "cake" left in e-commerce. The market seemed to agree with the concept and has high expectations for the venture. In early 2015, Wanda announced the closing of a funding round for the venture where the implied valuation for the venture exceeded $3 billion.

This joint venture was referred to by Tencent's founder Pony Ma as a "Smart Plaza", suggesting it was a platform that was open-minded to every possible retailing and O2O combination. Baidu's co-founder Robin Li described how smooth the future O2O purchase would be through the powerful consortium in the following example: One day a girl walks along the street and observes a girl with a new style dress; she can just take a picture of her, and know immediately which store in the nearby Wanda shopping mall is selling the dress. Then, the Baidu map will provide the directions to the store where she can try the dress on. When she decides to make the purchase, she pulls out WeChat Pay on her smartphone to close the transaction.

As part of the partnership (see Figure 5.6), Tencent's WeChat Pay was implemented at Wanda's shops, and it also

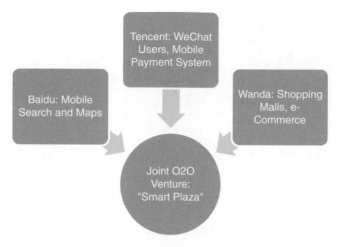

Figure 5.6   Smart Plaza – Combining O2O with Omni-Channel

brought in more than half a billion active WeChat users, while Baidu supported the users with location-based searches and maps. In addition, Wanda wired up all of its shopping centers with Wi-Fi and Bluetooth sensors so that shoppers could be monitored intensely. A new app was developed to ping customers with promotions and information as they step inside the malls. Consumers could peruse goods on the shelves but still pay on their mobile phones for purchases to save queuing, and have their goods delivered straight to their homes.

Some Chinese people jokingly referred to this joint platform as "three top rich people teaming together to challenge another big billionaire in e-commerce". However, some observers have cautioned that it may take some time for the new venture to become integrated and become a realistic challenge to Alibaba, as Alibaba has all its online resources under one umbrella. In fact, as explained in his 2016 New Year speech (see Figure 5.7), the future of e-commerce in the mind of Alibaba's CEO Daniel Zhang is essentially the same as the rationale behind the "smart plaza".

Back to the fight for New Year red envelopes: although it was a "Pearl Harbor attack" in the words of Alibaba Founder

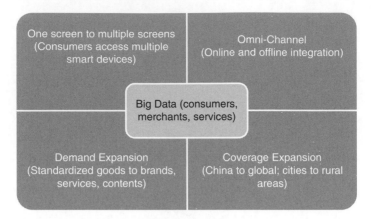

Figure 5.7   The Future Directions of e-Commerce

Jack Ma's warning to his staff, the outcome of that battle is far from determining the winner of the O2O war. Because of the mobile and social DNA of its WeChat app, Tencent has a unique advantage in online-and-offline e-commerce, but Alibaba is a similarly formidable contender in the O2O market with its dominating position in e-retailing and e-payment businesses. Meanwhile, both Baidu and Wanda have their distinctive core competence to compete for the O2O "cake".

Also, if the history of the Pearl Harbor attack is of any reference value, the addition of a new super-weapon, like the A-bomb, could change the balance of the war altogether. Therefore, each of the players has to continue innovating while vying for supremacy in the market for internet services, and the one with the strongest collective power will eventually win. That is why Japanese Admiral Isoroku Yamamoto, the commander-in-chief of the Combined Fleet, famously said after the successful Pearl Harbor attack: "The war still has a long way to go." The same is true for the war in the young O2O market.

CHAPTER 6

Mobile Entertainment

During the 2014 FIFA World Cup, China's national football team, ranked 103rd in the world, failed to go through to the tournament final in Brazil following the qualifying round. Despite this the mobile internet helped to create a time of celebration for hundreds of millions of fans as well as first-time watchers in China. In past World Cup tournaments, Chinese football fans simply watched the tournament on TV at odd hours (due to time differences) while drinking beer with friends. During the 2014 Brazil Soccer World Cup, people were active participants throughout the time that it was held. In addition to watching TV or online videos, they also interacted actively with their social networks to follow the games, played their own virtual games, and many used their smartphones to place bets on the games for the first time in their lives.

Gambling was generally illegal in mainland China, but provinces were permitted to run official sports lotteries that donate proceeds to charity. Reselling tickets for the sports lotteries run by provincial governments had become an industry in itself. In the 2014 World Cup season, China's internet firms operated as a platform on which the lottery centers could accept the placing of bets. Once again, the internet giants Alibaba and Tencent flexed their muscle in this mobile field, as they competed to build the most convenient and popular mobile lottery portals to help Chinese football fans participate in the World Cup.

Taobao, Alibaba's e-commerce site, promoted the World Cup lottery on its front page, and online shoppers could purchase tickets easily. Tencent naturally built up its interface around WeChat, the most popular social network platform in China. WeChat users could buy tickets while comparing information and thoughts about the teams with their friends. As a result of their mobile apps, soccer lottery purchases accelerated swiftly. Millions of Chinese were drawn in by the online betting platforms' ease of use and extensive marketing coverage on their mobile terminals. According to news reports, Taobao saw 4 million users bet on its online platform on the first day of the World Cup. Three days later that number had grown to 6 million. By July 5, three weeks into the World Cup and still way before the Cup final, China's National Sports Lottery Center calculated that $1.5 billion in "lotto tickets" had been purchased.

The new flow of money into online sports lotteries during the World Cup is only one example of the revolution in the entertainment industries in China when users embrace the mobile internet (a perfect example of "internet plus" into non-tech markets). In fact, the ultimate theme of the internet in China centers on entertainment and fun, which has a lot to do with the dominant component of young netizens (aged below 39) within the internet population (see Figure 6.1). According to CNNIC data, by the end of 2015 more than 75% of the internet users were between the ages of 10 and 39. Close to one third of the internet population is aged between 20 and 29 (29.9%).

Young internet users in China are more focused on entertainment services than the traditional forms of usage of the internet for information searches and email messages. For a large part of their time online, they play online games, watch videos of TV programs and movies, assume online personas in the virtual world and form online communities to have fun together. As smartphones have become the top channel for internet access in China, the young generation of users

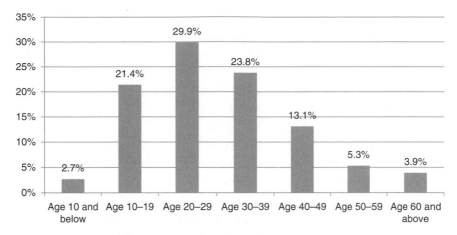

Figure 6.1   Demographic of Chinese Internet Users
(Data Source: CNNIC, December 2015)

enjoy themselves whenever and wherever, increasingly consuming, sharing and arguing about the entertainment content on their hand-held devices during their "fragmented time" (for example, during a subway commute or while waiting in line) throughout the day (vis-à-vis the fixed time before a PC).

It should be highlighted that the combination of mobile terminals and online content creates different and extra demand for content, not purely a shift of consumption from personal computers (PCs) to mobile devices. The reasons relate to two features of the mobile applications on smartphones. One factor is convenience. In the earlier example of sports betting on the 2014 World Cup games, the mobile interfaces built up by the internet firms were so convenient for customers to play that many of the lottery players were not actually enthusiastic soccer fans or people that had ever bet in the official sports lottery before.

The other factor is the efficient use of "fragmented time". For example, online literature can be read on mobile devices anywhere and anytime, which not only leads to a disruption in the physical book market, but also creates a different experience from traditional book reading (and subsequently a large group of new readers). On subways or at shopping malls, there are always people reading online novels on their smartphone screens when they have a few minutes of time available. The biggest growth potential for new demand is from people in smaller cities, who may not have PCs but are now viewing online entertainment content from smart devices.

For the internet firms, the hundreds of millions of entertainment consumers on mobile internet represent a huge business opportunity. In addition to selling physical products to those consumers, the firms are also selling digital content and entertainment, including novels, movies, TV shows and video games. But the online entertainment means more than an important vertical business line to the internet firms.

The bigger picture is that for China's major internet companies such as BAT (Baidu, Alibaba and Tencent), the entertainment business is a common strategic initiative for their respective ecosystems. When e-commerce in physical goods becomes more commoditized, unique content may become a distinguishing feature that draws users to a specific e-commerce empire and then keeps them hooked. The media content on their platforms could help keep their users engaged and prevent them from switching to competitors.

As such, all three internet giants have as their objective the building of an expansive entertainment platform that integrates online and offline entertainment. On the one hand, they compete to become "the top distributor" of content and entertainment in China, whether it is movies or TV shows, sports or gaming, music or novels. On the other hand, they become a major aggregator of content through licensing or partnership arrangements with global quality content owners, and in many cases, become producers of their own content.

As operators of powerful distribution channels, internet firms are making entertainment and services more accessible to users of smartphones and other gadgets like internet TVs. At the same time, they are becoming investors and producers of media content themselves (for example, movies and TV shows) as part of their mobile e-commerce strategy. For the existing entertainment industry players, internet firms are powerful allies and simultaneously enemies at-the-gate.

The year 2014 was probably the "breakout year" for China's mobile entertainment industry. Internet firms considered this content consumption field to be an important growth sector as China moves to a consumer-led economy, and their new capital investments led to unprecedented growth in mobile entertainment, both in terms of increased categories of content offerings and higher quality content from exclusive sources, such as partnerships with foreign content providers, for instance, HBO, NBA and Sony Music. The entertainment platforms of internet empires seamlessly cross-link online novels, publishing, gaming, animation, videos, filming as well as other derivative merchandise, with videos of movies and TV shows at the center.

Among all mobile content, driven by the wide use of smartphones, video streaming is soon expected to account for the majority of mobile internet traffic. Hence it is at the center of internet firms' entertainment platforms and also the focus of this chapter. However, internet literature is at the upstream of the flow of IP (intellectual property) rights in the industry, as it is the base for a variety of derivative content including publishing, gaming, animation, filming as well as videos. Therefore, in what follows the online literature business is introduced before discussion of the video streaming models in China.

Online Literature

Over the past 10 years, internet literature has grown from fun sharing into a booming business with proven profitability in China. Initially, many aspiring writers posted their works on online forums with little expectation of becoming full-time web-writers. Some were serious writers whose works were not accepted by publishing houses, so they looked to the internet as an alternative publishing platform with a lower access threshold. Many more were amateur authors who simply sought any readers for their novel creation. But today, digital reading – reading through a broad range of digital devices such as smartphones, tablets, laptops and desktop PCs – has become the main way for Chinese people to read a novel; and many authors put their work online first.

The most important catalyst for the boom is mobile devices. Smartphones and tablets are becoming pocket libraries for millions of avid readers in China, and their mobile reading apps make it possible for busy urban people to read wherever they are. The CNNIC data showed that there were nearly 300 million readers of internet literature at the end of 2014. Among all reading mediums – from printed books to computers to smartphones – 84.6% of readers used mobile smartphones to read works of literature, far ahead of the usage of other tools (see Figure 6.2).

Readers' migration to mobile devices has already led to industry consolidation. Until recently, the online literature market in China was dominated by three major players: Shanda Literature, Tencent Literature and Baidu Literature. Shanda Literature, a subsidiary of the Nasdaq-listed Shanda Interactive

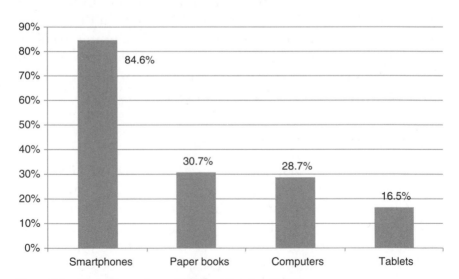

Figure 6.2 Usage Percentage of Different Reading Mediums
(Data Source: CNNIC, December 2014)

Entertainment Limited, used to own the most popular websites and nearly 50% of the market share. Launched in 2008, Shanda was a pioneer in enabling Chinese writers to publish online freely and monetize their work through micro e-payments from readers as well as rights and licensing deals.

Despite its leadership in content, Shanda Literature missed out on the development of the mobile reading market, and it was acquired in early 2015 by Tencent Literature, whose parent company, Tencent, has mobile entertainment in its corporate DNA. After the merger, the new entity Yue-wen Group ("Reading Literature" in English) became a superpower in the online literature field with approximately 70% market share. Synergies were expected as Shanda Literature had a lot of valuable copyrighted products and Tencent Literature could potentially link them with the mobile channels and huge related user groups within Tencent, such as WeChat and QQ.

The unique feature of Chinese online literature is that most works are serialized novels that authors write and post in installments. This online serial format proves to be a perfect fit for the mobile internet age. Every day, millions of young digital-reading users refresh their mobile apps, just to keep up with the latest daily updates of their favorite reads. For many people who do not have the time to read a book in hard copy, the novels on a mobile phone can be read easily whenever they have some spare time. Each serial installment typically has a few thousand words, so the reading can be done during any "fragmented time".

The installment format also helps the literature websites to implement a pay-for-content mechanism. When authors start to build up large readerships, the online portals offer them contracts and move their works off the free domain. The sites arrange for the authors to write a story in installments (typically with a total characters cap for each post), and readers then pay a tiny fee equivalent to a fraction of $0.01 to read each update, which is far cheaper than paying for hard copy versions from a book store. The development of mobile payment systems also makes it convenient for readers to make small repeat payments for their serial reading.

In addition to the factors above, the wish-fulfilment themes are a major reason for the enormous popularity of online novels among the young generation. While a big proportion of the readers are in China's smaller cities, calling themselves "diao-si readers" (losers) for not owning an apartment or having no girlfriend, the heroes are handsome, powerful and successful, and the sensational plots of the novels provide the readers with a way to dream of being the heroes themselves. **(See the "Diao-si Readers" box.)** For this, the internet authors have created many imaginary worlds for the enjoyment of their readership. The diao-si readers must feel even more empowered when they are able to change the direction of a writer's story by posting their feedback and recommendations (with charges definitely applying).

Diao-si ("Loser") Readers and Pu-jie ("Drop-dead on Street") Authors

The term "diao-si" appeared earlier in this book and in general it refers to unmarried young people who live on the margin in an otherwise booming economy. In the context of e-commerce, the term is related to having little spending power and cheap goods. For example, the users of non-premium-brand smartphones tend to call themselves "diao-si". In the context of online literature, the small installment payments for escapist content certainly fit the description. But when the online readers dub themselves diao-si, they are also highlighting their aspirations for a better life.

It turns out that some online authors enjoy no better living conditions than their diao-si readers. The millions of web writers in China are divided into multiple categories by their income and the number of fans. The lowest level is called a "pu-jie" author which can be translated into a "drop-dead-on-street author". Their fans are limited, their work is seldom recommended online and their annual income is below $150.

In contrast, the successful authors in real life are not diao-si at all. Some internet authors are celebrities both online and offline, as their popular novels have made their way into films and TV programs. Just like the stars on Google's YouTube, they leverage their online celebrity in various parts of the media market like publishing, filming and live events. The highest paid online authors are called the "the Supreme God" by the diao-si readers.

In addition to installment payments, most internet literature websites include a reward function, where readers can award the web writer money or credits at their discretion (for example, if a reader is especially satisfied by the story plot's change based on her suggestion). Some sites also publish periodical popularity rankings of online writers, which the readers must pay to vote for. The millions of online writers in China are categorized by their readers into five levels based on their income and number of fans. Except for the lowest rank, the "drop-dead on street" authors, all the professional writers in higher categories are called "gods". But they have different titles, like the deities of the Greek pantheon (see Table 6.1).

Table 6.1   The five ranks of web writers in China

Ranks	Number of Fans	Annual Income ($)	Number of Authors
"Drop-dead on street" authors	Few fans, only recommended occasionally	< RMB1,000 ($150)	Numerous
Xiao-shen (small god)	> 100,000	> RMB100,000 ($15,000)	Large number – foundation of sites
Zhong-shen (middle god)	> 500,000	> RMB500,000 ($80,000)	Several hundred
Da-shen (major god)	> 1 million	> RMB1 million ($150,000)	Hundreds
Zhi-gao-shen (the Supreme God)	Multiple millions	Multiple millions RMB (>$1 million)	20–30

(Data Source: 2015 survey by Beijing-based newspaper *Jinghua Times*)

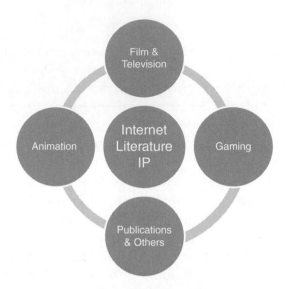

Figure 6.3   The Important Value of Internet Literature IP

Based on their online popularity among readers, many popular online novels have been adapted into traditional publishing, games, videos and blockbuster movies. As such, internet literature is the base of IP (intellectual property) rights for a variety of derivative content (see Figure 6.3). According to the data released at the 2015 Shanghai International Film Festival, by the end of 2014, 114 online novels had sold their copyrights to production companies, with 90 works being adapted into TV dramas and the rest into movies. The hit online video *The Lost Tomb,* which helped Baidu-owned video streaming company iQIYI's mobile app become No. 1 in the free app popularity rankings in the China Apple App store in 2015, was also a production based on an earlier online novel.

At the same time, devoted fans of literary works are not only readers. They are also inclined to be loyal audiences of dramas and movies adapted from literature, or players of games and fans of animation. Overall, online literature attracts a large digital-reading user base, has a proven profit model and has the upstream intellectual property (IP) rights for inter-linked entertainment products. Therefore, it is now a key piece of every internet firm's entertainment platform.

Video Streaming: From UGC to PGC

China's streaming video industry has grown exponentially in recent years, driven by the large smartphone population, the increasingly diverse selection of quality content, and the collective efforts by all stakeholders to reduce piracy. The CNNIC data showed that at the end of 2014 China had more than 400 million viewers of online videos. Among them, 71.9% of users watched online videos from their smartphones, making smartphones the leading terminal for online video access ahead of desktop computers and tablets (see Figure 6.4). The smartphone usage figure is expected to rise steadily as Chinese mobile carriers continue adopting faster fourth-generation (4G) networks that will further improve the video viewing experience on mobile devices.

The business model of the video streaming websites is mostly based on providing free content to gain user traffic and corresponding advertising income, although the revenue income from the fee-paying internet users' side is gradually catching up. In this ultra-competitive field, Alibaba-invested Youku Tudou and Baidu's iQIYI are the top two most watched video sites in China. As with the smartphone market, different market research firms' data have pointed to either of the two

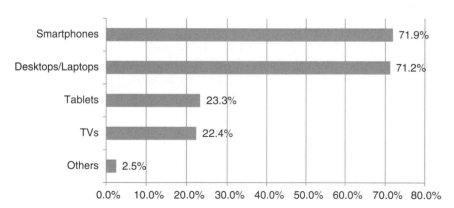

Figure 6.4   Terminal Usages for Internet Videos
(Data Source: CNNIC, December 2014)

Table 6.2   Relative speciality of the video streaming sites

Streaming Sites	Speciality
Youku Tudou	Watching and uploading UGC (user-generated content); Short videos
iQIYI	Full-length movies; Contents related to media industry and stars
Tencent Video	Imported contents (NBA, HBO, Fox Sports, National Geographic, etc.)
Sohu Video	Variety shows; TV drama series from the US

as the top leader at different times, and between the streaming sites themselves there is disagreement about each other's statistics on active viewer hits and fee-paying members. Other major players such as Tencent Video and Sohu Video are all within striking distance. Each of them had some unique strength in their early days (see Table 6.2), but as everyone rushes to build up their content library, the various video-hosting sites are becoming similar to each other in terms of content offering.

Youku Tudou is the combined company following a merger of the two earliest online video companies in China. Youku was established in 2006 and Tudou in 2005, so their combination created a leading position in terms of accumulated content. This competitive edge was most obvious in terms of user-generated content (UGC), because both had been rooted in user-generated, short videos. For many years these two websites were the "go-to" place for Chinese users to post self-made videos or to "shai" (show off) their experiences. As such, Youku Tudou has often been viewed as a Chinese version of YouTube. Alibaba acquired a 16.5% stake in Youku Tudou in 2014, before it bought the whole company for approximately $4.5 billion in 2015. This alliance has the potential to link e-commerce with video streaming for new businesses.

iQIYI is an independently operated subsidiary of Baidu. Baidu owned iQIYI in full before the smartphone maker Xiaomi invested to become a significant stakeholder of iQIYI in 2014 (which was part of a new "content and device integration" trend). Originally launched in 2010, it is considerably younger than Youku Tudou. But the search engine's backing has helped the subsidiary to amass a large user base quickly, because iQIYI's content is seamlessly integrated into Baidu's search and mobile services. In terms of providing full-length movies, iQIYI has something of a leadership position, because it is the first online video platform in China to focus on fully licensed, high-definition and professionally produced content. An additional speciality of iQIYI is the extensive content relating to the media industry itself along with the life stories of media stars.

Another major player is Tencent Video. Its advantage comes from the popularity of its parent Tencent's two messaging and social networking services, QQ and WeChat, which have hundreds of millions of users each. Social media and entertainment can complement each other very well, one being the catalyst for the growth of the other. The latest music and movies tend to be hot topics within the social platforms, which provides information on the content demand from the end-users, and many videos and music are being shared through the same platforms.

Meanwhile, Sohu Video (part of the internet company Sohu.com) is historically strong in variety shows, and it has also succeeded in licensing hit American TV shows for Chinese viewership. While domestic dramas and variety shows are still significantly more popular than foreign programs, American TV drama is probably the fastest growing content category in China, especially among young urban audiences. For example, *The Big Bang Theory*, an Emmy-award-winning show about nerdy scientists, was streamed more than 1 billion times in China. More recently, Netflix's political drama *House of Cards* was so popular in China that in the TV extravaganza celebrating 2015 Singles' Day, China's online shopping spree that took place on November 11, actor Kevin Spacey made a videotaped appearance in his US presidential persona from the series.

Generally speaking, the industry trend shows that video content is shifting from user-generated content (UGC) to professionally-generated content (PGC). In previous years video sites started as "sharing" sites, so UGC videos did help those sites to attract a large number of users and capture their attention. But after a few years of industry development, Chinese viewers became more sophisticated, and pure UGC could not fully satisfy their consumption needs. In CNNIC's 2014 market survey, user-generated content ranked near the bottom of the 10 categories of programs watched by mobile audiences (see Figure 6.5).

As Figure 6.5 shows, the most watched content category on the online video sites is TV programming. As a result, the prices for online syndication rights for hit serial TV dramas and top variety shows, such as *The Legend of Zhen Huan* and *I am the Singer*, have skyrocketed in the last few years. It may seem surprising that when people move away from their TV sets to watch programs on the internet, TV programs remain their favorite. The reason for this is that people's migration away from TV is due to TV programming as opposed to the content

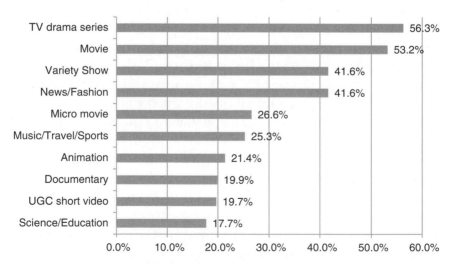

Figure 6.5   Popularity Ranking for Video Content Watched on Smartphone
(Data Source: CNNIC, December 2014)

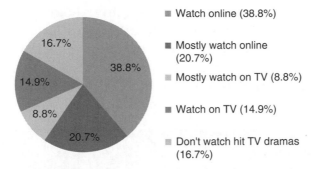

Figure 6.6   TV Drama Viewer's Migration to the Internet

itself. Programs on TV have fixed schedules, long advertisements and are difficult to record and replay; the viewers have no choice but to passively accept these realities. By contrast, internet streaming technology provides the viewers with more convenience and a better experience.

The CNNIC's 2014 data showed that a majority of TV drama viewers had moved to online (see Figure 6.6). Also, 80.4% of internet TV users used the "on-demand" function, while 67.3% used the "replay" function. More interestingly, CNNIC data also showed that after smartphones as the top video watching channel, 82.4% mobile video users preferred using computers to TV for watching movies and TV dramas. This illustrated that once the viewers develop the habit of watching videos "on demand", they are no longer willing to passively accept the pre-arranged programs on TV channels. They would rather spend far less time watching TV, potentially giving up TV altogether.

It is worth noting, though, that popular professionally generated content does not necessarily consist of blockbusters or big-budget productions. Nor do they have to be perfectly executed with an intelligent storyline. In fact, many TV drama series are denounced by Chinese viewers as "brain-dead drama" or "dog-blood drama", but people "watch and criticize" and then "watch more and criticize more". For the viewers of those programs, the focus is not on the show itself, but rather on getting together with friends and joking about the silliness of the content. In other words, the audiences for *My Love from Another Star* are different from those for *House of Cards*, but both programs can attract a large number of viewers. **(See the "Brain-dead drama" box.)**

Nao-can-ju (Brain-dead drama), Shao-nao-ju (Brain-burning drama) and Gou-xue-ju (Dog-blood drama)

It may be surprising to many that while an American drama like *House of Cards* has received high ratings on China's online video sites and gained popularity, TV episodes from China, Korea and Taiwan that received low ratings and are ridiculed as nao-can-ju ("brain-dead drama" in English) are still watched by large numbers of audiences.

As the name suggests, these "brain-dead dramas" are not intelligent productions but have superficial, naïve, or preposterous plots. They are represented by "young idol" romantic dramas, like *My Love from another Star* from Korea, which was a series about the love affair between a 400-year-old Harvard-educated alien and an arrogant actress. Chinese productions have their contributions too. For example, some episodes relating to China's war with Japan (1937–1945) included scenes where Chinese guerillas ripped live Japanese soldiers in half with their bare hands.

Nevertheless these "brain-dead dramas" have attracted big audiences, with the under-30s and women in their 40s apparently being the main viewers. *My Lover from another Star* was probably the most watched "nao-can-ju" in 2014. Many viewers imitated the main character's favorite pastime, i.e. watching TV while enjoying fried chicken and iced beer (with some unfortunate people having to be sent to the emergency room at hospitals).

This phenomenon is quite easy to understand: everyday work and life are so intense that people are not looking to learn or think deeply about something when they go online in their spare time. They are more inclined to relax in front of some nao-can-ju than use their brain power on **shao-nao-ju ("brain-burning drama" in English)**. The "shao-nao-ju" may be a tough task for exhausted people late in the evening, and even worse, many of those "shao-nao-ju" stories are simply pretending to be "intelligent".

Another similar type of low-rating, large-audience drama is called **gou-xue-ju** – the literal English translation is **dog-blood drama**. The term is mostly used to describe clichéd plots, where similar stories are endlessly repeated. Because the pronunciation of "dog blood" in Chinese is very similar to "dog shit" (gou-shi), many suspected that the term was originally meant to be "dog-shit drama".

For example, in all the dog-blood dramas, if someone enters a room without knocking, there are only two possible scenarios: either people are making out or someone is hanging himself or herself. And if a young girl pretends to be a boy, she is bound to be found out in one of four ways: her hat drops, she is seen in underwear while changing her clothes, she falls into water, or, the most dramatic – someone touches her breasts by accident.

Although the viewers' preference for professionally made content is clear (the next section will discuss the PGC content model in detail), it may be too early to declare user-generated content as being on the way out. The unique roots of Youkou Tudou's UGC, closely modeled on YouTube, may actually turn out to be a unique competitive advantage when the PGC available on competitor's websites tends to share the same characteristics. The original web-first shows made by amateurs can always potentially be turned into high quality programs once their value proposition is tested, proven and they have found traction in the market. Since movie theaters and TV stations are expensive channels, independent creative teams may first try out their production on an online platform such as Youku Tukou. In the past, low-budget original content was looked down upon by the professional industry; but in the mobile internet era, productions with online popularity quickly attract the attention of big internet companies and top studios.

For example, in 2013 a young couple from Beijing decided to take a world voyage on their 54-foot sailboat to celebrate their wedding, and they documented their trip on video in full detail. When they uploaded their 300 hours' worth of footage to the video site Youku, the website staff members were impressed by what they had recorded. Working with the couple, Youku created a documentary series entitled *On the Road*. The program featured their videos across the globe, and Youku claimed it as the first website-self-made original online reality show in China. The first season of this show, which consisted of 15 episodes that were broadcast once a week, reached over 100 million views on Youku within 6 months of its release. Its second season had similar success.

For foreign studios in particular, working with existing locally-produced shows is an easier and safer way to tap into China's booming online video industry. Take the self-made comedy series *Surprise* for example. The original online series *Surprise* involved a main character Dachui Wang who, like the heroes in many internet novels, was a diao-si guy who struggled through various hilarious scenarios of modern day life. It enjoyed explosive viewership on Youku before evolving into a more professional online video production and then a feature length movie production. With more than 2 billion cumulative video views since its 2013 debut, *Surprise* became China's top web comedy. In 2014, Hollywood's Dreamworks Animation joined forces with Youku Tudou to produce a spate of original online content based on *Surprise*, and Dreamworks further planned to use the partnership as a platform to develop more content customized for the youth audience.

PGC: In Search of Revenue (and Profit)

Currently, all video services sites in China essentially have the same business model, which is to provide free content to attract online viewers and rely on advertising income as the main revenue source. Revenue from fee-paying members remains relatively small. Given the general belief that "Content is King", all the major players compete to broaden their content offering. So far, the model has yet to prove profitable, but there are promising signs that the sector may be able to turn the corner in the near future.

No doubt, video streaming on mobile devices provides an interesting channel for consumer goods advertising due to its linkage to young Chinese customers. Young netizens are keen to try out new products, especially the ones they have seen in foreign movies or TV shows. For brands featured on quality programs, the positive impact has been substantial. The online video platforms may turn out to be a better deal than TV commercials overall; the latter can deliver large audiences, but the engagement with viewers is passive and measurement is inaccurate. Many brands have jumped on this advertisement channel bandwagon, including some wildly imaginative marketing campaigns through online videos. **(See the "Naked Subway" box.)**

Naked Subway

Online video advertising has prompted creativity from merchants. In September 2014, a Chinese company called Tidy Laundry designed a video advertisement based on sexy scenes on a Shanghai subway train. The video was posted on the major streaming video site Youku Tudou. The video undoubtedly captured viewers' attention online, but the story did not have a happy ending.

The storyline of the video was so wildly imaginative that most viewers were simply intrigued by the sexy content, yet had no clue about the punchline for the brand. In the video, two young women travel aboard a crowded subway in Shanghai before they start to strip down to their underwear without any warning or reason. The commuters in the subway car are shocked and ask them to stop, but to no avail. Then a man wearing a blue uniform enters the subway car and hands each of the two semi-naked girls a clean set of clothes. One of the two girls writes something in the man's notebook before they change into the new clothes.

Apparently, the punchline was the laundry company's uniform worn by the man, which had the company name on it. The man came to deliver clean clothes, for which the girl signed the receipt in his notebook. Then he picked up their discarded clothes and left. The advertisement message, at least in its planning, was that the company delivered excellent "service on call" at "any time". The video was designed in an exaggerated way to attract public attention, but the semi-naked scenes were so distracting that many viewers missed the marketing message completely and were baffled.

Nevertheless, this promotional video did gain some momentum on the video streaming site Youku Tudou. On top of the sexy scenes, the confusing storyline actually led to more viewers, similar to those "brain-dead drama" and "dog-blood drama" viewers. But the story ended with the Shanghai police showing up. According to news media, the company was fined for disturbing public order.

But for all the video-hosting sites, the cost of content acquisition has far exceeded advertisement revenue, because all the players try to own the latest and greatest content to keep users on their own domain. As a result, the professionally-generated content of the various sites is quite similar, and the cost of online syndication rights for quality programs has risen rapidly. Thus the competition for content has been escalated to a fight for "exclusive" content. For example, in January 2015, Tencent Video entered into an exclusive distribution agreement with the US National Basketball Association (NBA). For the first time in China, Tencent and NBA will launch "League Pass", a paid service that allows users to stream a full season of games live online. Just before that, Tencent Video had also become the exclusive online platform for HBO movies and Sony Music Entertainment in China.

Of course, unique high-quality content is the most expensive among all PGC. Therefore, the new strategy of the video sites is to look internally to find content exclusivity, either by partnering with media companies or setting up their own production units to create popular shows in-house. This homegrown content (also referred to as site-self-production) provides the sites with an alternative way – versus syndication or license from media companies – to stand out in distinguishable offerings, while keeping costs down on a relative basis. (In those companies' financial reports, homegrown PGC on the one hand reduces the cost for acquiring exclusive foreign content, but also increases operating expenses on the other hand.) For example, after the Korean TV series *My Love from another Star* became popular on the streaming websites, the sites decided to develop their own Korean-influenced shows to meet the demand for such content.

To put this into context, the difficulty in converting views into profits and the rising cost for quality content are felt by their US counterparts too. The most direct reference point is Google's YouTube. YouTube attracts more than one billion users each month, but according to news reports it still has not contributed meaningfully to Google's earnings. When the US streaming service provider Netflix expands into producing original content, it is similarly challenged by rising costs. Amazon has also been criticized by Wall Street for the rising costs of buying rights into HBO TV series and Disney films to build up its streaming video content business.

To increase their revenue income, the Chinese video streaming sites are shifting the free-content model towards the mixed "free-mium model". On the one hand, the video sites offer basic streaming content for free to attract advertisement income; on the other hand, they have a premium service for paid users offering exclusive content such as the latest Hollywood blockbusters and hit reality shows. However, while content cost is rising steadily, the revenue side of the video hosting industry remains uncertain and challenging.

First of all, as the major players increase spending into professionally-generated content (PGC), the issue of piracy becomes critical. Online piracy has long been a serious issue for the global entertainment industry, and China is no exception. For instance, even though China is the world's largest internet music market by users, according to the International Federation of the Phonographic Industry (IFPI) the digital music sales in China were at an estimated $82.6 million in 2013, which accounted for less than 1 percent of the $15 billion in global revenues made in 2013 by record companies (putting China at No. 21 globally). Part of the reason was that many small websites distributed unlicensed music downloads.

On the video side, before Tencent Video's exclusive online distribution deal with HBO in 2014, there was no authorized online distribution channel for HBO in China. But popular HBO shows such as *Game of Thrones* had already attracted a large number of fans, who posted their thoughts and comments on popular Chinese film review sites like Douban.com. This was because many shows were available on piracy video sites, and even on some major online video sites, users had posted unauthorized clips of HBO shows with Chinese subtitles (those posts were later removed).

The encouraging trend is that although copyright piracy still exists in China, the situation is definitely improving. In recent years, China's leading video sites have spent millions of dollars to buy licensed TV shows and movies. As a result they have proactively enforced their intellectual property rights to protect their investments. In 2013, several video platforms teamed up with the Motion Picture Association of the US to take legal action against Baidu and software company Kuaibo (QVOD) for providing access to unlicensed content. Both companies were fined by the National Copyright Administration of China an amount of RMB250,000 each (nearly $40,000), the highest penalty under administrative enforcement measures.

In addition, Kuaibo's peer-to-peer video sharing software also became the target of legal action. This software was the most convenient and popular software for individual viewers to exchange content, and it also enabled piracy vendors to distribute pirated movies and TV shows without paying expensive video bandwidth costs. In June 2014, the Industry and Commerce Supervision Administration in the city of Shenzhen issued a fine to Shenzhen QVOD Technology of more than $40 million.

Many people believe the industry has made significant progress in cleaning up piracy. Unlike a few years ago, most of the Western TV shows and movies on Chinese websites today are licensed. Although pirated content still exists, it is in fact difficult to find a pirated version of new Hollywood movies online. The crackdown on piracy gives the video sites more confidence to invest in more professional content, and it should also help the platforms to guide more users towards pay-per-view or subscription.

The second challenge for the video sites is to develop a stable user group, which is critical for both subscriber fees and advertising income. Under the current "free content + advertising revenue" model, all the sites are converging into similar content offerings, and in the case of hit variety shows, TV series or movies, the content from all video providers is the same. So if one streaming site updates the content too slowly or stops updating, the viewers can simply move to another site (and move back and forth among different sites), since the cost of switching between sites (essentially zero) is much lower than switching cable TV services.

This means that even with professionally-made serial content, it is difficult for any video site to develop a stable viewer base, due to the similar content available on multiple platforms. For user-generated content that is low in quality and lacks coherent themes, the video-hosting sites can only attract passing traffic. For merchants and brands, the commercial value of advertisements on the video sites remains to be fully proven; hence the growth of advertising revenue for the video streaming sites is far behind the rising costs of content acquisition. That in turn puts further pressure on the video streaming sites to spend more on acquiring unique quality content.

The third challenge is to develop paying customers. In the US, the popular method for watching online videos is already subscription-based streaming like Netflix, which involves paying a subscription and streaming as much as the user wants. Only a small percentage of downloads come from on-demand services like iTunes. In China, the pay-for-content habit needs to be nurtured by the video services sites as they expand.

Because of their advertisement revenue-centered model, major video streaming sites are filled with free content for Chinese users. Just like YouTube in the US, the Chinese sites have provided viewers the access – largely free – to nearly all the latest Chinese TV shows, movies, documentaries, professional chess games and so on. Through license agreements between these sites and American networks, even foreign TV shows are often available to Chinese viewers on the same day that they air in the US. Chinese users therefore have little motivation to pay for content online, unless the video-hosting sites provide unique content to get viewers hooked.

For example, in July 2015, iQIYI released its self-produced series *The Lost Tomb*, which was produced exclusively for online viewers and enjoyed enormous popularity in China. In order to watch the full series, a huge number of users downloaded the iQIYI app and purchased the subscription service. As a result, the company's mobile app became No. 1 in the free app popularity rankings and No. 2 among all the apps at the Apple App store in China.

According to the company's data, the number of user clicks on *The Lost Tomb* episodes surpassed 160 million within five minutes following the release of the series. Since the release, the episodes of *The Lost Tomb* have been viewed over 1 billion times. In addition, iQIYI was also encouraged by the fact that the hugely popular *The Lost Tomb* did not have a big budget like Hollywood blockbusters. It did not even use top-ranking Chinese actors; instead, most of the show's popularity was driven by the young "xiao-xian-rou" actors at lower costs. **(See the "Little fresh meat" box.)**

"Xiao-xian-rou" (Little fresh meat) Actors

The term "xiao-xian-rou" literally means little fresh meat, which refers to young men who are youthful, innocent and beautiful in both face and body. The term was coined by the media industry, and it is now also being used generally for similarly attractive figures in other fields, for example, young swimmers and professional dancers.

There are several important characteristics of "xiao-xian-rou" actors. First, they are young and energetic ("little"); second, they are relatively inexperienced in love and have caused no sex scandals ("fresh"); and third, they are fit and are enviably good-looking ("meat"). In addition to the concept of "meat", they should also have impeccable skin.

Clearly, the term has both lewd as well as commercial connotations. It expressively describes the physical embodiment of youth that is desired by older members of the opposite sex. But if "diao-si", a term based on the male genitalia, could become a widely-accepted term that occasionally even shows up in news headlines, should anyone be bothered by the "xiao-xian-rou" reference?

It would seem that no one is unhappy to be called by this term, because it is seen as praise of a person's youth, energy and beauty. In fact, some established actors have expressed the hope that they will remain as young as the new generation of "xiao-xian-rou" actors. In 2014, a main web portal invited internet users to vote to select "China's top ten little-fresh-meat" actors, and a movie was made in the same year titled *Love Affair 2: Little-Fresh-Meat*.

Thanks to the development of mobile payments and premium content, combined with the crackdown on unlicensed online content, the market has seen rapid growth in fee-paying subscribers since 2015. For example, with the help of the success of *The Lost Tomb*, iQIYI announced that the company's paid streaming subscribers had doubled since June to reach 10 million as of December 1, 2015. From iQIYI's perspective, it was hugely encouraging because it took more than four years to acquire the first 5 million paid subscribers, but it only took about five months to double that.

To put this in context though, iQIYI's executive conceded in related interviews that this premium subscriber figure was just "a small portion of our over 500 million users". In other words, although the growth rate of paid subscribers is strong, the number of subscribing members remains small. According to the *2015 Report on Development of China's Internet Audio-Visual Media* by the China Netcasting Services Association, advertising income still accounted for the majority of the sector's revenue (approximately 70%), whereas income from member subscription fees and other services accounted for approximately 30%.

Still, the trend is a cause for optimism for industry players. In relation to Tencent's *2015 White Paper on the Entertainment Industry,* Tencent executives claimed that for the major video streaming sites, the fee income from their paid subscribers had grown far more rapidly than advertising income. And it was estimated that the fee income side would catch up and provide a similar share of revenue to the advertising income side within three to four years. Alibaba's upcoming TBO (Tmall Box Office) should be an interesting test case for this. Alibaba announced in mid-2015 that it would launch an online video streaming service in China, similar to the streaming service company Netflix and the pay-television network HBO in the US, which would likely be the first test of a subscription-only model in China. Content quality and user experience would probably have to be perfect to make this experiment a success.

In summary, China's video streaming websites are still struggling to prove the profitability of the "Content is King" model. As piracy is reduced and intellectual property (IP) rights

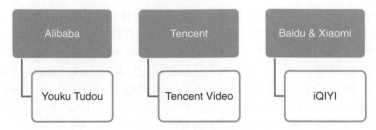

Figure 6.7   BAT and Their Respective Video Streaming Sites

become better protected, the viewer traffic flows will mostly be determined by high-quality, copyrighted content, which will force all players to invest aggressively in exclusive self-made or third-party video content. Therefore, the competition for premium content will continue and intensify, but the large market potential and rapid revenue growth offer hope that the companies will turn profitable in the long run.

As such, like many other mobile internet businesses, the ultimate competition among the video streaming sites comes down to one thing: capital. To maintain and grow its market share, each site would need capital on three fronts: to buy the content that will win the biggest audiences and the most advertising; to attract experienced online advertising salespeople; and to expand their streaming bandwidth from an infrastructure standpoint. Again, the market sees each of the three internet giants – Baidu, Alibaba and Tencent – running or backing its own online video platform's costly expansion, as they view the mobile entertainment business as of strategic importance to their internet empires (see Figure 6.7).

Multiple Screens, Multiple Revenue Models

Because the main theme of China's mobile internet centers on fun and enjoyment, internet firms view entertainment content as a similarly important channel to bring people to the online world as smartphones, mobile e-retailing, mobile search and social networks. Thus no internet firm can afford not to have a powerful entertainment platform centered on videos, both as a business line by itself for its revenue growth and as an online traffic hook to support the wider mobile commerce empire. This explains why all major players are investing aggressively in this sector even though it may take years before the video streaming business itself can turn profitable. At the same time, the internet giants are integrating the video streaming business with other parts of their respective internet empires in the search for more synergies.

The first aspect of integration is hardware. In the past, video streaming sites mostly used content to compete for users; now they are also investing in related smart devices as another way to engage viewers. In terms of entertainment hardware devices, the viewers' "old normal" was TV sets before they migrated to the internet. During the earlier years of online entertainment, the main terminal for video viewing was personal computers. Now in the mobile internet era, viewers go to smartphones as their first choice of screen. However, from the point of view of the viewer, the small screen of smart devices is a very different experience from the earlier big screens.

Because viewers still appreciate a big screen for a premium viewing experience, many leading video platforms are working with manufacturers to launch set-top boxes, smart TVs and other devices. In an interesting cycle of development, smart TV sets, equipped with browsers and internet access, are likely to become the "new normal" of living room entertainment in the near future. So far, the customer still prefers set-top boxes to smart TVs for reasons including the latter's higher price, the availability of alternative devices and the complexity of connecting smart TVs to home networks and the internet, but smart TV is quickly catching up in terms of market share.

At the same time, software programmers are trying to apply the same kind of creativity to big TV screens as they have with the small smartphone screens. In the future, TVs are expected to run apps as diverse as those available on smartphones. One can imagine that new apps could turn a smart TV into a multifunction command center for other home activities like food delivery and video calls. Thus, in the living room re-modelled with "Internet +", the big screen TV may remain as the main entertainment screen for households, and the smart TV and other mobile terminals may converge to collectively offer the same content and same entertainment value for users.

For instance, LeTV, originally a video streaming company that has been compared to Netflix, has expanded its hardware business into smart TV boxes, and then smart TVs, and more recently the smartphone markets. It boasts a content-centered platform, and its plan is to deliver premium content across the different devices within its unique software ecosystem. Similarly, Youku Tudou recently launched a new "Cloud Entertainment" business unit to develop hardware and services to make its content more accessible to users. The unit's first batch of hardware products consisted of a WiFi router, smart TV box and Android-system tablet.

This "content + device" convergence is further illustrated, in the opposite direction, by smartphone producer Xiaomi's $300 million investment in the online video platform iQIYI in late 2014. Apart from Xiaomi smartphones, Xiaomi also produces smart TVs (Mi TV) and set-top boxes (Mi Box), which may help iQIYI to grow its online video market share by reaching users of Xiaomi devices. As mentioned in earlier chapters, Xiaomi's vision is to develop a family of smart home devices that are seamlessly cross-linked under the Xiaomi "ecosystem", for which the entertainment content of iQIYI may serve as a common linkage.

Another aspect of integration relates to e-commerce. This connection may potentially turn more video viewers into online shoppers, which is referred to as T2O, or "to online". After its investment in Youku Tudou, Alibaba has started to place advertisements from Taobao and Tmall vendors within the online videos on the video-hosting sites. These videos are set up to have an advertisement cross-link that enables viewers to place orders for consumer goods that they see in the movies or TV shows.

T2O could be understood to mean "buying while viewing", but it remains to be seen whether the majority of TV watchers are interested in making shopping decisions while enjoying entertainment content at the same time. To avoid disrupting the entertainment experience, a new feature gives the viewer the option, when they see attractive clothes or electronic devices, to either place orders immediately or select the item and put it into a "shopping cart". In this way the viewer can handle the orders after finishing watching the program. The market, however, still needs more data on whether T2O truly creates a new, substantial source of e-commerce transaction flows.

The third integration is with other entertainment products on different screens. As introduced at the beginning of this chapter, internet literature works provide the upstream IP (intellectual property) rights for a variety of derivative content including publishing, gaming, animation, filming, as well as videos. The recent popular shows from iQIYI, LeTV and others, all adapted from popular online literature, were broadcast for both online viewers and TV watchers. In addition, some popular video shows like *The Lost Tomb* already had plans to produce related feature movies. In future, the video streaming sites may team up with local cable TV stations to offer subscription-based internet, cable and mobile entertainment content in a bundle as happens in the US.

All of the above represent a powerful trend where quality IP will be fashioned into various forms of content, which can then form seamless entertainment across multiple screens and formats, whether smartphones, PC computers, smart TVs, movie theaters and more. As shown by the emergence of Smart TV (and the boom in China's film box office to be discussed in the following chapter), consumer traffic flow between big screens (TV/movie theater) and small screens (smartphone/tablet) is not a one-way road to the mobile world, but a much more profound two-way flow.

The line between online and offline entertainment is also blurred. For instance, the interaction of online videos, social networks and movie theater-goers is a prevailing O2O value proposition in the film industry. The internet firms have to

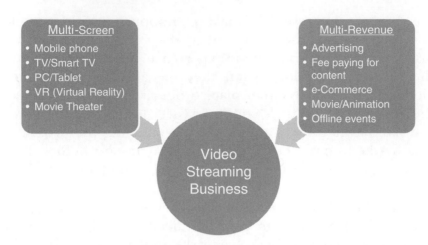

Figure 6.8   Multi-Screen, Multi-Revenue Model

capture and keep users' continuous attention no matter what screen they are watching, online or offline – and convince them to pay. As they compete to offer the most compelling content package, terminal devices and integrated platform, the "multi-screen, multi-revenue" model is the new game in town (see Figure 6.8).

7

"Internet+" Movies

Just like Xiaomi, the dark horse of the smartphone market, the movie series *Tiny Times* also had the Chinese character for "little" in its name, but it was one of the biggest domestic hits in the mobile internet age.

Tiny Times is a novel-turned-movie series that follows four fashionable college girls navigating their way through romance, work and friendship in Shanghai. As such it has been likened to *Gossip Girl* and *Sex and the City*. In the summer of 2014, the premiere of *Tiny Times* 3.0 raked in nearly $20 million, a record for domestic 2D films. It shocked both the Chinese movie industry and Hollywood when it unseated the US blockbuster *Transformers: Age of Extinction* to reach the top of China's box office charts during the first week of its official release.

It was remarkable that *Tiny Times* 3.0's origination, production and distribution were entirely shaped by social media, big data and internet financing, from beginning to end. The movie was based on a popular web novel, and the producer tapped into the novel's online fans and social network followers for suggestions on selecting the director and stars of the films. The distributors claimed that not a single advertising billboard was used across the country for marketing purposes; instead, promotion was done through the social networks of high school students and young adults. When the movie was criticized for its glorification of consumer culture, its fans – mostly young and female, like the heroines in the movie – rallied to its defense on social networks.

Tiny Times is a good example of a new generation of "internet+" movies in China. Similarly to restaurant booking and car-service hailing, the movie industry is seeing smart devices, ticket-booking mobile apps and related online movie streaming increasingly turning netizens into filmgoers at offline cinemas. At the same time, producers use big data technology to cater to the content demanded by modern Chinese youth, a group that had not been sufficiently addressed before by Chinese movies. For example, the luxurious lifestyle of high society girls in the movie, from fashion brands to exclusive clubs, clearly resonates with the young audiences' vision of success. Because of these new developments in the internet-related channel and content, the young generation who live with smartphones and tablets are turning themselves into movie-goers.

This trend may seem counter-intuitive at a time when online entertainment consumption is experiencing explosive growth. But it is truly a demonstration of the power of the internet, which keeps injecting new momentum into China's movie market. In fact, the movie business has quickly become one of the fastest-growing sectors in the O2O market. Not surprisingly, all the e-commerce giants are investing heavily in the sector, and each believes its respective online strength – search, e-commerce and social networking – will provide a powerful movie promotional tool. In addition, guided by the big data of audience behavior, each of the firms has set up its own movie unit to produce movies directly, especially those relating to stories about the young generation (who make up the majority of the Chinese internet population).

There is no question that these internet firms are the producers, distributors and exhibitors of the future. This explains why the head of distribution for a major China film group said at a recent industry conference, only half jokingly, that in the future all Chinese movie companies will work for BAT (Baidu, Alibaba and Tencent). At the same time, the internet giants are also expanding into overseas markets as studio buyers, content acquirers and distribution outlets, and this is creating both excitement and anxiety in Hollywood studios. This chapter will discuss how mobile internet has revolutionized China's movie market and why the Hollywood movies' strategy in China is also being challenged to transform.

The Big Screen Boom

Before discussing the profound implications of the mobile internet and mobile device screens, it is useful to look first at the phenomenal growth that the traditional movie industry in China has enjoyed lately. The most direct data point is the rapid growth of traditional cinema screens. Fueled by China's massive growing urban population, the number of movie screens has increased at a tremendous rate in recent years, and there is no sign of it slowing down. In mid-2015, the opening of the domestic comedy movie *Lost in Hong Kong* had an unprecedented 100,000+ first-day screen showings on nearly 20,000 screens, marking the widest release in global cinema history.

Although China has already surpassed Japan to become the second-largest film market in the world just below the US, its screen saturation (people per screen average) still has a lot of catching up to do. By the end of 2014, China had about 24,000 screens for nearly 1.4 billion people, versus the US which had 39,000 screens for approximately 300 million people. In other words, in 2014 China had about one screen for over 60,000 people and this is creating about one per 8,000 in the US. With the same level of saturation as in the US, China would have around 160,000 screens (close to seven times the current number).

Given that China has more densely populated cities than the US, one could argue that the US per screen average is not directly comparable to that in China. The neighboring Korean market might be a better reference, with approximately one

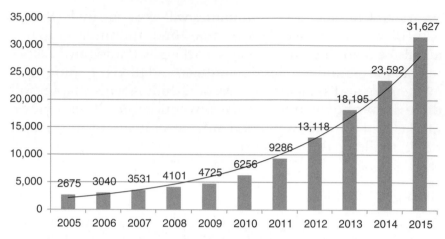

Figure 7.1   The Rapid Increase of Cinema Screens in China
(Data Source: China's State Administration of Press, Publication, Radio, Film and Television, 2015)

screen for every 20,000 people. Even at that level, China could be projected to have around 70,000 screens. According to the data from China's State Administration of Press, Publication, Radio, Film and Television, in 2015 more than 8,000 screens were added in China (roughly 20% of the total screens in the US, see Figure 7.1), at a rate of 22 new cinema screens per day. This expansion may continue for years to come, as movie screens continue to reach smaller urban centers across the country.

The expansion of big screen theater company IMAX Corp in China is a good example. China is a critical growth market for IMAX as many Chinese consumers, with new disposable income, are trying out IMAX theaters and 3-D films for the first time. According to company data in mid-2014, IMAX had built more than 170 theaters in China since 2004, and it planned to open more than 246 screens in the following five years. (In comparison, there were 340 IMAX screens in North America at the same time.) The China market is set to surpass the US and become the Canadian company's number one market globally.

Corresponding to the rapid increase of movie screens, box office receipts – an equally important data point for the industry – have risen rapidly in China as well. If the appetite of Chinese consumers maintains its growth rate, China will be on track to surpass the US to become the world's largest box office market in just a few years.

According to data from the Beijing-based film research company EntGroup, in 2014 Chinese box office receipts rose 36% from the previous year to reach $4.77 billion. The Chinese market's rapid growth in 2014 was a remarkable exception since the global box office was up only 1% from the previous year and global attendance was flat or declining in most markets around the world. In particular, the US and Canada saw their box office receipts fall by 5% and the key 18 to 39-year-old audience group shrink to its lowest levels in five years, according to a report by the Motion Picture Association of America. In 2015, China's box office takings leapt by nearly 50% from 2014, the fastest annual growth rate since 2011.

The rapid growth of the China movie market has not gone unnoticed by Hollywood. For years, however, the quota on foreign-made films imposed by the Chinese government was a major entry barrier for foreign movies. Historically there was a cap on the importation of foreign movies at 20 pictures per year, and the foreign studios only received a small share (13.5% to 17.5%) of box office revenues. In a positive development for Hollywood, in 2012 the Chinese government lifted the quota to allow 34 movies to be shown in China each year, provided that the additional 14 movies are in 3-D or IMAX formats. Foreign filmmakers' share of Chinese box office receipts (after costs) was also increased to 25%. "Co-production" movies jointly made by Chinese and foreign studios could be exempted from the quota and the foreign partner could have a bigger share in the box office proceeds. (This promising field is discussed in detail later in this chapter.)

For Hollywood, however, the goal is always to "further open up" the Chinese film market, or even to "completely open it up". This current quota system is part of a memorandum of understanding agreement between China and the World Trade Organization (WTO) concluded in 2012 and valid for five years. (Incidentally, this quota system is also being applied to TV programs from abroad, with video-hosting sites expected to register foreign content with the authorities.) This means the second round of negotiations will start around February 2017, and Hollywood and other foreign studios (such as those in France) have high expectations that the Chinese government will further relax its quota restricting foreign movie imports.

Since China is a major growth area in an otherwise flat or declining global movie market, the Hollywood studios have pursued it aggressively. The Hollywood blockbusters now have budgets often exceeding $400 million, so to be able to make $100 million or more at the box office in one market is really significant. (When *Avatar* achieved more than $200 million at the box office in 2010, China was no longer an afterthought as a market.) Instead, movie producers are going to great lengths to make sure their works appeal to both markets, and finding the quickest way to reach the greatest number of Chinese movie-goers has become one of their top priorities.

So far, the Hollywood studios have made significant progress in capturing the Chinese audience. As illustrated by Table 7.1, in 2014 six US studios managed to make more than $100 million at the box office in China. Partly shot in China and with the climax of the movie set in Hong Kong, Paramount's *Transformers: Age of Extinction* was the best-performing movie in China in 2014, and the $320 million which it achieved at the box office overtook *Avatar* to set a new record. Even more remarkable, the film's box office takings in China exceeded its North American gross figure of $245 million by a margin of $75 million (based on data from Box Office Mojo), marking a game-changing moment in the dynamic between the top two movie markets in the world.

The year 2015 also saw six Hollywood studios making more than $100 million at the box office from China's film market (see Table 7.2). Universal, which failed to reach that milestone in 2014, took the top spot in the market in 2015,

Table 7.1   Aggregate China box office receipts of US studios in 2014

Studios	2014 Rank	Aggregate Box Office in China ($ million)
Paramount	1	418
Disney	2	375
Warner Bros	3	358
Fox	4	310
Sony	5	164
Dreamworks Animation	6	122
Universal	7	52
Lionsgate/Summit	8	23

(Data Source: Pacific Bridge Pictures Research, 2014)

thanks mostly to the wild success of *Furious 7*. In only 8 days the movie grossed $250 million in China, and its total 2015 gross in China was nearly $400 million, making it the biggest film ever at China's box office. *Furious 7*'s success demonstrated that big budget, effects-driven, Hollywood action spectacular movies are still what the Chinese audiences love best.

The Chinese market is therefore at the center of global studios' future strategy. For years, foreign players have faced challenges when navigating the complex cultural, financial and

Table 7.2   Aggregate China box office receipts of US studios in 2015

Studios	2015 Rank	Aggregate Box Office in China ($ million)
Universal	1	711
Disney	2	532
Fox	3	285
Warner Bros	4	275
Paramount	5	259
Sony	6	121

(Data Source: Pacific Bridge Pictures Research, 2015)

political issues relating to viewers, partners and government in China. As a result, they look to local industry partners for a smooth entry into the world's second largest movie market. In the internet age, however, even domestic film companies themselves are searching for their new positioning. For one thing, the traditional film industry model is being disrupted by complex interactions between online firms and offline cinemas. For another, young, urban Chinese movie fans as the mainstream movie-going group are making their tastes known through social networks and mobile apps. So-called So-Lo-Mo trends are bringing new challenges and opportunities for both Hollywood and Chinese movie studios.

So-Lo-Mo (Social-Local-Mobile)

"So-Lo-Mo" is an abbreviation for Social-Local-Mobile, the three powerful trends reshaping China's film industry in the digital age. Until just a few years ago, China's movie industry resembled Hollywood in the 1930s, when studios controlled all business lines – from talent to production to theaters – before a 1948 Supreme Court ruling forced them to divest. In China this practice was called "being a dragon from head to tail", whereas the public audiences were passively on the receiving end. Today the internet element not only transforms the business model, but also has a huge impact on movies' content and production. For new films in China, their idea creation, movie production and marketing campaigns are increasingly shaped by big data and executed via social media (see Figure 7.2).

On "Social", the social networks provide a powerful link between movie-goers and movies at every stage in the life of a movie. It seems that in future movies will be triggered more by the "tail" (the end-users) via social networks, and mobile internet empowers movie fans to get involved in the whole life of a movie, from beginning to end (or as the Chinese saying goes, "from head to tail").

The importance of social networks is felt right from the idea creation stage. Before the internet age, it was very hard

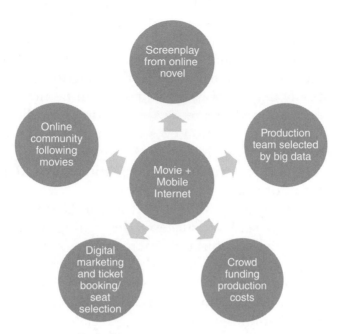

Figure 7.2   Mobile Internet Through the Life Cycle of a Movie

for young screenwriters in China to emerge, because a hand-ful of producers working with a small number of screenwrit-ers controlled almost the whole market. As discussed in the previous chapter, the internet has leveled the playing field for aspiring young writers, and many online novels have been adapted into feature movies. The popularity rankings of online literature provide movie makers with important information on potential movie-goers' constantly-shifting preferences for story-line and genre; hence more and more directors actively search the internet for potential hits.

In a more direct way, consumers increasingly make their preferences known to the directors and producers through social media. On a general platform like WeChat or a special-ized movie review site like Douban, movie fans comment on the latest movies and make suggestions. Rather like having dinner at a restaurant, they would prefer to have their favorite dishes made to order than wait to see what the chef is cooking.

Meanwhile, the studios are proactively using big data analytics to find consumers' focus areas. Even after a decision on a movie production is made, directors may still use social networks to interact with fans, because their feedback and comments not only help to polish the "base" online novel for the movie screen, but also create free marketing even before the movie is made. In short, the new studio model is: let us know what you like to watch (simultaneously we will try to figure out your taste preferences using big data technology), and then we will produce it for you.

For instance, starting with the 2011 hit *Love is Not Blind*, there have been a series of successes in turning online young adult novels into blockbusters, such as the 2013 drama *So Young*, which was adapted from the novel *To Our Eventually Lost Youth*. The *Tiny Time* series is by far the most successful example of all. Its author Mr. Guo Jingming was one of the top-tier online authors – the so-called "zhigaoshen" (the Supreme God) class of writers, with nearly 20 million followers. Based on social network popularity – of both the novel and Mr. Guo himself – the celebrity internet novelist turned his work into a movie. Within a short time, the movie caught on in China and exceeded all expectations to become a franchise.

Of course, the successful transition of *Tiny Times* from an online novel directly into a blockbuster hit was exceptional. In reality, while lots of film and television companies aggressively purchased popular internet content for production, not many films or TV series lived up to the quality of the original works. Usually, an online work is trialled in the form of a micro movie or web series before studios are convinced of its potential acceptance as a feature-length movie. Take the path of *Old Boys: The Way of the Dragon* as an example. The story of *Old Boys* was a sentimental tale of a pair of struggling amateur musicians in China who called themselves the "Chopsticks Brothers". It first went online in 2010 as a 43-minute micro online movie. After it received tens of millions of online views and its theme tune

Old Boys became popular, the story was turned into a full-length movie, which became one of the hits of 2014.

In addition to movie story choices, social networks also help to shape the choice of production team. Again, to use the example of *Tiny Times*, before Mr. Guo Jingming became a first-time producer-director, he checked with his fan base for advice. The production company also tapped into Weibo (the Chinese Twitter) for suggestions on the director and stars of the films from over 100 million Weibo followers. The feedback was somewhat unexpected because the fans suggested that Mr. Guo himself should be the director, an important reason being "to preserve the original flavor of the novel".

The new generation of movies are also increasingly using social networks for production financing. Movie crowdfunding has attracted the interest of many young audiences, and it is quickly becoming an important funding channel for movie production companies. (Detailed discussions relating to internet finance will follow in the next chapter.) When *Tiny Times* reached the third and fourth sequels, young fans were offered the opportunity to invest in the production for as little as $15. They were excited to be "co-producers" of the movie and appreciated the chance to visit filming locations, receive stars' autographed photos and even meet the stars.

Furthermore, at cinemas the "social" aspect is still visible when a movie is put on the big screen. Selected movie theaters in China have experimented with the "bullet screen" – a new model that enables viewers to chat about the films via text messages on the movie screen while they watch. **(See the "Bullet Screen" box.)** The "bullet screen" with social interactive features was invented in Japan, and was mostly used in the video streaming context to provide individuals with a virtual "watching together" experience (while watching online videos alone). However, as a testimony to the popularity of social networks in China, some movie theaters have boldly added this feature to the big screen, using the bullet screen in an already "physically watching together" setting.

"Dan-mu" (Bullet Screen) and "Tu-cao" (Spit and Criticize)

"Dan-mu" (bullet screen in English) is a new model of movie watching. The term may have originated from online warfare games, where intense shooting by canons fills the PC or smartphone screen with bullets. Likewise, some theaters in China have launched a pop-up commentary section on screen, where the audience can comment on the film and have their text messages projected for everyone to see and reply to. At any given time, those messages and comments scroll across the screen like bullets.

The "bullet screen" model was started at a video streaming site in Japan called niconico, and it has been adopted by major Chinese video sites such as Tudou and iQIYI. When watching a video on a mobile device, this technology allows viewers to send messages about what they like or dislike about the video, and all the people who are watching the video at the same time can see the message, respond to it or post their own comments.

In other words, the "bullet screen" feature of video streaming creates a virtual "watching together" experience, even though everyone is watching individually. The intense real-time social interaction among viewers provides an entirely different experience from the traditional web setting where viewers post their comments on the web page (not the screen) in sequence (not real-time). While comments can be so overwhelming that the content screen itself could get clouded, "bullet screen" proponents suggest the highlight of the experience is not the video itself, but to "tu-cao" (Chinese for "spit and criticize in a joking way") in a virtual social context.

Now the movie marketing people have bravely applied the "bullet screen" model to real cinema settings, and recent experiments have included major productions like *The Legend of Qin* and *Tiny Times 3*. Probably due to the self-selection of the audience attending those movies in the cinemas, the reactions to the trials were generally supportive. Many people seemed to be excited seeing their comments shown on the big screen. Some praised the model for combining watching movies and making friends at the same time. Some thought it was an especially good idea for boring or silly movies, so that instead of passively viewing the content, they could enjoy the social experience of "tu-cao". Some even suggested that the movie plots were occasionally hard to understand and the messages on the bullet screen provided insight for them when they were struggling.

Of course, opponents of the bullet screen, who were not interested in the interactivity with strangers in the cinema, found the social experience on the screen a distraction from movie watching itself. So the cinemas for *The Legend of Qin* took a middle path, where the audience messages were projected onto the two walls on either side of the screen. But that was not appreciated by many viewers because they believed that "a bullet screen had to be overlaid across the whole face to be exciting enough". For these young audiences, their approach to movie watching can best be summed up by the title of a 2010 Chinese action comedy: *Let the Bullets Fly.*

There is still debate about whether the bullet screen is simply a marketing trick or a major model revolution for the movie industry. For some audiences, the bullet screen is a distraction from movie watching; for others, it is an additional social interaction to enrich the overall movie watching experience. Most likely, the bullet screen is here to stay due to young audiences' strong desire to express their views. To them, while the director defines the storylines on the movie screen, the bullet screen is a parallel screen of their own to provide feedback on the movies. In future, specialized bullet screen cinemas equipped with cutting-edge technology may emerge, like the IMAX theaters, and it's likely that every cinema will set aside a special section dedicated to bullet screen viewers.

Finally, an important activity for young netizens after watching a movie is to comment on and discuss it on social networks. As a result, even after a movie's release the fans are still influencing its destiny through their movie reviews and comments on social media. For the movies they like, young Chinese fans may exhibit quasi-religious zealotry, whipping up a frenzy or defending it against criticism like an army of loyalists.

For example, when *Tiny Times*' emphasis on high-society life and material gratification stirred up controversy in China, its loyal fans on social networks – mostly young girls like the heroines in the movie – defended the film with fervent counterattacks. By contrast, the power of social networks is also obvious when viewers reveal their dislikes. In 2014, the 3-D film *Gone with the Bullets* was hotly anticipated because it was directed by Jiang Wen, whose 2010 satirical hit *Let the Bullets Fly* set box office records. But when negative reviews started spreading rapidly via social media, the film's box office suffered.

The second element is the "local" trend, which is both more subtle and more profound than the social network factor. With mobile internet providing Chinese consumers not only with more content, but also with more ways to find it, they have turned the tables, becoming "choosers" in consumption. Probably to the surprise of many, this does not necessarily mean that foreign content, in particular Hollywood movies, is the clear winner in "high quality content". In fact, local audiences are increasingly open to domestic productions, which for a long time had only a small market share due to the dominance of blockbuster imports from Hollywood.

Among the top 10 China Box Office performers of 2014, domestic and foreign movies were split 50/50 (see Table 7.3). The Hollywood blockbuster *Transformers: Age of Extinction* ranked No. 1, but it was the only foreign movie in the top 4. According to data from the State Administration of Press, Publication, Radio, Film and Television, in 2014 local productions took 54.5% of China's total box office.

In 2015, domestic movies gained even more ground and claimed 7 out of the top 10 box office spots (see Table 7.4),

Table 7.3   Top 10 China box office performers of 2014

Rank	Movie Title	Gross ($ millions)	Domestic/ Foreign
1	*Transformers: Age of Extinction*	320	Foreign
2	*Breakup Buddies*	187.97	Domestic
3	*The Monkey King*	167.84	Domestic
4	*The Taking of Tiger Mountain*	141.02	Domestic
5	*Interstellar*	121.99	Foreign
6	*X-Men: Days of Future Past*	116.49	Foreign
7	*Captain America: The Winter Soldier*	115.62	Foreign
8	*Dad, Where Are We Going?*	111.87	Domestic
9	*Dawn of the Planet of the Apes*	107.35	Foreign
10	*The Breakup Guru*	106.59	Domestic

(Data Source: Box Office Mojo, 2014)

Table 7.4   Top 10 China box office performers of 2015

Rank	Movie Title	Gross ($ million)	Domestic/ Foreign	Genre
1	Furious 7	390.91	Foreign	Action
2	Monster Hunt	381.86	Domestic	Fantasy/Comedy
3	Lost in Hong Kong	253.59	Domestic	Comedy
4	Mojin: The Lost Legend	252.01	Domestic	Action/Adventure
5	Avengers: Age of Ultron	240.11	Foreign	Sci-fi
6	Jurassic World	228.74	Foreign	Action/Adventure
7	Goodbye Mr. Loser	226.16	Domestic	Comedy
8	Pancake Man	186.35	Domestic	Comedy
9	The Man from Macau II	154.13	Domestic	Action
10	Monkey King: Hero Is Back	153.02	Domestic	Animation

(Data Source: Box Office Mojo, 2015)

amassing almost two-thirds of total box office receipts (61.6%). For three years in a row (2013–2015), domestic producers gained a bigger share of the market than Hollywood. It is worth noting that in 2015 only action and adventure movies from Hollywood made it to the top 10 box office spot, clearly suggesting that the new generation of movie-goers have strong views on the movies they like to see. Therefore, it is critical for Hollywood studios to better understand the new dynamics in China's market to ensure their movies remain relevant in the world's soon-to-be largest movie market.

The success of homegrown dramas illustrates a remarkable recent evolution in Chinese audiences' tastes. And it seems that Chinese producers have adapted more quickly to local audiences' preferences. (Of course, the US studios have to deal with scheduling issues. They are also sometimes given relatively short notice on release dates, making it more difficult to manage marketing campaigns.) The 21st century Chinese audience have seen enough spectacles, explosions and special effects from Hollywood movies. The challenge for the Western producers is to find something relevant to this generation that keeps them engaged, or to find something new that gets them excited. Most of the successful domestic movies have had some kind of social message that resonated with audiences.

Once again, possibly to the surprise of many, the mainstream "themes" of movies are not necessarily defined by audiences in the top-tier cities like Beijing or Shanghai. Instead, they are increasingly defined by "small town youths", a term that covers young movie-goers in tier 2, 3, 4 and 5 cities, essentially all youth audiences in urban centers other than the tier 1 cities. According to the *White Paper on Small Town Youths* by the Ent Group at the end of 2015, during the last few years movie-goers in tier 1 as a percentage of the total market had decreased steadily, while the smallest tier 4 and tier 5 cities were on the rise (see Figure 7.3). This growth is not that surprising when one considers the increasing penetration of mobile internet across the country.

The emergence of "small town youths" is an important reason for the "going local" trend in China's movie market.

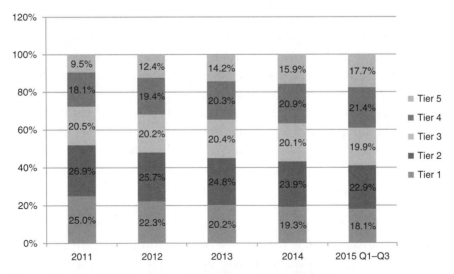

Figure 7.3   Tier 1–5 Cities' Share of Movie-Goers (2011–2015 Q3)
(Data Source: Ent Group, September 2015)

In the case of the *Tiny Times* series, the story centered on the individualistic pursuit of happiness and success, resonating with the young audience, with its exaggerated high-class life full of branded luxuries – everything young movie-goers dreamed of having, but doubted they would ever attain. In particular, the path of the film's protagonist was every Chinese college student's dream: She began the story as an ordinary university student, and then had to face things like job interviews and intimidating bosses in the workplace. But she managed to pull through and her life became better and better – she had a glamorous career, great friends and a handsome boyfriend.

Put another way, the storylines of *Tiny Times* and the like, which covered the aspirations, insecurities, struggles and stress of the new generation, had filled a void in the traditional domestic movie market. For a long time, at one end of the spectrum of available movies were the movies from the older authors and directors in China, to which young people could not relate or did not even try to understand. At the other end of the spectrum were foreign movies that appeared too remote and random for the "small town youths". The majority of the young audience like stories from authors of their own age, and they admire fashionable, popular and successful heroes that are also home-grown. To capture the market share in China, Hollywood movies have to adapt to the rapid increase of the "small town youths" at cinemas.

However, this new trend also raised questions about movie quality and the ultimate sustainability of China's movie market. Some film critics lamented that few of the movie hits in recent years had any real critical success, and they suggested that big data on consumer preferences may be skewed by the boom in the new audiences from China's smaller cities. In line with the critics, many hit movies of recent years, including *Tiny Times*, were selected by online polls to receive the Golden Broom Awards for "the most disappointing films, actors, directors and scriptwriters" of 2014 and 2015 (**see the "Golden Broom" Box**).

Golden Broom Awards and *Tiny Times*

Considered to be the Chinese equivalent of the Golden Razzie Awards in the US, the Golden Broom Awards were established in 2010 along with the boom in social network and online film reviews in China. At the beginning of each year, the organizer asks the public to select the country's worst film through online voting, and the final results on "the most disappointing films, actors, directors and scriptwriters" from the last year are announced at a ceremony.

The name "Golden Broom" was picked by the founders to symbolize "cleaning up", evidenced by the fact that not a single winner in the six years since the creation of the awards had ever attended the ceremony to formally accept their trophy. According to the organizers, the most recent contest among 2014 films has taken place amid "the most shameless, uncreative and dreadful" time in China's film history.

Tiny Times 3.0 swept the 2014 Golden Broom Awards, winning four awards in total. Its writer-turned-director Mr. Guo Jingming received both awards for "most disappointing director" and "most disappointing screenwriter". But he should have drawn some comfort from the fact that for the title of "most disappointing film" his film was in a tie with *The Breakup Guru*, which also ranked high on China's box office chart. And some online posts commented that it was so hard to make the 2014 choices "because there are so many bad movies".

Through the drama of the Golden Broom Awards, critics highlight that high box office revenues do not equate to quality films. The general public seems to agree, as reflected in the rapidly growing number of participants and sharp feedback during the voting process. For 2015, the nomination list was even longer than in 2014. Once again *Tiny Times* (the sequel 4.0 and series finale) was nominated for the most disappointing film category, but the award eventually went to some newer movie hits. As China's movie market continues its explosive growth, it is mature enough to take some constructive criticism with a sense of humor.

Finally, on the "mobile" side, the internet and smart devices are becoming the main medium linking the movie market and Chinese audiences. At the 2015 Shanghai International Film Festival, the organizing committee released its first ever report on the trend of "internet movies" in China, and its data showed that the internet had become one of the most important marketing channels for Chinese movies. 75.27% of

Chinese film viewers decided to watch a movie because they had read the original network fiction, played related online games or watched animations through the internet.

As such, digital marketing has become critical in China's increasingly competitive movie market. In smaller urban centers like tier 3 and lower cities, the internet may be the only cost-effective way to reach the potential audience. Mobile channels are especially important because for small town youths, their smartphones may be their only access to the internet. If young movie fans could be motivated to share movie information on social networks, a movie can potentially achieve far better coverage than by traditional offline advertising. These days the major social networks WeChat, Sina Weibo and Renren (a college-focused social network) are the main portals for online marketing. Meanwhile, specialized movie sites Mtime and Douban have also emerged as centers of movie reviews and scheduling information.

In the case of *Tiny Times*, for example, the film's producer and distributor Le Vision Pictures (the film arm of China's tech and media conglomerate LeTV), claimed that it did not put up one single advertising billboard across the country. Instead, knowing the fans are mostly high school students and young adults, it did most of the film's marketing activities through social networks. As a result, the production company not only saved a lot on advertising spend, but also claimed 85% accuracy in predicting box office returns by tapping into users of Weibo, Renren and Douban (an entertainment-focused social network).

In addition, mobile internet technology has also changed the way movie-goers pick a cinema nearby and book movie tickets in advance. It's a classic O2O connection between online activities (social network, screenings and location search) and offline activities (cinema going and popcorn promotion deals). As discussed in the earlier O2O chapter, the major O2O market players are approaching this sector from their different strengths – Baidu's mobile search engine, Alibaba's e-commerce big data, Tencent's messaging service and social media, and Wanda's shopping malls and cinema chains.

These big four are in a fierce price war to win the market share for online movie ticket sales. All three internet firms (BAT) have discount ticketing service subsidiaries, and Wanda has also linked interactive mobile apps with its theaters across China. Movie ticketing was an area where traditional movie theaters failed to provide convenient services in the past, due to a lack of investment in technology. Movie theaters used to post their schedule in the middle column or service page of local newspapers. Now the mobile ticketing service provides viewers with the most up-to-date movie schedules, location information of movie theaters, cheap tickets (thanks to the subsidies of the big companies) and seating reservation ahead of the showing. Collectively, the mobile apps have made an offer that movie-goers cannot refuse.

As a result, the market has seen a jump in the number of people using online systems and smartphones to buy movie tickets. In just a few years, online ticket purchases moved from zero to over 50% of the market and have become the main-stream channel. According to Baidu founder Mr. Robin Li's presentation in mid-2015, 55 out of 100 movie tickets were sold online, whereas in the US only 20% of movie tickets were booked online. Of course, the same question has arisen in the movie market as in other O2O sectors. There are concerns that the current discounted ticketing model is not sustainable because sooner or later major firms have to phase out their subsidies in the search for profit.

As with O2O dining services discussed earlier in this book, the core issue in price wars is about the "stickiness" of the new movie-goers, who are not necessarily avid movie fans, but are attracted to cinemas by the deeply discounted ticket price. For now, however, the enormous subsidies are also justified by the major firms as a way of gathering big data, which can potentially help them better understand audiences' preferences for movie productions. In fact, the big four players' ambitions extend beyond connecting Chinese audiences with domestic and

Hollywood movies, and they have all set up their own movie production units. They actively search for and team up with popular online novels to produce domestic movies. They have also entered into numerous partnerships with prominent writers, producers, actors, directors and studios from Hollywood to work on co-production movies for the Chinese market.

For example, Alibaba's film unit made its first-ever US film investment in Paramount Pictures' blockbuster *Mission: Impossible – Rogue Nation,* starring actor Tom Cruise. In fact, at the WSJ 2014 JD conference, Alibaba's founder Jack Ma said the company was already "the biggest entertainment company in the world", because Alibaba was involved in the entire supply chain from investment and production of content all the way to marketing and distribution of the movie. More recently, in early 2016 Wanda acquired Legendary Entertainment, one of Hollywood's biggest movie production companies for approximately $3.5 billion, and Wanda described the deal as "China's largest cross-border cultural acquisition to date".

It is worth highlighting that Wanda also has an unrivalled offline base for the movie business. Aside from being the largest owner of movie theaters and shopping malls in domestic China, it also acquired AMC Theaters, one of the largest cinema chains in North America, for $2.6 billion in 2012. Its more ambitious project, the Oriental Movie Metropolis (which aims to be the Chinese version of Hollywood), broke ground in 2013 at Qingdao City in Shandong province. This studio complex had a huge budget of $8 billion, which included film studios, movie theaters, a theme park, a film museum, a wax museum and resort hotels.

Therefore, whether "Content is King" or "Channel is King" is not a real question for the big players. With abundant capital, the "big four" are spending huge sums on both sides and positioning themselves as the global studios and distributors of the future. The related question, however, is on the sustainability of exceptional growth in China. In other markets, the low-cost entertainment options on electronic devices have led to less movie-going for young people. Is the Chinese market so different that it could buck the global trend? In China, will online entertainment screens eventually take away audiences from the big screen as has happened in the developed markets?

So far there is no data pointing in that direction, as Chinese movie fans seem to want both the cinema and the mobile-device experience. As big movie screens and mobile internet continue expanding their reach into small cities and rural areas, more "small town youths" are becoming movie-goers, and the market will likely see continued robust box office record-setting over the coming years. Of course, the film industry has already started working on ways to defend its market share. Cinemas equipped with bullet screens have tried to provide the same social interaction during movie watching as viewers have in the context of online video watching. The social and mobile components of movie watching, therefore, may soon blur the separation between big screens and small screens.

Hollywood's Changing DNA

The SoLoMo trends have not only transformed China's movie industry, but also had profound implications for Hollywood studios' business model in China. The internet-led boom in market size, together with more internet firms becoming movie studios themselves, provides more revenue opportunities and partner selections for Hollywood. At the same time, they need to have a better understanding of the DNA of the new "internet +" film business in China.

In particular, internet distribution and promotion channels have disrupted market dynamics, and Hollywood studios have to rethink their intellectual property rights at play in China in the new mobile, multi-screen context. Traditionally, Hollywood studios pay most of their attention to box office revenue in China, but online business is expected to bring greater revenue into the mix soon. According to industry estimates, although online revenue is currently much smaller compared to box office revenue, it may catch up with or even exceed the latter within the next decade.

Interestingly, the popularity of pirate DVDs in China may contribute to the development of the online movie market. In Western markets, movies go through a very clear "windowing" process. They appear exclusively in theaters for a period of time (traditionally a few months) before they move to DVD, and later to online distribution services. The major theater chains control the majority of movie screens in the United States, and they have aggressively opposed suggestions to shorten their release window for fear that audiences will be enticed to stay home instead. In China, windowing has not really developed, because the popularity of pirate DVDs means there is no legitimate DVD market.

Therefore, mobile internet players reason that the Western studios maybe be better off distributing movies online in China more quickly than before. The logic is that online channels can help to get the movies into the Chinese market before the pirates do, making it convenient for people to watch and pay. It follows that, by offering consumers a legitimate way to watch new films in a timely fashion, audiences may not bother looking for pirated products. (In the past, pirated DVDs were traditionally the fastest way for Chinese audiences to get access to a new movie.) Compared to a decade ago, new generation audiences are keen to enjoy the best movie watching experiences, so low quality pirated DVDs lose their appeal quickly if an authentic copy is available.

In other words, if content is distributed more quickly, audiences may be more willing to pay to watch it on mobile devices for the sake of convenience and quality rather than watching pirated DVDs. For example, in 2015 iQIYI charged just under $1 for Chinese audiences to watch new releases online, which was the same as the cost of a pirated DVD. Thus, if the mobile online distribution model is well utilized and managed, it could provide a good solution to the intellectual property issue, but the window period between cinema release and online distribution needs to be reduced or even eliminated in China. Otherwise, after a long window period, even a hit Hollywood movie may become an old movie by the time it is streamed in China.

(In all likelihood, a large number of Chinese audiences would already have resorted to another medium to view it.)

For example, when Tencent entered into a Netflix-style streaming service in 2014 with Warner Brothers (which has a minority stake in the joint venture), the two arranged to deliver movies to homes across China just two weeks after their US cinema release. The 2014 hit *300: Rise of an Empire* was among the first batch of titles available to rent in China when the film was still showing in cinemas in the US and other markets. In future, the "windowing" period in China may shrink further when one looks at Netflix in the US as a reference.

In August 2014, the sequel to the martial arts drama *Crouching Tiger, Hidden Dragon* and the four Adam Sandler movies were released simultaneously across the globe on Netflix and in IMAX theaters. It was the first deal of its kind, where major motion pictures make their debut on the streaming service and in movie theaters at the same time (that is, eliminating the theater window altogether). The US studios and cinemas were generally doubtful whether the loss of revenue from cinema patrons would be sufficiently compensated by the audiences watching movies at home, because movie ticket prices were substantially higher than the streaming price.

But some were more optimistic that the new model could potentially create a bigger pie. When Lionsgate launched its film *Arbitrage* simultaneously in theaters and on "video-on-demand", its chairman was reportedly happy that the movie "found two different audiences". Most likely more US stars, directors, studios and theater chains will accept straight-to-streaming deals in the near future, in the same way that Netflix has shaken up the television model. TV shows used to follow a similar "window" system, but they are now available for streaming immediately after or very soon after they are broadcast on TV networks.) When the window of theatre exclusivity in the US shrinks further, Hollywood studios should find it both easier and more profitable to embrace Chinese mobile viewers in a more timely way.

As the intellectual property rights protection of movies in China continues to improve (the same is true for videos, as discussed in the previous chapter), the market may see more direct cooperation in content production between Hollywood and Chinese movie studios. The biggest potential is in co-production movies, which have long been viewed by Hollywood studios as a new way to gain a bigger slice of China's booming film market. When officially designated as a US–China co-production, a movie can be treated as a domestic film to bypass China's import quota on foreign films, and the foreign producer could get a bigger share of the Chinese box office than with an imported Hollywood movie. Furthermore, working with Chinese partners helps distribution tremendously. The rumors and stories of local actors involved in blockbusters like *Transformers*, for example, created a valuable marketing opportunity even before the film's official release in China.

But it won't be easy for a movie to be all things to all markets. Around the world, almost every market focuses on two kinds of films – domestic films that resonate with local lives and Hollywood blockbusters. Due to cultural dissimilarities and the language barrier, finding subjects deemed suitable for both Chinese and US audiences has proved tricky. Over the past decade, co-production works have met with varying degrees of success, as the studios are still struggling to balance Chinese elements with international box office considerations.

Although some Hollywood blockbusters have added Chinese settings and co-stars, they have been at best Hollywood stories with Chinese sub-plots and arbitrarily inserted characters. *Transformers: Age of Extinction* in 2014 was one of the best-performing movies in China, but it was essentially two movies under one title. As the story developed, action shifted from Texas and Chicago to Beijing, with the final 30-minute all-out robot war taking place entirely in Hong Kong. The 2013 movie *Iron Man 3* was filmed in two different versions. The Chinese version had four extra minutes of footage featuring Chinese actors and locations, and another version with most of those scenes cut for international release.

In addition, for the purposes of co-production categorization, multiple product placement deals with Chinese consumer brands are also incorporated into the movies. This begs the question whether they pose challenges to the story's coherence (or become hilarious as in the case of *Transformer*). **(See the "Inserted from China" box.**) Market feedback has been clear: forcing "Chinese" elements into films is not the key to success. Even with Chinese fingerprints all over a film, its co-production is not organic if the elements are added in a random way, and the audiences can easily get tired of such awkward combinations.

Inserted from China

As a new normal, more Western films are incorporating multiple product placement deals with Chinese consumer brands. The challenge is to maximize commercial exposure without appearing too obvious. The latest *Transformers* movie is perhaps the most audacious trial of this trend.

In *Transformers: Age of Extinction*, all through the storyline of government espionage, robot war and endless explosions, numerous everyday consumer goods and services from China, from smoked duck meat ("Zhou Hei" brand), a power drink (Red Bull), to an online streaming set-top box (LeTV) and computers (Lenovo), found their way onto the big screen.

In one scene, actor Stanley Tucci played the billionaire inventor pursued by the CIA, who fled to the rooftop of a Hong Kong building. For no obvious reason, there was a refrigerator holding various food items. Stanley Tucci picked up a milk box with the "Yili Shuhua" brand and sipped milk for a good few seconds. In another scene, when the movie's other lead actor Mark Wahlberg withdrew cash in the middle of the Texas desert, the ATM machine happened to belong to China Construction Bank.

As one would expect in the mobile era, movie-goers took to the social networks to puzzle over the movie's numerous product placements. At the same time, some movie-goers, as Chinese consumers, found it interesting to see the daily commodities in a Hollywood movie. But more comments questioned whether the addition of Chinese goods had become excessive and whether the movie structure dictated by commercial factors is questionable.

Two-Way Co-Production

Along with the boom in the domestic film market, Chinese studios are moving up the value chain, helping to develop, design and produce world-class films and animated features. They are taking bigger roles, financially and artistically, in the creative process when collaborating with Hollywood than in the past. Naturally, their ambition is to make Hollywood-scale movies for global audiences. Thus an intriguing expectation is that China's film companies – both the traditional ones and the internet firms – will reverse the co-production equation to create Chinese movies with global appeal.

In a "reversing" co-production, the challenge is flipped accordingly. Rather than adding Chinese elements to a US movie, the producers need to find Chinese stories that could travel globally. Then they may also have to incorporate foreign elements and locations to attract overseas viewers. Such Chinese films will create storylines as a "Hollywood way of looking at China". Meanwhile, they have to learn about better storytelling from the established foreign film industry to have "a Hollywood way of presenting China". If that happens, China's movie market will not only surpass the US as the largest consumer of movies, but also emerge as a powerhouse of movie production in the world.

So far, China has yet to become a major exporter of film. Successful recent homegrown movies have had limited success in the overseas market, even though their box office numbers in the domestic market are already on a par with Hollywood blockbusters. The challenge for Chinese playwrights is to identify stories that will resonate with people from different cultures. To date, the situation in China's movie industry is similar to that in India, where the productions are mostly viewed within the country.

Take the 2013 hit movie *Lost in Thailand* as an example. *Lost in Thailand* was a contemporary comedy about a pair of co-workers competing to find their company's largest shareholder in Thailand to secure a contract for some coveted technology patent. With a preposterous plot and flamboyant characters, the movie presented Chinese audiences with exactly what they wanted: popular stars, funny dialogue and a subtle reflection on the ambitions and anxieties of China's growing urban middle class. For many new middle class people who feel confused and exhausted by the increasing demands of modern life, the movie resonated with them as a story about "losing themselves".

In China, *Lost in Thailand* was considered a comedy, presenting "contemporary China" in a jokey way. Even for Chinese audiences, this film style was a novelty. This low budget production (just under $5 million, according to news reports) was a big commercial success in China: it knocked *Life of Pi* off China's No. 1 spot in the month of its release and its box office exceeded *Titanic 3D*. When the movie was shown in US cinemas a while later, many had high expectations and even considered it a Chinese version of *The Hangover*. (*The Hangover 2* took place in Thailand as well.)

However, the domestic box office success of *Lost in Thailand* did not travel well; instead, the movie got lost in translation. At its weekend opening, it was reportedly shown in a mere 29 cinemas in the US and took less than $30,000 over the weekend. Maybe the humor of *Lost in Thailand* was simply too Chinese to connect with foreign viewers. But even before the box office consideration, the mere fact that the cinema chain distributor AMC decided to treat it as a niche movie and showed it on only 29 screens throughout the US provided important feedback: it may take some time before US movie distributors have strong confidence in Chinese movies' broad appeal.

What seemed to be promising, nevertheless, was the respectable performance of its 2015 sequel, *Lost in Hong Kong*. The state-side distributor Well Go USA released the film in North America on the same day as its Chinese launch, and although it was only shown in 27 theaters in a limited day-and-date North American release, it reportedly had solid success, earning more than $500,000. Also in 2015, another successful home movie *Pancake Man* had a successful premiere in North America over the opening weekend. *Pancake Man* was the tale of a poor street pancake vendor who gained miraculous super powers from the pancakes he served. Because the Hollywood film industry had long dominated the superhero movie genre, it was quite an achievement that a new superhero franchise from China could join the mix.

The most important reference point may come in the near future from a "reverse" co-production that is in the making. A fantasy adventure movie called *The Great Wall* is to be jointly produced in 2016 by Legendary Entertainment and Universal Pictures on the US side, and China Film Company and Le Vision Pictures on the China side. With a $150 million budget, *The Great Wall* is one of China's biggest productions to date, the largest film ever shot entirely in China for global distribution (a "reverse" from traditional co-production US movies).

In fact, the movie story is fundamentally China-centered. It is set in China hundreds of years ago, involving an army of elite warriors who must transform the Great Wall into a weapon "in order to combat wave after wave of otherworldly creatures hellbent on devouring humanity". Legendary described the story as "an elite force making a last stand for humanity on the world's most iconic structure [the Great Wall in China]", which has secrets hidden beneath the ancient stones. The IMDb website similarly has a one-line summary of the film for interested Westerners: "A mystery centered around the construction of the Great Wall of China".

The ultimate "reverse" probably results from the fact that the movie director Mr. Zhang Yimo is a Chinese native who does not speak English. Even though his prior productions including *Raise the Red Lantern*, have won international awards, this is Mr. Zhang's first attempt at a film primarily in English. That could be a challenge for the foreign partners, but the upside for the US production company Legendary Entertainment and Universal Pictures is that, with a Chinese director, together with the large Chinese cast, Chinese locations and Chinese capital investors, the movie easily qualifies as an official Chinese co-production rather than a Hollywood movie with some added Chinese flavors.

This movie is due for global release in November 2016 and US and Chinese film studios will watch it closely to see how enthusiastically the markets accept it. The fundamental risk is the same as for a typical co-production movie: that is, *The Great Wall* may be too Chinese for international audiences, but still too Hollywood and foreign for Chinese audiences. However, the special theme of the movie provides some cause for optimism. In foreign markets, Western cinemas can introduce the movie simply as an English-language movie with Matt Damon and monsters (perfectly Hollywood) that happens to have Chinese themes. In the Chinese market, action spectacular is the single genre that best resists the challenges from local movies. As shown by *Transformers* and *Furious 7*, Chinese audiences love to see movies featuring monster machines that race, fly and perform gravity-defying stunts to save the world.

If *The Great Wall* proves to be the global blockbuster it aims to be, it may become the template for future China–Hollywood co-productions, and it may further inspire other forms of collaboration between the studios. However, even if it is successful, it may not necessarily mean that studios will be keen to copy this model aggressively. Given the scale of the Chinese movie market itself, most domestic producers would be cautious about the foreign box office potential, because when they globalize their films, the foreign components will most likely dilute the movies' local flavor, and risk losing some domestic fans. Therefore, many producers may choose to ensure that their productions will appeal to and attract home-based fans first. As a Chinese proverb reminds people, "Don't drop a watermelon to pick up a piece of sesame".

Still, Hollywood movie producers should find co-production a promising adventure. No matter what the relative China and US content composition equation is in a movie, if it can become a hit in these two markets, it already controls a majority of the world's viewers. As internet giants like Alibaba, Tencent and Baidu invest their way into the movie business, they are set to be the new powerful movie studios in the digital age, as well as the dominating distribution channels of the future. Already their social networks, mobile applications and big data technology have led to an incredible boom in the domestic movie market, and their partnership with Hollywood may create the new generation Chinese movies – a blend of Hollywood standards and China's unique culture, tradition and history – that appeal to global audiences.

CHAPTER 8

Internet Finance

On January 4, 2015, the internet firm Tencent launched China's first internet-based bank "WeBank". One of the five privately funded banks approved by China's central bank, PBOC, WeBank in Chinese suggests a bank for "micro and many", reflecting its focus on ordinary individuals and small businesses and its linkage to the internet and social network. The ceremony was officiated by Premier Li Keqiang, and he pressed the "enter" button on a computer to send out the first loan of RMB35,000 ($5,400) by WeBank to a truck driver.

This first internet loan represented three important innovational aspects.

First, by providing microloans to the public, internet banks like WeBank addressed demands from individuals that were not adequately addressed by the existing financial system, with its focus on large companies.

Second, the internet bank conducted all operations online, so that the borrower did not need to go to an offline outlet to obtain the loan. WeBank first used Tencent's own version of facial recognition technology to verify the borrower's identity from a remote terminal; all of the loan processing was completed online.

Third, the creditworthiness of the borrower, the truck driver, was analyzed by utilizing big data technology, which effectively reduced the information asymmetry between the bank lender and the borrower. The driver was a member of a Tencent-invested logistics platform called Huo-che-bang (Truck Club), which links truck services with logistics companies. Based on the driver's driving history on the mobile app and his online profiles on other e-platforms, WeBank's financial model gave the driver a high credit rating and granted a loan carrying a 7.5% interest rate, without requiring collateral or a guarantee. In financial terms, WeBank's superior data sources and processing capability enable this internet bank to provide better priced credit to consumers. (Without sufficient information on the borrower, the interest on the loan would likely have been set higher by the bank.)

As summarized by Premier Li at the ceremony, "one small step for WeBank is a giant leap for financial reform". This statement was no exaggeration as online purchases were only made possible in China a decade ago by an escrow-like service designed by Alipay, the online payment system affiliated with Alibaba. e-Commerce in China started with a cash-on-delivery model, but Alipay and other internet payment platforms managed to build trust between consumers and vendors by serving as a sort of escrow service: when a consumer made a payment through Alipay, Alipay notified the merchant to ship the order, and Alipay released the funds to the merchant only when the consumer received the product. This innovative set-up led to a boom in online transactions in China.

Today a large part of the Chinese population has skipped credit cards entirely in favor of digital payments, just as people in many parts of China are skipping landline phones to buy a smartphone to access the internet for the first time. In addition, Chinese consumers are comfortable with using the internet to manage their savings and investments. As internet companies transform smartphones into a platform for financial transactions, China is way ahead of the rest of the world in terms of how widely internet finance is adopted.

The rising integration of internet and finance is closely linked to two imperfections in the financial system – and potential solutions stemming from the internet. One is the lack of investment choices for individual savers and investors. China's financial services sector is immature compared with developed markets, and it lacks the variety of products and services found in the US market. The two major investment channels – public stock and real estate markets – require large investments and a high risk tolerance. Meanwhile the deposit interest rates at banks are tightly regulated and currently set at low levels.

The other imperfection is the difficult access to credit by small and new businesses, because banks concentrate on the bigger and established companies because of their perceived lower credit risk. In response, internet firms have set up online investment platforms for individuals to educate themselves on capital markets and invest in financial products. New lending and equity financing models are also initiated for under-served individuals and SMEs (small and medium-sized enterprises), such as peer-to-peer (P2P) lending, equity-based crowdfunding and microloans based on big data.

In a short period of time, internet finance has fostered a more inclusive financial system where loans and equity financing are more widely available to consumers, start-ups, SMEs and whoever can put them to productive use. New players, many of which are private, internet-based and light on assets, have entered China's mostly state-controlled financial industry and offered innovative products and services. (See Table 8.1 for selected providers of internet finance to be discussed in this chapter.)

However, due to the lack of a market entrance threshold or business operation standards, many of these new offerings have evolved from regulatory "gray zones" and have grown rapidly "in the wilderness". For example, in the first half of 2015, there were more than 400 new cases of P2P lending platforms running into operational difficulties, according to data from P2P portal www.wangdaizhijia.com.

On July 15, 2015, China's central bank, PBOC, teamed up with other related regulators and jointly issued the long-awaited policy framework on internet finance in China, the *Guidelines on Promoting the Healthy Development of Internet Finance* (referred to as "the Guideline" in this chapter). The Guideline defined internet finance as "traditional financial

Table 8.1   Examples of internet finance in China

Product/Service	Providers/Brands (Selected)	Description
Third-party payments	Alipay, WeChat Pay	Support e-commerce, usage expanding into O2O activities, also used to pay utility and water bills
Crowdfunding	Demohour, dajiatou.com	A new financing channel for venture and movie investments, but estimated 75% capital flowing into "pre-market sales" relating to consumer products
P2P Lending	Jimubox, Renrendai, China Rapid Finance, Dianrong.com	Presently the dominant form of online lending, but there is a sharp rise in problematic platforms
Financial products sales	Ant Fortune (Alibaba), WeChat wealth management	Online money market funds, mutual funds sales, insurance sales, discount brokerage

institutions and internet companies using internet technology for payments, internet lending, public equity financing, internet fund markets, internet insurance, internet trust, and consumer finance". For the first time, government regulation defined the term "internet finance", and the new financing businesses such as P2P lending and crowdfunding were recognized and addressed.

Reflecting the exceptional complexity of internet finance – which covers numerous financial services under different regulators – a total of 10 government ministries and commissions jointly issued the Guideline. On the financial industry regulators' side, there were the central bank (POBC), the Ministry of Finance, the State Council Legislative Affairs Office and three regulatory commissions for the stock market, banking market and insurance market (CSRC, CBRC and CIRC, respectively). The internet industry was represented by the Ministry of

Industry and Information Technology, the State Administration for Industry and Commerce and the State Internet Information Office. In view of fraud and other crimes in this field, the Ministry of Public Security also joined the taskforce.

In terms of the regulatory responsibilities defined by the Guideline, the central bank would monitor online payments, the securities regulator CSRC would supervise crowdfunding and online sales of stocks and stock funds, and the banking regulator CBRC would oversee online lending platforms such as P2P lending. Based on this joint policy framework, the regulators would develop specific rules in their respective jurisdictions. As the topic of mobile payment has already been covered in the chapters on e-commerce and O2O markets, the following sections will focus on the new financing models (equity crowdfunding and P2P lending), the new internet distribution channels for asset management products and their related regulatory challenges.

Crowdfunding

Generally speaking, crowdfunding is a capital raising transaction involving a large number of people, with each person contributing only a small amount to the whole project. In China, the concept of crowdfunding has quickly become widely known precisely because of the "fun" focus of mobile internet. By allowing the average citizen to become a movie micro-financier, the application of crowdfunding to hit movies has educated the market and attracted wide participation (or at least, attention) from the public at large.

Crowdfunding has changed the way films are financed in China. Traditionally, Chinese films have been funded by studios, either state-owned or private, including the new ones set up by the internet firms themselves. In the digital age, crowdfunding campaigns are marketed as an opportunity for ordinary audiences to get involved in the glamour of movie making, since anyone who loves films or adores stars could become a minor investor and participate in movie production and promotion.

In September 2014, Baidu launched its movie financing product Baifa Youxi. Its funding site was a joint launch between Baidu, Taiwan's Central Picture Corporation, Citic Bank and DeHeng law firm in Hong Kong. To avoid the legal uncertainty around the crowdfunding deal structure (for example, constraints on public promotion and the number of investors), Baifa Youxi was set up as a trust for investment services, not a movie project to raise financing directly through crowds. The first movie project listed for investors at Baifu Youxi was *Golden Age*. Users could put up as little as RMB10 ($1.6) of their own money and receive yields (expected to be between 8% and 16%) based on how the films eventually perform at the box office.

Within hours the *Golden Age* crowdfunding product quickly attracted 3,300 supporters, who raised nearly $30 million, 120% of the movie's target. Since the investment capital from individual investors was small, the participants' financial returns would likely be small, but they were probably more excited about being able to claim that they had worked on the Chinese version of the Hollywood classic *Gone with the Wind* (which *Golden Age* was compared to in China). In other words, Baidu expressly positioned the Baifa Youxi as a fun experience rather than a serious investment product.

Similarly, Alibaba launched its own version of a movie investment product called Yu'le-bao in 2014. Owing to regulatory considerations, Alibaba also structured it differently from typical equity-based crowdfunding. The Yu'le-bao platform offers investment-linked insurance products from Kuo Hua Life Insurance Company, which investors could purchase from as little as RMB100 ($16), and the collective funds were subsequently invested in entertainment projects. (Yu'le-bao could be translated as "entertainment treasure".) Underlying the investment product was a range of projects from movies, TV shows and video games. As a way of gathering information on audiences' taste preferences, each investor was asked to choose a maximum of two investment plans from the list of projects.

As the above examples demonstrate, when putting their small fragments of capital together, the young netizens, who individually do not have a large amount of disposable income, can create a sizable capital pool. As "mini-producers", investors enjoy the opportunity to visit filming locations, get the exclusively issued electronic magazines and even meet the stars. Internet firms like Baidu and Alibaba, in addition to further familiarizing users with internet finance, also build up data on movie-goers' taste preferences. It may also serve as a marketing channel, because the investors are likely to be incentivized to mobilize people they know to watch the movies, increase box office takings, and subsequently receive higher returns from their investments.

In addition to the movies and stars, celebrities in other fields have also used crowdfunding for their unique projects. (And in some cases involving unique experiences, such as in the **"Harvard Education" box**, crowdfunding has turned ordinary people into public figures.) In March 2015, Yao Ming, the former National Basketball Association all-star with the Houston Rockets, started a crowdfunding campaign to invite wine and basketball enthusiasts to own a piece of his Napa Valley winery, for as little as $5,000 per person. Not known to many people before the crowdfunding campaign, Yao Ming's winery had been the biggest seller of high-end Californian wine in China by value in recent years. Driven by Yao Ming's adventure story as a Chinese player in the US NBA, basketball fans and curious investors rushed to participate, and he had met half of his funding target of $3 million within a day.

$15 for a Harvard Education

In the summer of 2015, a Chinese student was admitted by the Harvard Kennedy School of Government for graduate studies. The tuition fees and expenses for the master's program were expected to exceed $155,000, so he started a crowdfunding campaign on the biggest social network in China – WeChat.

The headline of his campaign was "Instead of buying me a lunch, have a walk with me at Harvard for a semester." For anyone who put up RMB99 ($15), he would add the person to his WeChat group for one semester. He promised to be online for at least two hours per week, including one hour for experience sharing and another hour for questions and interactions. In poetic tone, he wrote, "Together we walk into the US and into Harvard the symbol of US spirit. Together we understand the US, understand Harvard, and understand ourselves."

The campaign received mixed reviews from web users. Many users asked: "Why should others pay for your dream?" Some blatantly called the fundraising "begging", because they did not see much value in the experience sharing that he offered. Defending himself at a media interview, the student claimed that his parents had enough money to pay for his tuition fees, but he was inspired by many successful stories of online fundraising, and he hoped to be self-reliant by trying the crowdfunding.

After considerable controversy, the fundraising announcement was deleted from the WeChat account. But the student claimed that his fundraising target was RMB50,000 (about $8,000), and he reached that goal in just three days from nearly 400 investors. In that sense, his crowdfunding campaign was reasonably successful.

While these movie-related and celebrity-centered crowdfunding events feature in the news headlines, the majority of the capital in the Chinese crowdfunding market flows into those related to consumer goods pre-sales. For example, e-commerce sites Taobao (Alibaba), JD.com and Qihoo 360 Technology all have sizable "crowdfunding" platforms for consumer products. That really is the unique characteristic of the crowdfunding market in China. One possible explanation is the value of social networks: in addition to marketing, branding and inventory management, a crowdfunding platform provides a kind of social network for e-commerce players, especially if they do not have a WeChat (Tencent) or Weibo (Alibaba).

Because it lowers the cost of setting up a venture company for a specific product, crowdfunding helps to create a new entrepreneurial ecosystem. As a result, more entrepreneurs can engage in more experiments, and innovative start-ups can put their products out into the marketplace with few capital

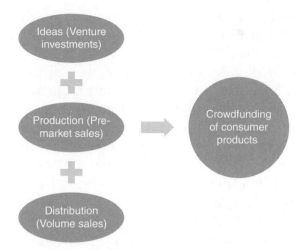

Figure 8.1   Crowdfunding of Consumer Products

barriers. Looking at the crowdfunding projects of consumer products, one could see them as a combination of venture investing (idea stage), pre-market purchases (product stage), and volume distribution (mature stage) throughout the different phases of a product's life cycle (see Figure 8.1).

Then the question becomes whether the crowdfunding model is too lenient on the project teams. Many projects arrive at the fundraising stage when they are only rudimentary ideas. In many cases, production is postponed, product quality is below expectation, or the product is not quite the same as planned. But there is very little that investors can do about it, because crowdfunding promotes innovation. Is that fair to the ordinary investor? To put it another way, is it appropriate for normal investors to behave like venture capitalists, taking on the risk of untested companies?

To that end, one of the largest crowdfunding platforms in China, Demohour, decided to transform itself. Set up in July 2011, Demohour was among the earliest crowdfunding platforms, and the movie project it facilitated which received the most support was a film called *A Hundred Thousand Bad Jokes*. Soon after, however, Demohour concluded that the existing crowdfunding models for consumer products had led to investments in too many companies that should not have been funded in the first place.

In April 2014, Demohour decided to end its crowdfunding business and turn the company into a "smart device pre-market sales platform". It vowed to select projects more vigorously before presenting them to the public investors. Also, to keep tighter control of the project, it would delay paying public funding to the project team until it saw substantive progress. (In the past, Demohour typically paid 70% of funding to the project team at the start.)

According to Demohour, in future all standardized product-related crowdfunding platforms will have to become "pre-market sales platforms", because conflicts among consumers/investors, project teams and crowdfunding platforms are increasing under the earlier model. Essentially, Demohour suggests that the crowdfunding money should only be paid out in pre-market sales, i.e. when a new offering reaches its production phase. The rationale is simple: ordinary people are not venture capitalists, and they should stay with what they are best at – being consumers.

Going forward, the greatest potential that crowdfunding offers is an equity financing channel for small and medium-sized enterprises (SMEs), but this is an area subject to tight regulation. In China, private companies must seek government regulators' approval before listing, and the qualification requirements for public issuance of equity are very rigorous. In short, it is really challenging for SMEs and start-ups to be eligible for the public issue of securities, and the costs for the listing process and the continuous disclosure filing requirements are prohibitively expensive for SMEs.

In this context, the important legal issue is whether a crowdfunding transaction constitutes a public issuance of equity, which is regulated by China Securities Regulatory Commission (CSRC), or whether it can be structured as a private placement exempted from registration requirements. Generally speaking, crowdfunding is a sort of equity issuance, where a start-up or established company raises funding from the public for its project. In return, the investors receive a portion of equity returns as reward. In fact, the name "crowdfunding" already suggests there is an inherent "public" element.

This question is critical because if a crowdfunding project is deemed to be a public offering of equity securities, then it must go through the full process of registration, application and approval before financing. Failing this, in the worst-case scenario it could constitute an "issuance of shares or corporate or enterprise bonds without authorization" under the Criminal Law of China. (Of course, this type of crime involves large amounts of capital and severe consequences, a very different scenario from typical crowdfunding transactions where individuals invest small amounts.)

The rational approach for SMEs, of course, is to keep their crowdfunding as private offerings of equity stocks. However, there are stringent requirements to comply with. For one thing, private offerings cannot be promoted in the public domain; instead they have to be offered to a number of specific investors. Most equity-based fundraising platforms set up a membership system for this purpose. Before potential investors can receive information on projects, they first have to qualify as members of the platform.

However, the definition of qualified investors for private placements remains vague under China's Securities Law and related regulations. Taking the concept of "accredited investors" under US securities law as a reference, a qualified investor needs to possess high net worth, ample investing experience and/or special knowledge of the issuer. By contrast, those looking at crowdfunding in China are mostly average people with little capital and limited investing experience. In fact, crowdfunding platforms often ask only for people's names and ID numbers for membership registration. Therefore, compliance with "know your customer" remains an issue.

The other hurdle to qualify for a private placement is that the number of investors must not exceed 200 in total. To this end, most platforms generally hold shares in the form of a

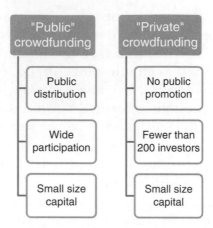

Figure 8.2   Two Versions of Crowdfunding: Public Offering vs. Private Placement

special purpose vehicle (SPV) as a means of "consolidating" investors. However, some recent CSRC regulations on private offerings seem to suggest that because the fundraisings often involve multiple levels of investors, the number of investors should be the total of all levels of the fundraising structure. This probably means that underlying investors in a SPV must be calculated separately, making the 200-investor limitation a critical issue for the ultimate fundraising size of crowdfunding transactions.

Finally, in the Guidelines for Internet Finance, the CSRC and other government ministries have formally determined that a crowdfunding of corporate equity characterized by "public distribution, small size, and wide participation" should be treated as a public offering of equity securities and is thus subject to regulation. (See Figure 8.2 for different standards for "public" and "private" crowdfunding transactions.) In other words, unless an equity-based crowdfunding by a corporation fits the standard of a private placement, it would be viewed as a mini-IPO (in the case of early stage start-ups) or a secondary offering (in the case of an existing listed company), subject to all the requirements of a public offering.

Due to the limitation on "small size (fundraising)", "public side" crowdfunding is not likely to be an important financing channel for corporations any time soon. The small sums of money raised by crowdfunding transactions, whether public or private, may not be sufficient for the financial needs of SMEs and start-ups. In fact, the capital raised may not even be sufficient to cover the offering cost in the case of a "public" crowdfunding.

Crowdfunding should, however, be here to stay because it plays into the "fun" theme of mobile internet. Apart from pre-market sales, crowdfunding in China in the near future will most likely focus on small investments for hit movies, social entrepreneurship and similar projects offering a unique experience. With little investment involved, the downside risk for investors is limited, and at the least they may have some fun and enjoy some interesting stories – or learn about Harvard – in return.

P2P and Internet Bank Lending

Similar to creating new equity financing channels in the form of crowdfunding, the internet has also revolutionized the lending market. Online peer-to-peer (P2P) lending is the practice where ordinary consumers lend directly to individuals and small businesses using online platforms, without using a traditional financial intermediary such as a bank. Historically, commercial banks found small size loans too costly to cover, but these days digitally mediated transactions are reducing lending costs and leading to a boom in financial activities.

While crowdfunding attracts many "diao-si" investors who make a small investment for the sheer joy of participating, P2P lending appeals to a smaller group of wealthy investors who are far more willing to take risks in large amounts. P2P has exploded in popularity in China over the last few years (see Figure 8.3), and China has already surpassed the level in the US (where the model was first developed) and become the world's largest peer-to-peer lending market since 2015. Across the country there are estimated to be more than 3,000 P2P platforms focusing on four industry segments: consumer lending, small business lending, auto loans and real estate lending.

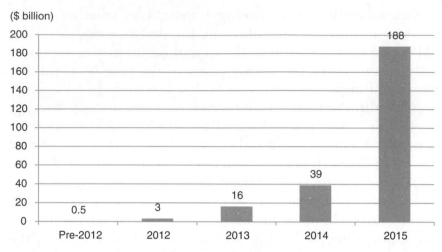

($ billion)

Figure 8.3   Growth in Chinese P2P Online Lending (2011–2015)
(Data Sources: Wangdaizhijia.com, Wind Information)

The P2P lending business is part of the shadow banking market in China, as many P2P lending websites gather funds from the public and then lend funds to individuals or small companies, instead of simply serving as an information platform to facilitate lending and borrowing between parties. A general shortage of credit in the Chinese banking system, combined with banks' preference to lend to large SOEs (state-owned enterprises), drives individuals and SMEs to online lenders. Attracted by the rapid growth and business potential, venture capital and major internet firms have flocked to the P2P platform start-ups (see Table 8.2).

Table 8.2   Major Chinese P2P platforms and their investors

Chinese P2P Platforms	Investors (Domestic and Foreign)
Renrendai	Tencent
ppdai.com	Sequoia Capital
Yooli.com	Softbank China Venture Capital, Morningside Group
jimubox.com	Xiaomi, Temasek, Matrix Partners, Ventech Capital, Magic Stone Investment
Penging.com	Shenzhen Hi-tech Investment Group

The essence of "peer-to-peer" lending is to use network technology to achieve equal positioning by both the borrower and lender in four aspects: information disclosure, risk appetite, term structure and rights and obligations. In China, however, P2P is understood to be "person-to-person" by some market players. Their P2P platforms aim to allow anyone with money to become a lender, and anyone who needs money to apply for a loan. Without a proper setting, the online lending business is ripe for abuse. Recently there have been a number of Ponzi scheme-like scandals where lenders have pooled funds from investors without matching them to borrowers.

To better protect investors' interests, the new Guideline has clarified two critical issues relating to P2P lending. As a result, the market has seen a complete shake-up of the existing business model, and the breakneck pace of P2P lending growth has slowed dramatically. The first requirement of the Guideline is that P2P platforms can only serve as information channels to match borrowers with lenders. The Guideline bans P2P sites from "enhancing borrower credit worthiness" (that is, providing security or guarantees for the loan). In other words, P2P lending platforms are now defined as information intermediaries (brokers) rather than credit intermediaries (banks).

This clear definition is a blow to many P2P platforms. In developed markets, the government's credit bureau has data on individuals' credit history, from which the P2P operators can supply a score for the potential borrower, on which potential lenders can base their decision about whether to enter into the transaction. (In fact, internet firms like Alibaba and Tencent are using their online big data to develop new credit score systems to fill this gap in China, which will be discussed later in the chapter.) But in China this type of credit data system is not fully developed, making additional types of credit support, such as collateral or guarantees, necessary for P2P business.

For example, to attract investors to try out their innovative loan offerings, new P2P platform entrants typically provide high expected return figures. But first-time investors tend to worry about the inherent high risk related to high returns, so the P2P platforms often implicitly guarantee "principal amount protection" to appease investors' concerns. The reality is, however, that Chinese laws prohibit the salespeople of investment products from guaranteeing "principal protection" or investment returns, except for bank deposits or government bonds (because they are essentially risk free).

For smaller P2P businesses, they will likely have difficulty finding customers if they are not permitted to provide any credit support (such as guarantees or collateral) to win over investors' confidence. Even before the 2015 regulatory guideline, repeated fraud-related bankruptcies or sudden website closures had already highlighted the risks of the smaller P2P operators. The recent online fraud cases involving high profile P2P platforms further shook the confidence of the public. **(See the "P2P Fraud" box.)** Therefore, a consolidation of businesses is expected, where only the P2P platforms backed by large companies with trusted reputations can survive.

P2P Fraud – Buried and Cremated

Information disclosure is at the core of P2P lending, but many platforms share very little information with retail investors. With limited information disclosure, the users – especially those who are not sophisticated in finance – are not necessarily fully informed of the risks involved. Often the investors are given an expected return figure, but do not have access to information that allows them to determine the level of risk of a loan. For example, some P2P platforms in China operate under the model of cash pooling, in which funds are collected into a pool before being lent out to borrowers with investment projects. From time to time, operators run away with funds put in by investors.

In December 2015, Beijing police started investigating a major Chinese P2P lender, Ezubao, for illegal operations. According to news reports, the company raked in funds from nearly 1 million investors by promising annual returns as high as 15%, and its total loan volume exceeded $1 billion at the end of 2015. In February 2016, the police announced 21 arrests (including that of the Ezubao founder), and the company was shut down.

The local officials on the case found out that more than 95% of the investment products that Ezubao listed on its platform were fake projects, and the company executives went to great efforts – including literally burying the evidence – to conceal the Ponzi scheme. They buried some 1,200 documents nearly 20 feet underground at a site on the outskirts of Hefei, Anhui Province, where Ezubao was based. The local police had to deploy two excavators to work for 20 hours to dig them up.

But the closure of another P2P platform was even more dramatic. In February 2016, Tongxin Venture Investments, a P2P platform based in Taian, Shangdong province, made an "official announcement" online that consisted of only two photos. One photo was a certificate showing that the company's owner had been "cremated". The other was the death certificate of the owner, with the cause of death listed as "heart suddenly stopped beating".

The second important requirement in the Guideline is that internet finance players like P2P platforms must entrust their users' funds to the custody of licensed brick-and-mortar banks. In the past, most P2P platforms kept the funds at third-party payment institutions, and the market believed that was a major flaw leading to cases where P2P operators fled with customer funds. To comply with the new rules, P2P platforms are reaching out to banks to set up custodian partnerships.

This custodian relationship is likely to accelerate commercial banks' entry into online lending. China's commercial banks had kept a close eye on the enormous custodian business for P2P and other internet finance businesses, but the regulatory uncertainties kept them from making major moves. With the new Guideline in place, commercial banks will speed up their entry into the P2P custodian business, and they may acquire quality P2P platforms to strengthen their internal capabilities for internet finance activities. However, due to reputation and credit risk considerations, banks may not accept small P2P operators as custodian clients, which should lead to further consolidation of the P2P market in favor of the larger players.

In this context, a licensed internet bank can be viewed as a formally registered P2P platform with a full banking license to provide legitimate online deposits and lending services. WeBank, which is 30%-owned by the internet giant Tencent, was the first licensed privately-owned internet bank to start operations. Zhejiang Internet Commerce Bank (also called MYBank), a subsidiary of Ant Financial Services Group and closely affiliated with the Alibaba Group, completed its registration a few months later and launched similar web-only banking businesses in mid-2015. Before the arrival of these official internet banks, internet firms had already provided financing services for e-commerce merchants in the form of microloans or supply chain financing. With their experience with individuals and vendors in mobile commerce, they are well placed to serve the under-banked consumers and small businesses at a low cost.

Traditionally, most of the state-run banks in China favor lending to big institutions for two reasons. On the one hand, the major commercial banks have had long-term relationships with and knowledge of the big companies in China. On the other hand, historically the banks have limited data tools for credit risk evaluation of individual consumers and SME businesses, and the transaction costs for those small loans under the brick-and-mortar banking model are prohibitively high. By contrast, internet banks run branchless banking operations that can serve customers 24/7. Their cloud-based model requires much lower operational costs than the traditional brick-and-mortar banking model. In addition, their parent companies' substantial databases of consumer behavior from internet businesses allow them to compile credit risk data in unconventional and innovative ways.

The internet banks are therefore able to provide financial solutions for a gap in the consumer economy, i.e. providing small amounts of credit to people that cannot be reasonably priced within the formal banking system to fill their special needs. Again, take the first internet loan by WeBank as an example. For the loan to the randomly selected truck driver, Tencent's WeBank used internet-linked data mining tools to assess the credit background of the potential borrower. The driver was a club member at the Tencent-invested logistics platform called Huo-che-bang ("Truck Club"), which linked logistics operators that needed to ship cargo with truck driving companies.

At the time of the loan, this platform had one million drivers with 650,000 truckers as members, and it was serving more than 160,000 logistics company customers. For each club member trucker, Tencent's platform had a large amount of information, such as total distances travelled, total cargo volumes transported, the scope of orders handled and so on. Some drivers had to pre-pay cargo freight, but commercial banks were not set to process such small loan amounts of that nature. WeBank, however, could refer to the data from the driver's operations on the mobile app, develop its own analytic model and evaluate the potential borrower's creditworthiness.

There is no doubt that the branchless bank concept is a major revolution from the existing banking model. Besides lower operating costs, it brings a lot of convenience to the users: there is no need to search for the locations of branches, no travelling required and no queues. Concerning the regulatory requirement on personal identity verification, however, the fact that they are branchless has been the biggest obstacle for internet banks to be fully functional as planned.

Under the current rules of China's central bank, PBOC, when individuals open a banking account, they must visit a real bank outlet to have their identities verified by a bank employee. Similar regulations on personal loans require bank employees to visit every loan applicant at the person's work or business, and then personally witness the signing of each application. Internet-only banks, however, by definition have intentionally eliminated these face-to-face encounters for the sake of efficiency and cost saving.

The solution offered by the internet firms is biometric identification at remote terminals. Among the possible options, facial images have been the top choice by internet firms, ahead of fingerprints, palm prints, retina images and other alternatives. One obvious consideration is probably cost: with the cameras on desktop PCs and smartphones, the marginal cost of taking a digital picture for identification is close to zero. Also, the facial characteristics read by the technology can be compared with the photos at the personal identification card information center and those in police databases. This type of technique means that online facial recognition can leverage offline security agencies' authoritative databases, whose information has been developed by strict face-to-face settings.

In January 2015, WeBank demonstrated Tencent's own facial recognition technology at the first pilot internet loan, where the truck driver verified his identity from a remote terminal. Shortly thereafter, one of its executives commented in a public interview that their facial recognition technology was quite mature and had lower error probability than the verifications done by human eyes. Supported by strategic cooperation between Tencent and the National Citizen Identity Information Center, which was affiliated to the Ministry of Public Security, its accuracy rate reached 99.65% at that time.

A few months later, Alibaba's founder Jack Ma unveiled Alibaba's own version of facial recognition at the CeBit conference in Hanover, Germany. He pushed a "Buy" button on an app that he called "Smile to Pay", matched his face with a white outline, and took a picture of himself. That information was transferred to the Alipay server and verified. With that, he bought a 1948 vintage souvenir stamp from Hanover as a gift for the mayor. According to media reports, Alibaba's face scanning system (called Face++) had an accuracy rate of around 99.99%. In addition to remote verification for banking, Alibaba's aim is to apply the facial recognition to all e-commerce, so that within a few years there will be no need to enter a password.

So far, China's central bank is not fully convinced of the accuracy and security of the facial recognition technology. In 2015, the central bank, PBOC, decided that "the conditions are not yet mature for using biometric technology as the primary means of verifying the identities of depositors". According to the Guideline, biometric identification cannot be used officially until a national standard for its use is developed in the financial sector and the related financial regulations are amended accordingly. Since WeBank's initial loan made remotely to the truck driver, the personal loan service remains in the testing phase. Similarly, Alibaba's MYbank is operating with limited offerings because the physical presence requirements for the opening of accounts are not lifted yet.

The controversy around facial recognition technology illustrates the fine balance that China's financial regulators have to strike. In the Guideline, the authorities have recognized the efficiencies of online banking, the new services it offers to customers and the innovations it brings to the financial industry. The challenge for regulators is to keep pace with technological change and strike a delicate balance that allows innovation to flourish while mitigating risk.

Internet-based Wealth Management

While only a small percentage of the population goes into crowdfunding and P2P lending in China, the majority have embraced internet finance to manage cash (including payments and short-term savings) and access standardized investment products. The latter is a much bigger market (trillion dollars) for internet firms than the former two business lines. For a start, online short-term deposit products from internet firms have been the best example of financial innovation in the mobile economy.

In June 2013, the first Internet Money-Market Fund (I-MMF) product, Yu'e-bao, was launched by Alibaba's financial arm Ant Financial (formerly known as Zhejiang Ant Small & Micro Financial Services Group). The Yu'e-bao I-MMF was offered to internet users as an alternative to traditional short-term deposits at commercial banks.

By the end of 2013, the Yu'e-bao product had already attracted more than 120 million investors and accumulated more than RMB100 billion ($15 billion) assets.

To put the numbers in context, the Yu'e-bao product made the underlying asset manager, Tianhong fund management company (in which Alibaba has a majority stake), the first investment fund in Chinese market history to exceed AUM (assets-under-management) of RMB100 billion within 6 months of launch. By mid-2014, Yu'e-bao's AUM exceeded

RMB600 billion (more than $90 billion), standing as one of the largest money market funds globally. Months after Yu'e-bao, Tencent launched its version of I-MMF, "Licai-tong", which also attracted a large volume of AUM in a short period of time.

The exceptional popularity of the I-MMF products is the result of internet firms identifying and solving several structural issues of the financial market in China with the help of internet tools. First, Chinese households have one of the highest savings rates in the world, so they have trillions in cash in bank deposits. They are not happy with the low returns from the deposits, but they are not necessarily comfortable with the risks of public stocks or real estate. Therefore, Chinese investors are constantly in search of risk-controlled alternatives to demand deposits.

The interesting twist was that Yu'e-bao provided investors with higher returns than typical bank deposits. Its premium return, to a large extent, actually came from Yu'e-bao investing in bank deposits itself. By drawing a big pool of money together, Yu'e-bao's manager Tianhong could negotiate higher deposit rates when it put the capital into the interbank market. In the summer of 2013, the interbank market saw tight liquidity conditions, represented by the skyrocketing borrowing rate (the Shanghai LIBOR rate). As a result, Yu'e-bao was able to offer much higher rates than direct bank deposits. For example, in July 2013, the 7-day rate on Yu'e-bao on an annualized basis floated around 4.6% for a period of time, more than 10 times the benchmark bank deposit rate (0.35%).

Second, Yu'e-bao and similar products have managed to accumulate a large amount of "leftover capital" via the internet. (In fact, "Yu'e-bao" can be translated into "treasure in residual amounts".) As seen in the internet literature business from earlier chapters, celebrity online novelists are supported by a large number of diao-si readers who pay a miniscule amount to read an installment. Similarly, Yu'e-bao has no investment threshold (which is required by most wealth management products sold at banks), and its minimum initial investment is as low as RMB1 (15 cents in US dollars).

Third, the I-MMF products have high liquidity because of simple online procedures, and they can easily be processed on smartphones and other gadgets. I-MMF products like Yu'e-bao can generally be redeemed on the same day and in many cases within the hour. By contrast, traditional money market funds (MMF) require two to three days to complete the redemption process. In other words, I-MMF products like Yu'e-bao have the high-yield benefit of a MMF but maintain the same liquidity as a bank deposit.

The explosive growth of Yu'e-bao and similar I-MMF products shocked the commercial banks. At the inception of these I-MMF products, the banks saw customers moving out deposits at an alarming rate; meanwhile, they had to finance the interbank market at a high cost. To put it differently, commercial banks experienced a lower asset and liquidity base (the decrease of cash deposits) and higher operating costs (the financing costs to buy liquidity at the interbank market) when challenged by I-MMF products. In a somewhat drastic response, some banks set limits on their customers' daily transfers of cash to I-MMF services like Yu'e-bao. Soon the major commercial banks started to launch their own internet MMFs that could be redeemed on the same day (T+0).

From a different perspective, the essence of the remarkable success of Yu'e-bao is simply using the internet as a better information channel and a more convenient transaction platform. In the past, banks were the most important channels for funds' marketing because of their large number of brick-and-mortar branches. Money market funds are readily available at banks and other financial intermediaries, but many ordinary people do not know about them, and the banks as the distribution channel are not incentivized to promote them. Now financial products on the internet have eliminated such information asymmetries. At traditional commercial banks customers also have to go through a separate process to invest in MMFs, while the I-MMFs have simplified the process so much that the customers can transact on smartphones in a few minutes.

Table 8.3   Various "Treasures" and products from Ant Financial/Alibaba

Name	Investment Profile	Risk
Yu'e-bao	Cash management (liquid)	Lowest
LeYe-Bao	Insurance coverage for company staff	Low
Yu'le-bao	Similar to crowdfunding, invest indirectly in entertainment projects like mobile games, movies and TV shows	Moderate to High
ZhaoCai-bao	Fixed-term wealth management products, Alternative assets	Moderate to High
Stock Funds	Public stock market exposure	Moderate to High
Stock Trading	Direct exposure to individual stocks (to come)	High

Building on the momentum of Yu'e-bao, Ant Financial has developed itself into a distribution platform for investment products covering various asset classes and different risk/reward profiles (see Table 8.3). In August 2015, it launched a dedicated wealth management app "Ant Fortune" (in parallel with the e-payment app Alipay Wallet). To advertise the app and to help the majority of the population to become familiar with financial products, Ant Financial offered the funds at zero commission fees during the promotion period. In addition, it reduced the redemption period from 3 days (T+3) to 1 day (T+1).

However, the ambition of Ant Financial does not end with being a channel for money market funds or investment funds. It aims to develop a broad-based mobile financing system based on the big data and cloud computing capabilities from the whole Alibaba Group. The Alipay Wallet app, Ant Fortune app, and more mobile services that Ant Financial plans to launch in the near future collectively have the potential to take control of the majority of the population's money transfers, savings, investing and everyday spending in China, if the commercial banks and other financial institutions do not react quickly.

As outlined in the earlier chapters on e-commerce and O2O, Alipay has dominated the mobile payment market. It not only processes e-commerce transactions, but also handles many other types of online payments like utility and water bills. With O2O businesses rising, Alipay has spread into numerous offline payments as well, such as taxi hailing, restaurant services, and movie ticketing. After more than 10 years' development, Alipay (started in 2003) has completely dominated the PC terminals. At the mobile terminals, even with the increasing competition from WeChat payment based on the social network, Alipay's market share remains at a staggering 80% level according to market research firms' data.

The main reason for having Ant Fortune as an asset management app that is independent of, rather than integrated with, the Alipay Wallet app is to prevent Alipay from becoming too "big and burdensome" as a platform, which would have a negative impact on users' experience. This illustrates the enormous scale of the services represented by each business line. When its micro financing business, represented by MyBank, takes off, Ant Financial will most likely launch a separate mobile app for that as well. (See Figure 8.4 for the e-money empire that Alibaba is building up.)

With existing leading positions in the above three areas in domestic urban markets, the greater potential for Ant Financial's future growth is in rural China and global markets. In rural areas, the internet services could likely fill a role similar to the community banks in the US – serving clients the big banks do not cover and providing small size loans that the big banks' business model cannot justify from a cost perspective. The internet may also be the best medium to educate a large part of the Chinese population about capital markets and financial investments that they have never dealt with.

In the global markets, by mid-2015 Alipay reportedly had more than 17 million overseas users and supported settlement transactions in 14 foreign currencies. Relating to cross-border e-commerce, Alipay has developed services like overseas tax rebates, overseas O2O, international money transfers and so on. Meanwhile, Ant Financial is also reaching out through

Figure 8.4   Ant Financial's e-Money Empire

foreign partnerships. In early 2015, Alibaba acquired a 25% stake in the parent company of the major Indian online payment platform and e-commerce firm Paytm. Significant internet finance growth may come from bringing financial inclusion to those emerging market populations that have long been left out of the mainstream business world, as in rural areas of China.

The Future of Internet Finance

By applying mobile technologies to the finance industry, internet firms surprised the traditional financial institutions by offering innovative and convenient services to consumers, which truly put consumer experiences front and center. However, it remains to be seen how disruptive internet finance can be for traditional banking. In the digital age, traditional banks have quickly adopted internet data and analytics capabilities, and every financial institution is incorporating mobile internet technology into its traditional banking and asset management operations.

Take mobile payments as an example. In this field, the difference in user experience between Alipay and banks' online payment services is continuously decreasing. In addition to commercial banks catching up quickly, internet firms also face new challenges from foreign peers. In February 2016, Apple officially launched its much anticipated Apple Pay service in China through a partnership with China UnionPay (CUP), the only domestic bank card organization. (Samsung is also expected to reach an agreement with CUP soon to bring the Samsung Pay system to China.) Using Apple devices, the customers of 19 major Chinese banks are able to link their bank accounts to Apple Pay, which supports both mobile app and in-store payments. The users can complete transactions at e-commerce sites that accept the payment system or at offline merchants that have compatible point-of-sale (POS) machines from UnionPay.

Although Alipay is the default payment method for e-commerce transactions on Alibaba's e-commerce marketplaces, the payment setups at offline storefronts vary significantly. For O2O activities, consumers generally find a product or merchant before selecting the corresponding payment method (instead of picking the payment method first and then finding a transaction). The customers have to go with the payment method used by the merchant or platform behind the transaction, where Alipay may only be one option. For example, Apple has already listed Carrefour, 7-Eleven, Burger King, McDonalds and KFC among the merchants accepting in-store Apple Pay in China. As a result, Alipay may not always be used by customers when alternatives are readily available and equally functional.

Furthermore, the "big four" state-owned commercial banks have fully developed internet channels and platforms for their customers. For example, all of the major banks have web-based "direct banking" services, which not only offer traditional banking services like credit card repayments and account management remotely via the internet, but also cover expanded services like wealth management and money wiring services. According to a presentation by a major commercial bank executive in 2015, more than 85% of banking business is now being processed through e-channels, a substantial jump from less than 20% ten years ago. Similarly, securities firms and insurance companies are building online and mobile channels to reach more potential customers with specialized products.

Among the industry players, there are radical disagreements on whether the arrival of internet firms is bringing about a revolution in the finance industry, or if the industry is simply going through a rebalancing process after the adoption of internet technology. If the internet only brings a new distribution channel to the finance industry, then internet financing will fall short of a revolution, particularly because the traditional institutions have quickly incorporated the internet channel into their existing large balance sheets and broad branch presence. The "heavy infrastructure" that the banks have accumulated and developed for decades may turn out to be a major competitive advantage in the internet finance war (see Figure 8.5).

Therefore, in the same way as video streaming sites have to use unique entertainment content to keep viewers loyal, internet finance companies have to provide special value and services to maintain user loyalty. Otherwise, internet finance firms like Ant Financial may find it difficult to justify their high valuations based simply on their exploitation of the internet as a channel to market. (Ant Financial was valued at more than $40 billion in its 2015 private fundraising round, among the most valuable start-ups in China, like the smartphone maker Xiaomi).

For example, in the summer of 2013 when the I-MMF product Yu'e-Bao was launched, the capital markets had tight market liquidity. Yu'e-Bao benefited from high interbank rates and thus was able to offer much higher yields for customers than bank deposits. As a result, it accumulated users and assets-under-management (AUM) rapidly. However, since 2014

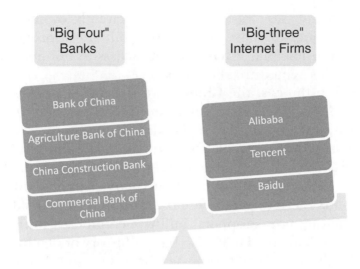

Figure 8.5   Banks' "Heavy Infrastructure" Likely a Competitive Advantage

China's central bank has steadily injected cash into the banking system, and the interbank rate has decreased correspondingly. By mid-2015, the yield offered by Yu'e-Bao dropped to half of the yield at inception, and its AUM decreased to a fraction of its peak amount.

To provide unique value to users, the most promising area for internet firms may be to offer small loans to Chinese individuals and SMEs. These under-serviced customers collectively have a huge need for credit, but it is challenging for the commercial banks to acquire (1) a large number of (2) small-scale borrowers (3) with good credit quality (4) at a low cost. Because the majority of the 1.4 billion population has had no credit spending experience or even any interest in borrowing from financial institutions at all, there is no well-developed credit scoring system in China, similar to the FICO scores and other consumer credit record services in the US.

The big data capabilities of internet firms, derived from e-commerce transactions and social network activities, have provided them with a huge competitive advantage. In early 2015, Alibaba launched Sesame Credit Management Group to develop a credit-scoring system primarily based on online data.

Sesame Credit was one of the eight privately owned credit-scoring businesses that received preliminary approval from China's central bank, PBOC, and its access to online transaction data has been unrivalled to date.

While in the past the Chinese were using Alipay simply to shop on Alibaba's Taobao e-marketplace, these days the payment platform is so ingrained in China that its hundreds of millions of users access the platform to pay nearly all their household bills. The wealth management platform Ant Fortune also has hundreds of millions of users who manage their savings and investments there through Yu'e-bao and other financial products. In addition to shoppers' online e-commerce transaction records, Taobao and Tmall also have a history of dealings with tens of millions of small businesses that sell or source goods on the two marketplaces.

All this data on retail consumers enables Sesame Credit to work with those who may have little credit history at traditional credit agencies. As more merchants adopt the Sesame credit score system, "Sesame" opens the door for Alibaba in two directions (see Figure 8.6). On the one hand, Sesame Credit can facilitate access for more consumers to new borrowing services such as home loans, car loans and other types of installment credit. For example, Mobile Loans, a P2P lending website that has partnered with Alibaba, announced that loan requests from

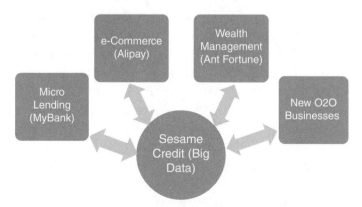

Figure 8.6   Two-way Data Flow between Sesame Credit and Digital Businesses

borrowers with high credit scores at Sesame would be processed much faster than others. On the other hand, more credit transactions bring more data to the Sesame Credit database, which can serve as a foundation for Alibaba's many other businesses such as O2O business lines.

Tencent, on the other hand, is applying a social network-based methodology to the credit evaluation of internet users. On Tencent's social networking platforms like WeChat and QQ, more than half a billion people have registered their personal data with effective identity certification. Just like the trucker's operational record on the logistics service app relating to the pilot microloan, Tencent believes that user behavior and history on the social networks also provide sufficient data for the evaluation of creditworthiness. The logic is that the more someone uses social networking services, the more likely that person is to be conscious of and concerned about his or her reputation.

In addition, at Tencent's gaming platform the users' transactions on virtual goods and online game points are also useful variables for internet data mining. Some of these parameters used by Alibaba and Tencent may seem unconventional, hard to quantify and somewhat arbitrary, but they are all valuable inputs for the big data approach.

According to news reports, P2P lending site China Rapid Finance had used the social network data provided by Tencent WeChat and gaming data to rate 50 million Chinese consumers for creditworthiness by mid-2015.

By contrast, commercial banks generally take an asset-based approach in credit assessment. It is hard for individuals and SMEs to get the loans if they do not have collateral or assets. As a result, while hundreds of millions of the new middle class are now financially active consumers, the existing financial system has not sufficiently covered the majority of the population. Many young, employed people do not have credit scores. That is an enormous vacuum that needs to be filled quickly as China moves into a consumption economy, and the internet-based big data approach may be the only efficient way to resolve it.

The biggest uncertainty around the seemingly unlimited potential of internet finance is industry regulation. China's rapidly expanding internet finance sector is coming under increased scrutiny from Chinese regulators due to the rising numbers of P2P scandals. As discussed earlier in this chapter, regulators have resisted approving facial recognition technology for opening full-service online bank accounts without visits in person to bank branches. As commercial banks rapidly build up their own internet channels, the explosive growth of Yu'e-bao is not likely to be repeated frequently in other areas of the financial markets.

Furthermore, when internet firms dive directly into the underlying finance businesses (in addition to being a new channel), their operations will be subject to the same supervision as traditional banks and institutions, their products will be similarly examined and regulated, and their corresponding compliance costs may turn out to be much higher than they have anticipated. Again, the banks' existing operational infrastructure, as well as their extensive compliance experience, may provide them with a significant edge in the war of internet finance.

But there is no doubt that internet finance firms can be a source of inspiration and transformation for traditional financial institutions with their pioneering business models and consumer service culture. China is at a crossroads with internet finance and – given the immense potential value to consumers – should move promptly to place it on a sound footing. In particular, commercial banks can refer to the way internet lending platforms innovate through their collection and analysis of consumer data for credit and risk management. As a wave of financial sector liberalization sweeps through China, internet finance may experience a breakthrough from a comprehensive upgrade of the existing regulatory framework.

Going Overseas: A Bumpy Road

Few had expected the Golden State Warriors basketball team to reach the US National Basketball Association's (NBA) 2014–2015 season title with a rookie head coach and a roster filled with young talent that had little playoff experience. It was a huge achievement for the franchise that had not won a championship for 40 years. However, the even bigger winner of the NBA Finals was a Chinese smartphone manufacturer that sponsored the team, whose brand name became increasingly well known in the US thanks to marketing campaigns like the one with the Golden State Warriors.

No, that Chinese smartphone brand was not the widely talked about young smartphone start-up Xiaomi. Nor was it Lenovo, the PC giant that once acquired the IBM PC division and more recently the Motorola mobile phone division in the US. Furthermore, it was not the aggressively expanding Huawei that did better than any other Chinese player in terms of moving into high-priced models. The Chinese company was ZTE or Zhongxing Telecommunications Equipment Corp.

Although ZTE was a major supplier of telecom gear used by carriers around the world, its name was still unknown to many people outside of China. In recent years, Xiaomi, Lenovo and Huawei were in a neck-and-neck race in the domestic smartphone market, and globally they were also competing for the world's third largest smartphone vendor position behind

Samsung Electronics and Apple Inc. But in the US market, ZTE was ahead of them. In fact, ZTE was the only Chinese manufacturer with a sizable market share in the US.

By the end of 2014, it had become the fourth largest smartphone brand in the US – behind only Apple, Samsung and LG, and it was the second largest in the prepaid (no contract) market. ZTE's partnership with the NBA was part of the company's plan to increase its brand awareness in the US market and worldwide. For the latest 2015–2016 season, ZTE signed up further new deals with two more leading NBA teams – the Chicago Bulls and Cleveland Cavaliers, its basketball sponsorships reaching five major NBA teams in total.

ZTE's solid presence in the US is one example of Chinese smartphone makers expanding overseas and challenging market leaders Apple and Samsung. The broader trend is that the major internet companies in China are moving beyond the saturated domestic market to compete on a global stage to maintain their growth. Their presence has been felt abroad as they send their products and services overseas. They also actively partner with or directly invest in foreign companies to accelerate their expanding reach. However, as will be seen in the examples in this chapter, it is not an easy task to break into the US and other foreign markets. Many companies have tried and struggled to work out their strategy beyond the home market. Perhaps ZTE has made a fast breakthrough in the US smartphone market, but for all the Chinese internet companies expanding into global markets, the task is no slam dunk.

"Tomorrow Never Waits": ZTE in the US

Although China is the largest smartphone market in the world by number of users, the US market is equally significant. The US smartphone sales figure is about half of that in China in recent years, but because the US average price per unit is much higher than in China, the US market's total dollar size is neck and neck with China. Apple and Samsung are considered to be the two dominant players in the world partly because they have leadership positions in both China and the US market.

In the Chinese market, domestic brands like Xiaomi, Lenovo and Huawei have emerged to compete directly with the two leading foreign brands. However, they need to achieve a meaningful foothold in the US before becoming true global players. Another aspect of the US market's importance is that if one can build a successful brand in the US, this brand value can be applied to worldwide markets. Therefore, the Chinese smartphone brands have a lot at stake when they compete with the two leading foreign brands (and among themselves) for market share in the US: ZTE reaching a top three Android phone maker ranking is thus highly significant.

ZTE was founded in 1985 at the tech metropolis of Shenzhen city in Southern China. Traditionally its main business was supplying telecom equipment and network services to global telecommunications carriers. Recently, the consumer device business including smartphones has been a new growth area for the company. Just a few years ago, ZTE was one of the most important domestic brands in China. In fact it once ranked first among the top four brands of "ZTE, Huawei, Coolpad and Lenovo" (known as "zhong-hua-ku-lian" in Chinese). However, Xiaomi, Huawei and Lenovo have adapted to the Chinese market's special needs and characteristics much more quickly than ZTE. As a result, ZTE's market share and leadership position in China have declined amid intensified competition in recent years.

The main reason for the decline of ZTE's smartphone market share in China is its heavy reliance on its partnership with carriers. Even in 2013 when competition for the domestic market was hot due to new entrants like Xiaomi, who marketed their phones almost exclusively on the internet, ZTE's carrier-based phone sales still accounted for about 80% of total business, with social network-based sales at only about 20%. With the carriers' subsidies decreasing, the weakness in ZTE's marketing model became obvious, and ZTE realized that it urgently needed to transform itself. Learning from its competitors, ZTE expanded its online sales channels and responded to users' comments and suggestions in the internet forums.

In the US market, however, ZTE's deep relationship with carriers is a huge advantage. Unlike in China, the sales channel for smartphones in the US market is dominated by the carriers. This means that for any smartphone manufacturer to enter the US market, its first priority is to establish a relationship of trust with carriers. ZTE entered the US in 1998 and established partnerships with many of them including AT&T, Verizon, Sprint, T-mobile and so on. As illustrated by the sales figures in 2014, the company's smartphone shipments to the US had a growth rate of more than 50% in 2014, far exceeding its overall growth of 20% globally.

In the past, ZTE supplied unbranded "white label" phones in response carriers' demands, so the products were at best "handsets assembled by ZTE". Strictly speaking, ZTE was not even an OEM (original equipment manufacturer) of smartphones, let alone a phone brand for the US market. ZTE's first break was between 2010 and 2011, a period when US customers were actively upgrading their phones. While all the manufacturers were focusing on the post-paid (contract) market, ZTE brought a high quality, larger phone screen to the prepaid (no contract) market. The ZTE Warp phone exceeded 1 million units in sales, a major milestone for ZTE.

According to ZTE's data, between 2010 and 2015, its US business increased approximately 20 times. Meanwhile, its phones moved from "having no logo" to "carrying the ZTE logo". With the trust of the carriers, more than 95% of ZTE device testing is now performed at ZTE's own labs. By contrast, years ago ZTE had to test its devices at authorized third-party labs, which was costly both from an expense and an efficiency perspective. In 2015, ZTE stated that it had 68 types of device available for US sales (although not all carried the ZTE brand), and it boasted that its phones could be found at any carrier.

As the company aims to strengthen its own brand power, ZTE has decided to scale down production lines by offering only two series of smartphones, "Axon" and "Blade". With the addition of the "Nubia" brand produced by a subsidiary, ZTE currently owns three smartphone series, which, interestingly, can be abbreviated as the "NBA" series, taken from the initial letters of Nubia, Blade and Axon. **(See the "China's First Lady Chooses ZTE" box.)** As it launches more high-end and innovative products, ZTE is distancing itself from the fierce price competition among Chinese brands selling phones at close-to-cost prices. (Of course, in a bid to target a variety of carrier relationships and consumer groups, ZTE remains flexible in providing handsets with customized features and distinct specifications.)

China's First Lady chooses ZTE, not iPhone

During President Xi Jinping's European trip in early 2014, the First Lady (Madame Peng Liyuan) attended a soccer match between Chinese children and their German peers in Berlin, Germany. Soon a picture of her taking photos with a mobile phone during the game appeared on the internet. The photo sparked a hot social media theme: which brand was she using?

Although the picture only showed the back of a white smartphone, without any logo readily visible, the tech-savvy online community in China quickly discovered that the phone used by the First Lady was a Nubia Z5 mini handset, a sub-brand from the Chinese manufacturer ZTE Corp., which had a retail price of around $300.

ZTE was definitely thrilled by the unexpected boost. On ZTE's website, it included a news clip about the story, titled "'Nubia', not iPhone, is Chinese First Lady Peng Liyuan's Latest Choice of Smart Phone". According to Chinese media reports, the Nubia phone's upgraded version, the Nubia Z5S mini, enjoyed three times more sales than usual in the two days after the photo hit the internet. (The news report quoted the sales numbers from the online retailer JD.com, which served as the sole retailer of ZTE's Nubia Z5S mini.)

Before that, First Lady Peng's fashion choices had similarly created internet crazes and driven up sales for various Chinese brands. For example, when she made her debut at President Xi's trip to Russia, her choice of dresses created a nationwide frenzy for domestic apparel. According to media reports, the black handbag she carried led to eight million searches for "Peng Liyuan handbag" on Alibaba's shopping site (and the bags quickly sold out).

In addition, ZTE's extensive portfolio of patents is also an advantage for its expansion in the US market. At the corporate level, ZTE has made the commitment to license standard essential patents on fair, reasonable and non-discriminatory (FRAND) terms (or as ZTE executives put it at public interviews: "We're paying our fair share"). ZTE entered into cross-licensing arrangements with major patent holders like Qualcomm, Microsoft and Google, and over the four years from 2011–2014, it paid more than $17 billion to US companies in licensing fees and royalties.

At the same time, ZTE has spent large amounts in research and development to build up its own patents. According to the data from the World Intellectual Property Organization (WIPO), by the end of 2014 ZTE was the only Chinese company that ranked in the top three worldwide in patent applications under the Patent Cooperation Treaty (PCT) for five consecutive years. According to ZTE's estimate, it held 13% of the world's 4G-specific handset-related patents. As will be seen later in this chapter, the lack of a patent portfolio is a major challenge for Chinese tech companies' overseas growth. In ZTE's case, its own patent portfolio and broad cross-patent licensing arrangements provide a solid foundation for its entry into foreign markets.

Furthermore, ZTE's targeted brand marketing, supported by distinguishable design and features for the target population, has made an important impact in the North American market. At the 30th anniversary of the company in 2015, ZTE introduced a new logo and a fast-speed tagline "*Tomorrow Never Waits*", emphasizing the new focus on transformative mobile technology solutions for its consumers and carrier partners. To some extent, the new brand image can be viewed as a correction from its earlier practice, which was relatively slow to incorporate the internet value into its business lines. As mentioned previously, the company reacted later than its competitors to the fact that many Chinese consumers had moved to buying new smartphones online a few years ago. But in the context of its new corporate value, ZTE has repositioned itself as a consumer-oriented smartphone brand, and consumer needs are now paramount for the company.

In the North American market, ZTE has worked hard to change the conventional perception that Chinese brands represent cheap prices, low quality and poor service. Instead, the new brand identity of ZTE is youthful, fun and sporty. ZTE's branding partnership with major NBA teams comes at a time when smartphone technology is fundamentally changing the way fans are experiencing sports such as NBA games (with photo taking, sharing on social networks, following players' Tweets, etc.). The NBA has a large number of fans in the US, and the games are also broadcast in China and many other parts of the world. Players' Twitter accounts are being followed by fans worldwide. The games' global outreach to the potential targets – young people and sports fans – is a perfect match for the ZTE phones' new brand identity. (**See the "ZTE's Winning Picks" box.**)

ZTE's Winning Picks

During the 2014–2015 NBA season, ZTE selected three teams for its marketing campaign: the Golden State Warriors in San Francisco, the Rockets in Houston and the Knicks in New York City. San Francisco and NYC are the two cities in the US with the longest history of Chinese immigration and the largest population of ethnic Chinese residents. The Houston Rockets have developed a big Chinese fan base since the 7-feet-3-inch center Yao Ming was acquired from China, and it became the most broadcast team in China. More recently, the American-born Chinese "Linsanity" Jeremy Lin also played for the Houston Rockets after playing for the New York Knicks.

Under the partnership deal, the ZTE brand was promoted around the arenas, on the courts and using giant LED displays outside of the arenas. The players were not necessarily required to use ZTE phones, but they got one if they asked for it. For example, when Jeremy Lin was with the Houston Rockets, he took a selfie with a ZTE phone, which led to a YouTube video "How to take the perfect selfie with Jeremy Lin!"

The Golden State Warriors and Houston Rockets were among the top winning teams for the season, and both went to the Western Conference Finals. Hence, that series was already a big win for the ZTE brand. After eliminating the

Rockets, the Golden State Warriors went to the Finals and won the NBA championship, bringing priceless marketing presence for ZTE. The New York Knicks did not have a winning record, but they had the ultimate all-star of all-stars: New York City. Every day there were more than 1 million people passing by the ZTE LED sign outside Madison Square Garden, the arena for the Knicks' games.

Those endorsement deals with the NBA teams turned more successful than even the ZTE executives had ever dreamed. For example, according to data released by ZTE, the Houston market only represented 5% of the US population, yet it contributed more than 8.5% of ZTE's smartphone users. Total product sales in Houston exceeded those in a similar size market without sports-based marketing by more than 40%.

To match its new marketing theme, ZTE has teamed up with a large number of software makers and technology partners to develop distinguishable designs and features for its target market. One good example was its Axon phone released in July 2015. ZTE went to great lengths to incorporate advanced tech specifications into the model to make sure it could live up to the company's new brand positioning as the "affordable cutting-edge phone". The phone included a "lightning-fast processor" with 4GB of RAM and a long life battery, and it had a dual microphone designed for high fidelity sound recording, which ZTE claimed to be "the first true high-fidelity phone available in the US" with "amazing high-fidelity sound playback". In addition, the phone was equipped with full biometric authentication features including fingerprint, voice and retina recognition.

The most important feature, however, related to its camera and that played into the company's new focus on the sports theme. The Axon phone had dual rear-facing cameras that could shoot 4K HD videos. There was an 8-megapixel front-facing camera, and the sub-camera is used to speed up the auto-focus or for depth-of-field effects. According to ZTE, the front camera had "incredibly fast auto-focus" (ZTE's term), and it would allow the user to take selfies simply by smiling, a testimony that this new phone's camera is perfect for sports fans to catch fast-moving objects and scenes.

In today's market, however, almost all the brands' new versions are equipped with better cameras and screens, more powerful processors, cooler designs and higher quality metal materials. ZTE's plan is to surpass LG to reach the top three in the US market within the next three years. Maybe the real test for ZTE in the US still lies ahead. It is worth noting that at the ceremony to add the Knicks to its list of team partners, the CEO of ZTE's North American operation, Lixin Cheng, was awarded a number 8 jersey to celebrate the deal. (In Chinese society the number eight is the luckiest number of all.) For ZTE's next major breakthrough, good luck may be as important as its technical superiority and smart marketing.

Xiaomi: Into the Emerging Markets

Competition among the Chinese smartphone brands in the domestic market is truly fierce. In 2015, according to data from the market research firm Strategy Analytics, six of the top 10 smartphone brands worldwide were Chinese manufacturers, with a few of them selling handsets only in China. Another firm, Canaccord, estimated that there were about 1,000 smartphone brands globally, with several hundred of them in China. This data certainly demonstrated the significant size of the Chinese market relative to the rest of the world, but it also explains the price war among the Chinese brands and their razor-thin profit margins.

At the same time, since 2015 the Chinese market has started to experience slowing growth. The research firm IDC estimated that smartphone shipments during the first quarter of 2015 were 98.8 million, down 4.3% from a year earlier. That was the first decrease in new orders in six years. But this was not completely surprising when put into context, because IDC also estimated that more than 800 million people were already using smartphones in China.

Therefore, the Chinese smartphone makers are looking for more opportunities outside China, particularly in emerging markets. Compared to the Chinese market, robust growth in smartphone demand is still expected in the emerging markets in Asia, the Middle East, Latin America and Africa, where many consumers are replacing their basic feature phones with smartphones. As happened in China a few years ago, many people in emerging market countries will skip landline phones and move directly into the mobile phone era. With ever increasing technologically advanced capabilities, smartphones may also replace personal computers (PCs). Therefore many customers in those markets who have never owned a phone or a computer may leapfrog directly into a low price and high performance smartphone.

As a result, the domestic competition among Chinese brands is extending into the global markets, where Xiaomi and others will also need to fight with both globally established brands like Apple and Samsung and local start-ups from those countries. For Xiaomi, the immediate test is whether its low-cost business model can translate into success in overseas markets like China. Xiaomi's current model is to sell smartphones at near cost to develop a user base quickly before focusing on more profitable services at the next stage. Its low-cost strategy looks for markets where the price of a smartphone constitutes a large part of a consumer's income. According to Xiaomi executives, after China, Xiaomi's priorities will be India and Indonesia, followed by Brazil and Russia. These countries all have large populations of people who may become first time smartphone users in the coming years.

In particular, India is the most sizable and fastest-growing market. First, it has a population size comparable to that of China and is still growing. Second, with more than 200 million Indians online, India has the third largest number of internet users in the world, and it is projected to overtake the US in second place soon. Third, although India already has hundreds of millions of people using mobile phones, the smartphone penetration rate in the country remains low. Therefore India is probably the most promising smartphone market in the world, with hundreds of millions of potential new customers.

But Xiaomi's India entry has not been an easy one. To some extent, its hard work there resembles what foreign brands like Samsung and Nokia have experienced in China. The Indian market is intensely competitive. To start with, many home-grown entrepreneurs in India have been inspired by the success stories of Xiaomi and similar smartphone manufacturers from China. They are launching internet and mobile technology ventures themselves to capitalize on Indian market potential. Equipped with local knowledge about customers and distribution, some indigenous companies are among the best-selling brands in India. (Samsung as a foreign brand is also among the top sellers.)

In addition, Xiaomi's low-cost strategy is challenged by the broad range of the "low spending power" class in India. India's local brands like Micromax and Karbonn have already offered the local market smartphones comparable to Apple and Samsung specifications at much lower prices. To reach all Indian consumers, the top-selling local brands release a high number of phone variants to cover a large price range, with the low-end spectrum set at extremely low price points for mass appeal.

For example, some of them even design phones for customers who have so little spending power that they cannot afford 3G connections, and these ultra-cheap smartphones are sold at about $50 or even just a fraction of that. These products have no ambition to win over brand-conscious consumers in the big cities, but they have proved to be popular among those Indian consumers who have modest budgets and are happy to have a "just functional" smartphone for the first time.

Correspondingly, the distribution side is similarly more fragmented than in China. When Xiaomi first entered the Indian market, it successfully launched an online flash sale as had been done in China, which offered limited batches of phones to drive up demand and build brand cachet. For the broader market, however, many Indian customers still buy phones from the corner shop. So local brands can play out their local contacts and knowledge further. For a nimble player like Xiaomi that traditionally only sells phones and seeks feedback online, managing and building brick-and-mortar retail presence is a new challenge.

Another implication of offline distribution is that Xiaomi has to deal with traditional advertising as well. In the Chinese market, internet-based marketing has allowed Xiaomi to pass substantial advertising savings on to consumers. But in the Indian market, Xiaomi went "old-school" in July 2015 and bought an entire front page of *The Times of India* to run a national advertisement. After Xiaomi global VP Hugo Barra showcased the advert on Twitter, some news stories speculated that that was the first ever print advertisement taken out by Xiaomi.

Furthermore, features required by local customers also increased production costs, creating another challenge to the low-cost strategy. For example, it would be a huge task to make the mobile phone systems compatible with India's 20 plus official languages and additional dialects. Local brands have already developed software features to support local languages. As reported, Xiaomi has gone to great lengths to provide local customers with interfaces in India's languages. Its Mi 4i phone, for example, supported six Indian languages, but inevitably cost more than quite a few rivals (about $200). The cost may rise even higher when Xiaomi works with local engineers to cover more languages.

Finally, without much of a patent portfolio itself (and hence few cross-license arrangements), Xiaomi has to deal with lawsuits from competitors. In India, it has already been sued by Swedish telecom company Ericsson in late 2014. Ericsson accused Xiaomi of failing to pay licensing fees on patents. The local Indian court issued an injunction against Xiaomi, blocking both sales in India and the importation of devices. The case went up to the Delhi High Court, and legal proceedings are still ongoing. But the implication for Xiaomi goes beyond India, because the case may have alerted other IT giants to search for potential patent infringement claims against Xiaomi.

To put all this into context, Xiaomi's success in China has a lot to do with particular Chinese user preferences and market characteristics. There is no guarantee that the model could be replicated easily elsewhere. For the Xiaomi model to work, the company will likely target markets with large populations, a developed e-commerce culture, and weak telecom service providers. All these factors are important because Xiaomi needs volume to lower its own operating costs, and subsidies from telecom carriers may easily upstage Xiaomi phone's price advantage. Such perfect market conditions are difficult to find globally, and where they do exist, in India perhaps, Xiaomi has to prepare to compete head to head with foreign as well as other Chinese brands.

Besides, local rivals Apple and Samsung are formidable competitors in different ways. Apple's iPhone has distinctive brand power at the high end. The risk to Xiaomi and other lower cost brands is that their high quality phones may be bought by the broad population as a first time device, but most of those people still dream of having an iPhone for its brand value and related symbolic social status. In other words, the lower-priced models may get Indian users familiarized with and attached to a smartphone, but ultimately they may become Apple customers.

Samsung is one of the market leaders in India, and its product specifications are similar to Xiaomi's offerings. But the more interesting link between the two players is whether Samsung's rise and decline in China provides a reference point for Xiaomi's experience in India. (**See the "Samsung in China" box.**) In India and other emerging markets, Xiaomi is challenged to react to local market dynamics and consumer needs. The "Samsung in China" case shows that premium foreign manufacturers of smart devices can quickly lose market share and profit share to local rivals, when the latter's products match technological specifications, provide lower prices and better serve the special preferences of local customers.

As mentioned, some Indian brands specifically positioned themselves for the low price category, without even attempting to compete in the top-tier cities where consumers favor high-status foreign brands. The same is true for Southeast Asian markets, where local brands as a group have rapidly secured a solid foothold in a market among the world's fastest-growing category (next only to India). In the Philippines, for example, local brands have already grabbed more than half of the market share. The Philippine manufacturers "think and behave like Filipinos", and they develop devices in light of the feedback they receive from local users, much as Xiaomi tweaks its phones based on Mi-fans' feedback. Like Samsung in China, Xiaomi (and other Chinese brands) risks being squeezed from two sides in the foreign markets – between Apple's iPhone in the premium product category and the commoditized Android smartphones in the low price product category.

Samsung in China – A Reference Point for Xiaomi in India?

Samsung entered the Chinese market in the early 1990s. As an early player, Samsung built up extensive distribution networks from the sales of its televisions and traditional mobile phones. That gave Samsung an early mover advantage over other foreign brands like Apple when the Chinese market moved into smartphones, as many Chinese consumers bought their phones at consumer electronics retail outlets rather than through carriers.

Samsung traditionally positioned itself as a high-end product. But as the Chinese market became more developed, Apple has become the single dominant player in the premium market, while local brands like Xiaomi and others aggressively priced quality phones (comparable to Samsung's products) near cost to gain market share. In addition, local manufacturers are also more sensitive to local customers' needs, offering Chinese-oriented features such as big screen sizes, optimized connectivity for China and dual SIM cards.

As a result, Samsung saw itself being squeezed from both ends but was slow to react. In order to maintain its premium brand, it did not reduce prices to match the Chinese brands. That strategy mostly failed: Samsung suffered from a huge inventory of unsold devices, and the Chinese brands all gained market share at the expense of Samsung. As the first time buyers' market continues shifting to smaller cities (fourth- and fifth-tier cities) and rural areas, the squeeze from lower priced Chinese products becomes even stronger. For one thing, in those areas, the Samsung brand does not necessarily have more glamour than domestic ones. For another, Samsung's existing channels in the cities have little value for new consumers in small towns and rural villages.

Samsung in China can be an important reference point for Xiaomi's venture in India. A few years ago, Samsung rose in China when the once-dominant mobile producers Nokia and Motorola declined. But soon Samsung lost market share to the new local players like Xiaomi and Huawei, because it struggled to find the right positioning in the market.

The intriguing question is: will the Chinese brands eventually be forced to become another Samsung in the new competition, on a path of decreasing market share and profit share globally? The bottom line is that in the highly matured market for Android system-based smartphones (see Figure 9.1), it is increasingly difficult for smartphone manufacturers to differentiate their high-end products. Hence, the possibility for any company to become the premium brand within the Android system family and to challenge the status of Apple's iPhone is quite low.

In a different context, however, there is still room for competition. The mobile internet era sees consumer preferences and habits change rapidly, so dominance in a single product may not last forever. The ultimate competition is to create a firm that turns consumers into believers in the company's value and culture, who then become deeply and intensely attached to the company and treat that brand as an identity that remains continuously relevant in their life for a long time. The true

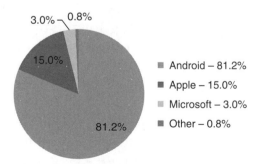

Figure 9.1 Smartphone Operating System's Global Market Share, 2014
(Data Source: Strategy Analytics)

winner has to be decided in the ultimate multi-device world, which is "Smart 2.0" in ZTE's words, "convergence of telecom and IT" as described by Huawei, and "all-inclusive ecosystem" to use Xiaomi's term. All these Chinese players are seeking to tie users to an expanding family of devices and services, and the global war on smart devices will eventually be decided on a much bigger battlefield than the smartphone market alone. (The next chapter will continue this discussion in connection with Chinese-led innovations.)

Lessons from Overseas Expansion and Acquisition

In recent years, more and more Chinese tech and internet companies have started testing the waters of overseas markets. However, they often face formidable challenges and suffer serious setbacks when they expand into unfamiliar territory. Even for BAT (Baidu, Alibaba and Tencent), the three internet giants that have dominated the Chinese market in their respective fields, their journeys into foreign markets have not been completely smooth, either.

For example, in 2014 Alibaba launched a US shopping website 11Main on the home turf of e-commerce giants Amazon.com and eBay, but in just a year, Alibaba sold 11Main to another US e-commerce business OpenSky. (Alibaba kept a 37.6% stake in the combined entity after the transaction.) At the start of 11Main, Alibaba envisioned a shop window for small-time US merchants that may opt out of the US marketplaces, but it didn't take too long for the merchants to complain about a lack of support for their growth.

The other two internet giants have had their setbacks too. Tencent's WeChat messaging app has achieved more than 1 billion users worldwide, but most are in the Greater China region. After having solicited 100 million overseas subscribers – most of them from Southeast Asian countries – WeChat has hit a bottleneck in further expansion of the user base. In addition, it still has little impact in the English language-based social landscape dominated by Facebook or in local-language-centered markets such as Japan (controlled by a local service called Line). For China's leading search engine Baidu, its search service in Japan did not attract significant attention after years of trials, and its Vietnamese online forum, Tieba, launched in Vietnam, apparently tripped over social network regulations there before it was shut down.

Strictly speaking, few Chinese tech and internet companies have developed into truly global players. The Chinese companies generally have the majority of their customers in China (with limited foreign customers), earn almost all of their revenue income from the Chinese market (with limited foreign revenue sources), and have few brands recognized worldwide (with limited brand awareness in foreign markets). Part of the reason, of course, is because of the fast growth and enormous size of the Chinese market itself, which has kept the Chinese companies focused on domestic market share for a long time. At the same time, Chinese companies face many more challenges when they move beyond the home court.

The first challenge is a lack of patent holdings and potential intellectual property-related lawsuits. Xiaomi's lawsuit in India illustrates that it is critical for Chinese tech companies to secure an intellectual property (IP) portfolio in overseas markets. In the case of ZTE, its extensive existing portfolio of patents provides the company with considerable bargaining power in foreign markets, because ZTE's own patents allow it to enter into numerous cross-patent cross-licensing agreements with companies such as AT&T, Qualcomm, Siemens, Ericsson, Microsoft and Dolby. But such an IP portfolio is the result of ZTE's investment and accumulation over more than a decade. With fewer internal resources, younger start-ups like Xiaomi are more likely to face tougher challenges.

While all Chinese companies have to continue investing and innovating to fight the IP war globally, the bottom line is that they still have to prepare themselves for patent litigation. Take ZTE, for example. Because ZTE is one of the fastest growing smartphone vendors in the US, a great number of nuisance patent suits have followed. According to ZTE's own data, ZTE is facing more than 50 cases at any given time for patent infringement. At times these patent cases are brought by entities that have no intention of actually manufacturing the products. In response, ZTE has invested in hiring legal experts in-house and engaging with top class external legal professionals. With its own patent portfolio and cross-licensing arrangements with other major players, ZTE is not scared of going to court.

Between 2013 and 2015, ZTE consistently defeated InterDigital Inc. four times in investigations relating to Section 337 of the Tariff Act of 1930. In December 2013, the United States International Trade Commission (ITC) rejected InterDigital's allegation of violations of Section 337 of the Tariff Act of 1930 based on seven patents, with three of the patents ruled as invalid. This ITC ruling was later upheld by the US Court of Appeals for the Federal Circuit in February 2015.

In a separate ruling in August 2014, the United States ITC issued a final determination rejecting InterDigital's allegation of violations based on three other patents. Later, in April 2015, the jury in the US District Court for the District of Delaware decided that ZTE did not infringe any of InterDigital's claims relating to US patent 7,941,151. These legal proceedings are meaningful wins for ZTE, because it is rare for a Chinese company to succeed consistently in Section 337 investigations. For many other Chinese companies with few patent holdings and limited overseas legal capabilities, such patent lawsuits can present serious problems.

Another major hurdle is branding. When Chinese companies launch more high-end products in developed markets, they have to change the stereotype that Chinese products offer cheap prices, low quality and poor service. Few Chinese technology companies have established the same brand recognition globally as the products from their Asian neighbors, such as Samsung and LG in South Korea, or Sony and Canon in Japan.

The direct solution, of course, is to get affiliated with a North American brand, or more directly, to acquire one. For example, in the US market the Lenovo brand has an advantage over other Chinese brands thanks to its PC business. The brand is well known for acquiring IBM's ThinkPad division in 2005. Similarly in its global mobile business, Lenovo made two major US acquisitions in 2014: Google's Motorola Mobility and IBM's x86 enterprise server division. To a large extent, Lenovo's success in the global mobile business will depend on how much it can benefit from these two major acquisitions, especially the Motorola assets.

Motorola was a pioneer in mobile phones and a household brand in China many years ago, but it collapsed due to disruptive technologies and changing consumer behavior. After the merger, Lenovo decided to run both brands in the Chinese market. But young Chinese consumers have no memory of the earlier glory days of the Motorola brand in China, because Motorola had largely departed from the Chinese market some years ago.

Rather than trying to revive a last generation brand in the Chinese market, Lenovo's main rationale for the $2.9 billion acquisition of Motorola Mobility probably lies in the new channel that the Motorola brand may provide for the overseas markets. Motorola is strong in the carrier markets of North America and Latin America, which gives Lenovo important access to those markets.

As opposed to acquiring a brand directly, a more opportunistic way for a Chinese company to build up a strong brand in North America is to invest in "designed in North America" research capabilities. For example, during the decline of Canadian company RIM in recent years, ZTE recruited a team of BlackBerry engineers to give its North America R&D capabilities a substantial boost. **(See the "ZTE picks up BlackBerry" box.)** As a result, in 2014 ZTE (Canada) released a new smartphone called Grand X Plus, which was designed for Canadians out of the company's R&D Centre based in Ottawa, Canada. The brand value from a "designed in North America" product like Grand X Plus is not limited to the US and Canadian markets. Because the North America market is considered to be "high-end", the brand value can later be transferred to other parts of the world (including the Chinese market itself).

ZTE Picks Up BlackBerry

Research In Motion (RIM) was once the pioneer of the smartphone segment with its BlackBerry device, and for many years the company was one of Canada's gems. But in recent years BlackBerry's market share was quickly gobbled up by Apple and Android phones. In 2013, the company experienced serious financial distress and went into restructuring.

During the restructuring process, RIM announced multiple rounds of layoffs, and many tech companies including ZTE, Huawei, Samsung and TCL all paid close attention to the departing research team. In March 2014, RIM announced a round of layoffs including the senior engineers for chip design and product design from its Waterloo headquarters and the BlackBerry products research center in Ottawa.

ZTE was so determined to expand in North America and to acquire those talents that it created a special department inside Human Resources dedicated to that recruitment task. In the end, ZTE beat the competitors and succeeded in cherry-picking more than 20 engineers from BlackBerry. The fresh troops from BlackBerry were mostly based in Canada, but may later move to the US or China to play greater roles for ZTE.

The best-known know-how of RIM lies in communication security, which explains why the BlackBerry devices and services have been widely used by corporations, and even the Pentagon and NATO. In the hyper-connected mobile internet era, the security issue is more important than ever, and ZTE may potentially distinguish its products with additional security features.

The third hurdle is the different consumer culture and tradition that Chinese firms have to adapt to in foreign markets. Many Chinese companies have selected emerging markets as their overseas journey's first stop because of the overall similarities between those markets and China. As happened in China a few years ago, some emerging markets have a young and mobile-first population where smartphones are taking off in a big way. In addition, the customers there are generally as cost-conscious as those in China. Therefore, the general perception is that emerging market entries can play to the strengths of Chinese companies.

In practice, consumer behavior in different markets does exhibit some similarities. For example, the flash sales – offering a limited amount of products at extremely low prices for a limited time period – can be applied universally to foreign markets to stir up some quick consumer interest. But aside from the similar cost-consciousness among customers, there are a lot more local factors that are new to the Chinese players. Chinese firms are good at identifying and satisfying their customers' needs in the home market, but few of them have deep experience selling across different cultures.

As mentioned earlier in this chapter, when it ventures into the Indian market, Xiaomi has to tweak its products to adapt to the 20 plus local languages there. But when new language features are added, its product cost goes up, challenging the company's low-cost corporate strategy. On the distribution side, Xiaomi may have to acquire physical storefronts or enter into distribution deals in India, which can be expensive and difficult to manage. (In China, Xiaomi has smartly avoided that with its online sales model and its loyal Mi-fan group.)

When the product is inherently culturally sensitive, such as social networks and messaging services, the barrier is enormous. For example, Tencent has promoted WeChat in numerous overseas markets for new users. Conscious of the cultural differences, Tencent even signed up Argentine football star Lionel Messi for a TV advertising campaign in mid-2013. (The rationale was that sports are universal across cultures.) However, the reality is that the Japanese and Korean markets respectively have their own version of competing products in their own languages, and in the English market users have fully invested themselves in Facebook and other networks. As a result, in 2015 Tencent executives stated that its new approach to WeChat expansion is to further develop it in China, adding unique features and building an ecosystem to attract new users globally.

Fourth, investing in foreign markets is no less challenging than business expansion. Generally speaking, overseas mergers and acquisitions of established foreign firms are more direct way than business expansion to gain market entries, new customers and global market share. However, transactions in the capital markets have a different set of issues for Chinese companies.

Increasingly, Chinese firms are interested in acquiring cutting edge technology development by investing in start-ups, especially in Silicon Valley which is viewed as the innovation capital of the mobile internet. Many US start-ups are researching the same tech issues as Chinese firms, and their breakthroughs in the US are most likely applicable to the Chinese market as well. Among Chinese internet companies, Alibaba is perhaps the most active buyer in the global M&A market (see Table 9.1).

The key issue for Chinese buyers is that they have to get many things right to ensure that their acquisitions are adding value. Lenovo's earlier acquisition of IBM's ThinkPad division

Table 9.1   Alibaba's investments in US tech companies

US companies	Business sector	Amount ($ millions)	Date
Groupon	Group discount deals	Undisclosed	Feb 2016
Grindr	Worldwide #1 gay social network app	93	Jan 2016
Snapchat	Mobile messaging	200	Mar 2015
Peel	Smart TV mobile app	50	Oct 2014
Kabam	Mobile gaming developer	120	Aug 2014
Lyft	On demand ride-sharing	250	Apr 2014
TangoMe	Social messaging	280	Mar 2014
Shoprunner	Members-only e-commerce	206	Oct 2013
Quixey	"Deep" search engine for information in mobile apps	50	Oct 2013

(Data Sources: News Reports and Public Disclosure)

has successfully firmed up its global leading position in the PC business, but it took Lenovo almost eight years to fully integrate the IBM business it acquired. The Lenovo/IBM case is just one of the few successful precedents of Chinese companies' overseas acquisitions. Even with its earlier deal experience in the US, there is no guarantee that Lenovo's recent purchase of Motorola Mobility from Google can repeat a successful integration. In short, an investment transaction is only the start of a long journey. To realize synergy value from a successful integration requires a lot of hard work after a merger or acquisition deal is closed.

The biggest challenge to integration lies in the differences and even tensions between the two sides' business processes, governance structures and corporate cultures. It forces the Chinese firms – which have a proven model in China – to develop and execute a balanced and sustainable global operating model. From the process aspect, overseas acquisitions call for global standardization balanced by controlled flexibility in specific markets. From a governance aspect, Chinese headquarters need to empower overseas managers and build channels for easy cross-border communication. For example, according to news reports, the disappointment of 11Main businesses was partly caused by the fact that its limited scale resulted in inadequate attention and support from Alibaba headquarters.

Another related challenge is to find the right people and team to execute cross-border integration. Needless to say, a few trips a year by headquarters executives alone are not sufficient for local integration. A successful integration requires a global team from the very top, including Chinese members who are absolutely clear about headquarters' culture and strategy, while hiring and incentivizing local talent to deeply localize day-to-day operations. The tension between different cultures is usually highlighted by the composition of the working team. On the one hand, Chinese firms may feel uncomfortable incorporating a completely new local team to manage their overseas assets; on the other hand, it can take years for a Chinese buyer to build a management team and related network of local stakeholders from scratch.

These days a new challenge emerges as the competition for frontier technologies intensifies. There are many great start-ups in Silicon Valley, but at the same time there is already so much capital, as well as so many great investors. It is therefore a very crowded marketplace, even before the Chinese firms and capital move in. Despite their financial power, the search for the right acquisition target is no easy task.

What troubles Chinese firms is that no matter how success-ful they are in their home market, they are not necessarily automatically networked into the start-up community of Silicon Valley. They still need to build up a network and earn trust. In particular, some unique Silicon Valley cultures may not be obvi-ous to foreign firms who are not sufficiently local. For example, start-ups may not view large internet firms as preferred business partners, because the perception is that they tend to require more paperwork. In relation to Chinese capital, the stereotype may also involve slow decision-making and additional regula-tory hassles.

Of course, Chinese buyers have one trump card in addition to their financial capital: the enormous size and rapid growth of the Chinese market. They have the opportunity to prove that they are the preferred business partner for foreign tech compa-nies to create new values together. As is often said in the M&A market, the best way to find more good investments is to make a good investment first.

For example, in October 2014 Baidu bought a control-ling equity stake in Brazilian online discount company Peixe Urbano for an undisclosed sum. (As mentioned, Baidu has one of the top Chinese group-buying sites, Nuomi, and has invested aggressively in the Chinese O2O (online-to-offline) market, including online deals/offers). After the acquisition, Peixe Urbano management had extensive exchanges with Nuomi on O2O businesses and replicated Chinese practices in the Brazilian market. According to Baidu's information, Peixe Urbano's market share increased from 35% to 55% within one year of the Baidu acquisition.

What is really interesting is that the challenges that Chinese companies now face in overseas markets are very much the same as those encountered by US companies such as Amazon and eBay when they ventured into China earlier. More than a decade ago, those American tech firms were similarly intrigued by the Chinese market's large user base and fast market growth. Yet the cultural, language, political and technological factors turned out to be more complicated than they expected. As a result, they chose to focus mostly on the North American market.

However, the bottom line for Chinese firms these days is that their overseas expansion is a must rather than an option. While there is always more growth to be found within China, the fastest growing market in the world will inevitably slow down, and the top Chinese tech companies must search for and find their next billion customers. Their journey into foreign markets is full of hurdles, challenges and competition, but with their overseas listings and significant foreign shareholder ownership, one may expect Alibaba, Tencent and other Chinese companies to manage cultural differences better than the US firms did in China a decade ago.

Similarly, the US firms also have to tackle the Chinese market in order to win the battle for global domination. Maybe Western companies today can do better in China as the country's mobile internet ecosystem has become more developed, sophisticated and globalized. Going forward, direct fights between Chinese and US firms will be seen in both markets. The next chapter will examine the opportunities and challenges that foreign firms are facing in the Chinese market.

10

Launched in China

No one would have imagined that Amazon in China could become a customer of its local competitor, Alibaba. But since Amazon opened a flagship store on Alibaba's online marketplace Tmall in early 2015, it has become just that. Tmall offers virtual storefronts and payment portals to merchants, such as Amazon, who use its site in order to access end customers. In return, Amazon pays a commission on each sale on its Tmall outlet.

For Amazon, which is struggling to expand its independent e-commerce operation in China, setting up an online store on Tmall represents a major shift to its strategy. In the US, Amazon is synonymous with e-commerce, but since entering the Chinese market about a decade ago, the company has been fighting an uphill battle with local contenders, such as Alibaba and JD.com. Currently its domestic rivals Alibaba and JD.com control about 90% of the e-commerce market, which means that the world's largest internet retailer is a small player with less than 2% of the total market share.

From its online shop on Tmall, Amazon caters to Chinese consumers' rising appetite for imported products. As one of the first major non-financial companies to set up operations in the Shanghai Free Trade Zone, Amazon promised customers competitive pricing, relatively fast shipping and a guarantee of the authenticity of the imported goods that it sold, all of which played to its strength as a true global brand. While foreign retailers are unable to compete on price vis-à-vis domestic suppliers, they may win over higher income bracket consumers who are keen to buy authentic branded goods that are simply not available domestically.

The Amazon China case demonstrates that in China's fast growing but highly competitive e-commerce space, it is critical for even highly successful overseas players leveraging their global resources to create a localized strategy. Amazon is still far from posing a serious challenge to Alibaba or JD.com, but its new move helps it to provide a differentiating service to Chinese consumers. As will be illustrated further in this chapter, Uber and other US internet firms are entering the Chinese market employing various localized strategies and tactics, including separate Chinese offices, local employees, local investors and local partners.

The business dealings between Amazon and Alibaba also illustrate that the Chinese and foreign internet firms are increasingly interconnected. The Chinese market not only has an unrivalled internet user group, but is also the largest mobile-first and mobile-only market in the world. As a result, new mobile applications often achieve scale more quickly in China than elsewhere. This chapter will also examine the innovation ecosystem in China, which is quickly becoming a source of unique features, products or business models that can be adapted by foreign companies. The Chinese market is poised to be the trend-setter in the near future, rather than the trend-follower, particularly in next-generation mobile device and application innovation.

Uber: Localization in the Chinese Market

Uber, the San Francisco-based car-sharing app company, was a latecomer to the ride-hailing service market in China. Uber began tests in China in late 2013 in the southern cities of Guangzhou and Shenzhen, offering a service in which customers could hail rides from licensed limousine companies. Its official full-scale expansion in China did not occur until

December 2014, when Uber sold an equity stake to China's search engine giant Baidu and integrated its service with Baidu's map application and payment system.

However, Uber has been an undeniable hit in China, and Uber's explosive growth in China may be the best performance by a US tech company in years. Uber CEO Travis Kalanick disclosed at a September 2015 Beijing event that Uber's Chinese unit operated in almost 20 cities. Five of Uber's top ten cities by ride volume were in China, and Uber China counted 1 million rides a day in the country. Furthermore, it planned to enter 100 more Chinese cities over the next year, doubling the company's own expansion goal (of 50 cities) that was set just three months ago.

According to the *2016 Chinese New Year Cross-border Travel Report* released by Uber China, Chinese Uber users traveled to 319 cities around the globe during the Spring Festival holiday week in February 2016, more than twice the figure reported in 2015. China's financial hub, Shanghai, reported the largest number of Uber users choosing to travel overseas, followed by Beijing, the southern metropolises of Guangzhou and Shenzhen, and then East China's Hangzhou and Southwest China's Chengdu. (It is worth noting that Chengdu replaced New York to become Uber's most successful city globally in terms of daily ride volumes in October 2015.)

As background, as is the case in many cities around the world, the demand for cross-town transportation is at the heart of an urban lifestyle in modern China. Although more individuals have begun to own their own cars, the demand for taxi service is increasing even more quickly, as the population in many cities has exploded due to relentlessly fast-paced urbanization. Local governments in Chinese cities limit the base fare that taxis can charge customers. In places where the government-mandated taxi fares have been kept low or even reduced, the taxi drivers strike from time to time, making hailing a taxi next to impossible.

Partially in response to the demographic trends and partially in response to the dysfunctional nature of the market, car-hire apps emerged in 2012 to allow smartphone users to book and pay for taxi rides or limousine services using mobile apps. Their emergence has changed the way that the Chinese travel around their cities. In this area, Uber's main competitor is Didi Kuaidi, a combined entity resulting from the merger of two specialist start-ups in taxi-hailing that were backed by two of China's biggest internet companies Alibaba and Tencent, respectively. Before their merger, Alibaba invested in Kuaidi (translatable to "finding a taxi swiftly") and Tencent invested in Didi (which denotes the "honk honk" of a taxi).

After their launch in 2012, the Kuaidi and Didi apps caught on instantly with China's urban residents. The already large, expanding and congested cities, with their inadequate public transit networks, and the relatively large fleets of inexpensive taxis make the Chinese market perfect for taxi-hailing mobile services. But trying to get taxi drivers in China to use taxi-hailing applications was not easy. Early on, both companies had to find creative ways to attract, train and convince taxi drivers who were not tech savvy nor wanted to be. They competed head-to-head on the streets to promote their respective apps and corresponding mobile payment systems (Alibaba's Alipay and Tencent's WeChat Pay).

Both Didi and Kuaidi spent huge amounts of cash on subsidies to incentivize passengers and drivers to try out their services. In addition, they set up customer support centers near the spots where taxi drivers gather to have a cigarette or tea during shift changes. Some app managers were based in those centers to facilitate registration and to teach hundreds of taxi drivers how to use the app. At one point, the service centers offered free beer to taxi drivers to register themselves and bring along more of their colleagues to sign up (after completing their shift of course!). Then the drivers would be divided into groups on the app, with the idea being that the drivers could exchange information on traffic and road conditions within the group, which might also encourage the drivers to stay logged onto the app even in the absence of hailing customers.

After a price war reportedly involving more than $300 million in total rebates to taxi drivers and customers, the two companies did entice many taxi drivers and, as a result, permitted Didi and Kuaidi to penetrate the market in a really meaningful way. (In fact, almost all taxi drivers in big cities now have multiple smartphones and tablets installed in their taxis each devoted to servicing specific apps.) And, of course, because it became convenient to have access to at least one app, a large portion of urban residents installed e-payment apps on their smartphones and linked their bank accounts to them, so that they could complete mobile payments directly at the conclusion of their taxi rides.

Unfortunately (or perhaps obviously) the cumulative cost of the subsidies proved to be too much for the internet firms. In February 2015, these two largest taxi-hailing apps decided to enter into a $6 billion merger that effectively put an end to the price war. (Possibly as a symbol of "marriage" and "good will", the merger news was announced by the founders on Valentine's Day.) At the time of the merger, Didi Kuaidi reportedly employed 4,000 people, compared to the 200 who were working for Uber in China. The combined company had a near monopoly on mobile hailing of traditional taxis, and it also controlled more than 80% of China's private car-hailing market, according to the estimates of research firms.

Didi Kuaidi's taxi-hailing model is different from that of Uber. The internet companies make no money from taxi rides, and the hailing app is simply a tool to acquire customers for other ride-hailing services. Over time, of course, Didi Kuaidi has moved to monetize its giant customer base with what it calls a "freemium" model, in which Didi Kuaidi broadens its offerings to include premium car services and carpooling, both of which have been the main business lines of Uber globally. For example, in the summer of 2014, Kuaidi launched a luxury limo service in 20 cities that competed directly with Uber's high-end black cars.

The key to Uber's rapid growth in China is its commitment to localize its services to suit the Chinese market. In CEO Travis Kalanick's own words from his interview with Chinese media Caixin: "[We] have to go above and beyond in becoming truly Chinese." Uber understands that the complex and swiftly changing business environment in China is fundamentally different from the rest of the world, and has taken several important steps to adapt its business model to these unique conditions (urbanization, growth, swift demographic change, etc.).

First, Uber set up Uber (China), an independent entity with a separate management structure and separate headquarters. In fact, Uber China was the only instance in which Uber set up a separate company in a foreign company. And it demonstrates Uber's determination to make its Chinese operation embedded in the Chinese market. To that end, Uber China has also engaged with strategic investors that could help guide them to become "more Chinese". This has included building local management teams, interacting more closely with regulators and the government, and campaigning extensively to acquire more customers and drivers. According to the company's disclosure in early 2016, Hainan Airline Group, Guangzhou Automobile Group, Citic Securities and the insurers China Taiping and China Life are among "a long list of Chinese firms with investment in Uber".

Among all the Chinese institutional investors, Uber's relationship with Baidu is probably the most critical. For Uber, at least three things about its business in the Chinese market are different from its business in the rest of the world, both from a technology as well as a product perspective. One is about the mobile payment systems in the retail market, which is dominated by its primary competitor's two major investors (Alibaba and Tencent). Another is about maps and location services (because Google Maps still does not work in China at the present moment). The third factor is the reliance on and interconnectivity with social networks, as social apps in China are more thoroughly embedded and often work differently from those available in English-speaking markets.

As summarized by Figure 10.1, the investment relationship with Baidu provides Uber with all three indispensable components – the leading map service in China, a payment system independent from Alibaba's Alipay and Tencent's WeChat

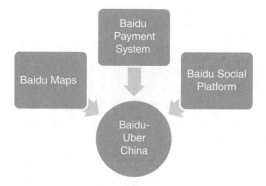

Figure 10.1   Critical Baidu Support for Uber's China Expansion

Payment, and social network based marketing on the Baidu platform, which is an important alternative to the WeChat social network. (In fact, Uber's public account was blocked by Tencent's WeChat social network in 2015.)

Uber is acutely aware of the fact that the majority of Chinese consumers are extremely sensitive to price. They aspire to the same services and goods they observe in the developed markets, but they always look out for free stuff or bargains as their incomes are comparably low. As a latecomer, Uber has offered huge subsidies to win over market share, sometimes doling out bonuses that are up to three times the amount of an average ride fare. In 2015, Uber China reportedly invested $1 billion in order to expand its market reach (while Uber was increasingly driving for profitability in the US market).

Interestingly, Uber's discount and subsidy strategy looks very similar to Alibaba's successful attempt to challenge the then-dominant eBay in China a decade ago. Taobao, Alibaba's main C2C (consumer to consumer) e-commerce marketplace, opened in 2003 without charging users fees. For a few years, it maintained a no fee model, while eBay in China continued to charge sellers and so lost market share steadily. Alibaba did not start charging transactional fees until it fully dominated the market. As Uber (China) raised nearly $2 billion in the second half of 2015 (with the latest round of fund raising reportedly boosting its valuation to more than $8 billion), the company is expected to put more subsidies into play in 2016 to continue its aggressive expansion.

Unlike many Western tech firms that mostly rely on expatriate managers, Uber hired local management and empowered them to run city operations. That move is critical for solving local issues in the complex and very challenging car-hiring business environment. For example, because Uber offers a large amount of cash as bonuses to Chinese drivers to get them on board, some drivers game the system by employing specialized software to cheat in reporting rides or their duration.

The local managers are quick to identify and deal with local scams that are detrimental to Uber's business. **(See the "Patients, Nurses and Safe Shots" box.)** Had Uber simply stuck to the tried and tested formula of hiring expat managers, it is likely that its ability to respond to such local challenges would have been slower and less effectual.

Patients, Nurses and Safe Shots

In 2015, Uber paid out a significant amount in bonuses to Chinese drivers to build its brand awareness and expand its market share. An unintended consequence was that groups of fraudsters developed specialized software to get paid for fake rides. As a result, Uber's reported performance of having captured 1 million rides a day was questioned.

For example, one driver might have received a job at the airport, but he still wanted to get paid for the trip there while the car was empty. He would go into one of several invitation-only online forums and request a fake fare from the fraudsters. The drivers referred to themselves as "patients", and the professional ride-bookers were referred to as "nurses" because their task was to use specialized software to issue an "injection", a location-specific ride request (from a fake customer), near to where the driver was.

After the "injection", the "patient" (driver) headed to the location selected remotely by the "nurse" (fake booker), and then completed the trip while the booker monitored remotely to ensure the fake journey showed up on Uber's GPS tracking software. After all was said and done, the driver could collect the fare and a bonus which may have been up to three times the fare, while the "nurse" was paid the actual fare charged and a small fee in recompense for helping the driver cheat the system.

Alternatively, the driver could do the operation himself. In order to do this, he needed to invest in a modified smartphone that could operate with multiple phone numbers and multiple corresponding Uber accounts. He could use one number to act as a rider, request a lift, and then accept it from his own driver account. These Uber driver and rider accounts were also for sale, and were advertised on e-commerce marketplaces, also promising to be able to circumvent Uber's background checks.

On these online marketplaces, the listed offerings even included modified smartphones that could be used to pretend to be a new user each time they placed an order. It could show unique 15-digit identity numbers to make Uber's software believe they were different phones every time the modified phone was used. With this feature, the users could "permanently" enjoy the "first ride" promotion (an additional credit for first time users). Of course, Uber (and its competitors) worked hard to crack down on the scams. Software upgrades released in late 2015 apparently closed many of these loopholes permanently.

The local management team is also critical to Uber's China operation because the overall regulatory regime remains in flux. Many car-hire app users have applauded the mobile app businesses for the convenience it offers in being able to find a car (whether a taxi or private car) that has a friendlier driver than in a standard taxi. But as in many places where Uber operates, there is also rivalry between its car-hire drivers and the established taxi drivers who are also plentiful in most Chinese cities. The profits made by taxi drivers have been squeezed by the services provided by unlicensed, private drivers, and they complained about the unlicensed nature of the business, attacking it by raising safety concerns.

Generally speaking, Uber and other car-hire app companies that link passengers to private drivers still operate in a legal gray area in the country, as policymakers mull over ways to regulate the industry. The central government has not yet developed nationwide regulations for car-hire apps, but some local municipal authorities have developed regulations that prohibit unauthorized private car owners from using the apps to pick up passengers. Uber's local managers are effective in communicating with the municipal governments. And they have, on occasion, managed to find government officials who are willing to support this innovative technology and service in their cities.

Uber China has also done well in understanding how to play into local users' special interests and preferences in order to differentiate itself from the competition. For example, in the summer of 2015 Uber China launched a promotion that gave the users the chance to meet eligible bachelors through its app on the eve of Qixi Festival. (The Qixi day is the seventh day of the seventh month in the lunar calendar. In a fairy tale, a celestial weaver and a cowherd on earth fell in love but were separated by heaven's rules. They were only allowed to meet on that one day each year.) In the cities where Uber operated, special buses picked up users who booked places in order to mingle with other singles.

The campaign helped to provide an experience for Chinese Uber users that was both fun and local. On Chinese social media, Uber was lauded as playing matchmaker on the nation's equivalent of Valentine's Day. There were even jokes about Uber having accumulated a convenient, self-selecting pool of potential husbands for single women. In short, the local management teams of Uber China understand what Chinese people need, and they were empowered to acquire users by adapting to local preferences, instead of attempting to impose marketing and publicity techniques simply because they worked in other markets.

Of course, the competition between Uber, Didi Kuaidi and other homegrown car-hiring app companies is far from over, with Uber set to expand its offerings and footprint, and the local players expanding to premium services. Whereas Uber offers marquee black car service in major cities, it has also launched less expensive services such as a ride-sharing service to allow private individuals to pick up passengers. It tries to gain mass appeal in China by offering a higher standard of rides for a modest premium. Conversely, the challenge for the Chinese companies will be to move up-market with new paid services that compete with Uber's successful premium service.

Inevitably, Uber and its local rivals in China are on a collision course in the world's largest car-hiring market. In an interesting parallel to Uber's China's expansion, Alibaba, in 2014, made a sizable investment in Lyft, the main competitor to Uber in the US. In 2015, Alibaba-backed Didi Kuaidi also invested in Lyft, leading to a complex web of partnership and competition among the internet giants in China and Silicon Valley (see Figure 10.2). In fact, it may be a harbinger of more direct competition between the Chinese and US internet firms in their respective home territories. Their fierce rivalry may result in lower prices for customers, creative business models and possibly further revolution in technology.

To add a new twist to their intertwined competition in both the Chinese and US markets, Uber and Didi entered into merger discussions regarding their China operations in August 2016. Such a merger would potentially create a cross-holding alliance. In the proposed transaction, Uber would sell its China operations to Didi in return for a 5.89% stake in the combined company along with "preferred equity interest", which would be equal to a 17.7% stake. Uber China's investors, including Baidu Inc, would receive a 2.3% stake in the merged entity. Didi

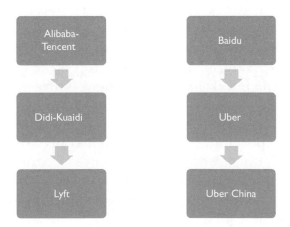

Figure 10.2   Interconnected China and US Internet Firms in Ride-Hailing

founder Cheng Wei and Uber Chief Executive Officer Travis Kalanick would join each other's boards.

This proposed merger was viewed by the market as a form of truce, bringing to an end a costly price war between the two companies who were vying for leadership in China's fast-growing ride-hailing market. By selling its China operations to its fierce rival Didi, Uber would be free to focus on other markets and possibly an initial public offering of the Uber group. However, China's Ministry of Commerce, the antitrust regulator, found that the two announced their agreement to merge without filing an application with the Ministry in advance, and, thus, without obtaining formal clearance.

According to the Ministry of Commerce, based on the antitrust regulations in China, "business operators need to file an application on their merger deal if their combined revenues reach a certain amount." In September, the Ministry announced at a news conference that it was investigating whether the merger between Didi and Uber's China unit could lead to a potential monopoly. In other words, the vast scale of Uber's operations in China, along with its rapid expansion in this market, may become an obstacle to its planned merger with the major local player.

Uber's success in obtaining substantial market share in China, when contrasted with other non-domestic technology companies, can be viewed as unique. However, what's even more interesting from the perspective of this narrative is the fact that Uber's service has taken off in China much faster than it did in the US. For example, Uber's top three most popular cities worldwide purely in terms of ride volumes – Guangzhou, Hangzhou and Chengdu — are all in China. Of course, the enormous scale of the Chinese market is the primary reason. An equally important factor is the high concentration of city residents following central government's urbanization push. There are about 200 cities in China with more than a million people, which are perfect places to develop "shared economy" business models.

Chinese customers are ready adopters of social network technologies. They socialize online and actively re-distribute information on new products or new services to their contacts. The mobile internet and smartphones have created a new social coordinating mechanism, and what the market sees is a seemingly endless potential to put goods, labor, and in the case of Uber, cars that are less than fully utilized, to productive use. The implication is profound: new mobile applications probably can receive market feedback and achieve meaningful scale more quickly in China than elsewhere, because new technology based on "human infrastructure" tends to spread faster in China. In fact, Uber has found that even when it comes to the initial number of customers in a region – the first 1 million users in a city – its growth in China has been much faster than what it has seen elsewhere.

That's probably why Uber CEO Travis Kalanick calls China one of "the largest untapped opportunities for Uber, potentially larger than the US". For foreign tech companies, the Chinese market is not only important for its enormous market size and the fast pace of technology adoption, but also valuable because of the unique innovation arising from it. As the subsequent sections will illustrate, the emerging innovation ecosystem in China is creating a remarkable wave of innovation that challenges the long-held perception of "Made in China" being simply synonymous with cheap imitation. Going forward, the Chinese market may well be a source of innovation for international companies.

A New Innovation Ecosystem

Few people know of the Zhongguancun Science Park in Beijing, which is one of the major innovation hubs for China's tech industry, and probably even fewer would compare it to Silicon Valley in the US. However, it is the home of established Chinese internet players including Lenovo and Baidu, and it also houses the Chinese headquarters and research center for world-renowned technology corporations such as Google, Microsoft, Intel and Oracle.

Located in the capital city of Beijing, Zhongguancun is filled with angel investors, hedge funds and venture capital firms that have helped fuel the breakneck growth in online and technology based businesses. Zhongguancun is also close to a group of top Chinese universities, national academies and corporate research centers. According to the data from the Ministry of Science and Technology, the Zhongguancun district gave birth to 49 start-ups on a daily (!) basis in 2014. The main section of the Zhongguancun Science Park, the nearly 200-meter-long Inno Way (or "the Innovation Street"), had attracted 2,000 angel investors and investment organizations as well as 4,000 entrepreneurial teams in a year since its June 2014 opening.

The Zhongguancun Science Park, together with numerous high-tech development zones that spread across the country, constitutes a national infrastructure for innovation that is strongly promoted by the central government as well as the local provinces and cities. In his public speeches, President Xi Jinping emphasized that innovation, economic restructuring and consumption should be among the top priorities of China's next stage growth (the 13th Five Year Plan for 2016–2020). Premier Li Keqiang suggested at the 2015 central government work report that, in addition to the existing RMB40 billion (nearly $7 billion) government fund earmarked for China's emerging industries, further funding would be made available for promoting business development and innovation.

The government initiatives include building up the innovation clusters, where the administration system is more user-friendly for businesses to get started (for example, faster corporate registration). Local governments also launch venture funds at provincial and city levels, whose funding and subsidies help early-stage entrepreneurs feel more comfortable with taking a little bit more risk. In dozens of cities like Beijing and Shanghai, university graduates and young professionals are frequently rewarded with preferential tax treatment for their start-up endeavors.

Also, incubator facilities are established to provide entrepreneurs with inexpensive or even free office facilities, assistance with business services, and common spaces that connect the budding startups with potential investors. They also serve as community centers, where entrepreneurial minds can bounce ideas off each other and start-ups' owners meet angel investors to present projects. In addition, they are also education centers. Various lectures on entrepreneurship and capital markets are held daily, where seasoned professionals share their experiences with the "wannabes".

There are more than 20 incubator facilities (also known as service centers) on the "Innovation Street" at the Zhongguancun Science Park. For example, established in 2011, Garage Cafe was the first service center at the district where entrepreneurs could work on their projects for a whole day at the cost of one cup of coffee. Today the 3W Café is by far the most famous among all the coffee shops, because Premier Li had coffee there with start-up owners and entrepreneurs in May 2015, tangibly demonstrating the government's support for entrepreneurship and innovation. (**See the "Premier Li's Cappuccino" box.**)

Premier Li's Cappuccino

The "Innovation Street" at Beijing's Zhongguancun Science Park is famous nationwide for edging out other places in attracting the most ambitious and forward-looking entrepreneurs. Young start-up owners from all over the country visit the place to find brainstorming peers, business partners, angel investors and industry backers. But when Premier Li walked into the 3W Café in May 2015, the community received an unprecedented "spiritual boost" from the government's endorsement for entrepreneurship and innovation.

The vanilla cappuccino that Premier Li ordered has since been known as the "Premier's coffee", and the 3W Café has turned into a tourist site of sorts. Outside the coffee shop, people wait to take photos against the backdrop of a big screen that shows Premier Li Keqiang drinking coffee with young entrepreneurs.

Near the coffee table where the meeting took place, a wall is now covered with banners calling on people to start their own businesses.

According to media reports, at the 3W Café Premier Li stopped to read the phrase printed on one of its walls: "Life is limited, but zheteng is not." (Zheteng is a contemporary Chinese term that means to toil and bustle around something with vague prospects.) "Ah, zheteng," the Premier commented, "That really sums up innovation."

"Zheteng" is a common theme of the internet industry as well as the overall start-up community in China. The 3W Café certainly embodies the meaning of the term: the coffee shop itself is a start-up. It is the first crowdfunded café in China, and it has an ambitious plan to open 100 stores in 10 major cities across the country.

In 2015, according to data from the Ministry of Science and Technology, China had more than 1,600 technology incubator facilities. With government endorsement in the background, a dynamic ecosystem of entrepreneurs and start-ups is organically being built up (see Figure 10.3). The network of established internet firms and their seasoned entrepreneurs,

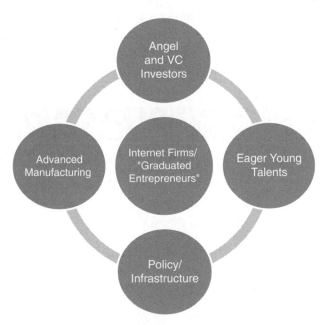

Figure 10.3   China's Innovation Ecosystem

endless eager talents, abundant angel investors and venture capital, and a sophisticated manufacturing system are collectively making China one of the most interesting centers of innovation in the world.

For an illustration, one need look no further than the last decade's track record of Chinese "unicorns", the early stage tech firms that are valued at $1 billion following an initial public offering (IPO), sale or publicly announced private funding rounds. According to data compiled by Atomico, the London-based venture capital group led by Skype co-founder Niklas Zennstrom, among the 134 tech start-ups that reached the billion-dollar mark during the 10 years of 2004–2014, the number of "unicorns" from China (26) exceeded those from Europe (21), and was only behind the innovation superpower of the US (with 79, of which 52 came from Silicon Valley). (There were none from Africa, Latin America, or the Middle East.)

What is remarkable is that, unlike in the past this new innovation ecosystem cultivates cutting edge ideas for the global technology and media industries. The first generation of Chinese tech companies were mostly copycat versions of Western sites. However, in the new digital economy, the second generation start-ups are about Chinese users' booming online consumption and the rapid adoption of mobile applications. They are creating a remarkable wave of innovation in business models and product features that challenge long held perceptions and is very likely going to represent a successful source of exports to the rest of the world.

The core of this ecosystem is a network of "graduated entrepreneurs" from established tech firms at home and abroad. Many of them had previous successful careers at the three leading internet firms (Baidu, Alibaba and Tencent). Their BAT resume provides them with immediate credibility in the market. Their alumni network not only provides industry talent to partner with or recruit, but also supplies a pool of seed investors. In some cases, the BAT companies themselves may become a significant strategic investor.

More start-up founders are emerging from other origins as other companies besides BAT have reached significant business scale and multi-billion valuations (Xiaomi being only one example). Equally important, some founders are former Chinese employees of global technology giants such as Microsoft, Hewlett-Packard and Yahoo (either in the US or in their Chinese operations). The trend cuts across the pay grades of the major companies as the most innovative, irrespective of seniority, can replicate the success of the companies they work for, but now as owners or founders rather than as employees.

Either as a senior executive who is financially secure enough to take a major career risk, or as a newly-minted young employee who feels that she does not have much to lose, the aspiration to create a Xiaomi or Didi Kuaidi is everywhere. Hundreds of start-ups have been created in the past three years by former employees of Alibaba and other major internet firms. As previously described, two former employees of Alibaba's Taobao marketplace founded Mogujie, a social shopping website specializing in women's fashion, and it has already become a unicorn itself (with a valuation exceeding $1 billion). This development resembles the multiplying effect seen in the Silicon Valley ecosystem in the last few decades, where the generations of innovators from Intel, Netscape, Google and Paypal have created wave after wave of start-ups.

Along with the growing number of "graduated entrepreneurs", there seems to be an endless supply of young and eager talent. More than half a million engineering students a year graduate from Chinese universities. At the business schools, more MBA candidates than ever are taking entrepreneurship courses with ambitious plans of launching start-ups. (Years ago, investment banking and management consulting jobs were the top two career tracks.) And an entire generation of young Chinese students are returning to China for mobile internet opportunities following their undergraduate studies in the US and Europe.

At the 3W Café and other entrepreneurship-themed community meeting places, the "graduated entrepreneurs" are mentors and angel investors to the younger start-ups. Driven by those former internet firm employees, there is an increasingly active angel investor community which is keen to invest in the next big wave of information technology ventures. In recent years, both the amount of angel capital and the number of projects that could be invested in have increased multiple times. According to Zero2IPO Research, during the first half of 2015, there was $743 million angel capital invested in 809 projects, with the average investment per deal nearing $1 million per transaction.

Another important factor in this booming ecosystem is an unprecedentedly large flow of venture capital (VC) – from both foreign and domestic funds – into start-up projects. As would have been expected, businesses that focused on mobile consumers have dominated VC capital-raising in recent years. With the emergence of angel investors, who tend to invest in even earlier phases than the venture capitalists, the VC firms are also moving their involvement forward. (In extreme cases, "investors are in line even before the business is functioning in any meaningful way".)

In 2015, according to data from consultancy Preqin, in 2015 venture capitalists invested a record $37 billion in Chinese start-ups, more than double the previous year's number. The doubling of venture deals last year came after a tripling in deal value the year before, demonstrating the immense appetite of the VC industry for Chinese innovation (see Figure 10.4). Although not necessarily counted as venture capital, the investment arms of established internet firms (such as BAT and Xiaomi) are also aggressively chasing investment opportunities. Because they are disruptors themselves, they are constantly on the lookout for the next big thing – some new development that can fundamentally change the ecosystem or even the landscape in which they operate. As a result they diligently make investments into new ideas across all sectors.

The pace of VC deals slowed in the fourth quarter of 2015 because there were concerns that too many start-ups had been set up in certain sectors in China, leading to costly price

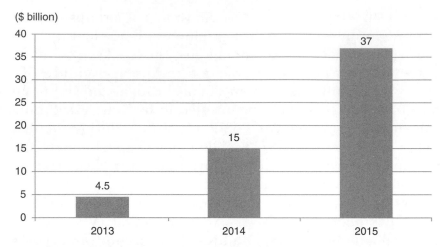

($ billion)

Figure 10.4   Total VC Investments in China (2013–2015)
(Data Source: Preqin)

wars among them to compete for customers. For example, in the O2O (online-to-offline) service market, many apps often started in a single niche (such as flower delivery and wedding services) and used venture capital to fund subsidies to attract customers and suppliers, rather than focusing on the development of innovative solutions or the scaling of their current platforms. As a result of this, some venture firms have started holding back on new investments, particularly as concerns are rising that the market was saturated with start-ups trying to solve identical problems. Too much competition between these made the risk of business failure very high indeed.

However, Meituan-Dianping (the leading O2O company for restaurant booking and movie ticketing analyzed in Chapter 5) raised $3.3 billion at its latest private fundraising round in early 2016, shrugging off such worries, at least for the present moment. The investors in Meituan-Dianping (valued at more than $18 billion at this fundraising round) included venture capital firm DST Global and Singapore Sovereign Wealth Fund Temasek. The $3.3 billion Meituan-Dianping fundraiser topped an earlier $3 billion round raised by the ride-hailing company Didi Kuaidi to become the single largest funding round on record for a venture capital backed start-up.

In fact, the fundraising by Meituan-Dianping in the January 2016 round sets all records globally for a venture capital fundraising round. And, overall, China is narrowing the gap with the US, the global center of modern venture capital. (According to Preqin data, the value of US deals in 2015 was $68 billion, up from $56 billion the previous year, which represents a smaller increment than that of comparables for China.) The country is, in effect, emerging as a legitimate and serious challenger to the US for leadership of the technology industry.

Also notably, moving beyond "Made in China" does not mean that the sophisticated manufacturing infrastructure is of no use; instead, it is an indispensable part of this ecosystem and a distinctive competitive advantage over other innovation hubs worldwide. China's economy modernization started with manufacturing connected to the import-export businesses. After decades of continuous development, it has a seamless web of sourcing, manufacturing and logistics services that is second to none. The electronic manufacturing sector is by far the most advanced globally. For example, the southern city of Shenzhen is arguably the best place for hardware start-ups. Once a small fishing village next to the powerhouse of Hong Kong, following three decades of development Shenzhen is now home to domestic tech giants such as Huawei and ZTE, and it has become an electronics manufacturing center for the global tech industry.

With easy access to parts and manufacturing know-how, this smart hardware hub provides young companies with an edge over foreign competitors in terms of production timelines. Also, having the supply chain in such close proximity means that early stage inventors can easily tweak their pilot products at factories, giving them more opportunities to calibrate the finished product. In fact, China's massive electronics supply chain, still robust in the aftermath of the "Made in China" era and still becoming increasingly sophisticated, is invaluable in the new convergence between hardware and software.

In summary, the new dynamic ecosystem in China is creating more tech start-ups that cannot simply be described as the Chinese version of US or other Western firms. The new generation of companies are more innovative in terms of products and technologies specifically designed for local market needs, more willing to accept outside investors, and have a more global outlook from their inception. In particular, many are using the mobile internet to challenge inefficient domestic incumbents.

In fact, it is quite possible that in the near future China will have more billion-dollar start-ups than the US, although given Silicon Valley's lead, the US is likely to continue to have more firms in the highest bracket of valuation. China's top ten highest valued start-ups (see Table 10.1) are almost all related to mobile commerce. Their high valuation not only reflects their dominance in the world's largest mobile commerce market, but also factors in the investors' optimism in the special business models or product features that they are pioneering.

Cross-Pollinating Innovation

Today Chinese companies are moving to the forefront of global technology innovation, particularly when it comes to hardware. For example, when President Xi Jinping visited Tajikistan during the Shanghai Cooperation Organization (SCO) Summit in September 2014, the smartphone from China's domestic brand ZTE was on his list of national gifts.

The specific ZTE model used for national gifts was reputed as one of the world's most secure handsets (perhaps thanks to ZTE's recruitment of Blackberry's research team after the Canadian company's recent financial distress related restructuring). Historically, China used traditional artisanal products such as silk, porcelain and painting as national gifts in the diplomatic context. Using domestically produced smartphones as "national gifts" is intended as a demonstration of the progress China has made in the technology sector, and it also demonstrates China's determination to transform itself from the "world's factory" for low-tech manufacturing into a global technology exporter.

Table 10.1   China's top ten highest valued start-ups (as of January 2016)

	Company name	Valuation (US $ bn)	Latest funding (valuation date)	Business description
1	Xiaomi	45	December 2014	Leading manufacturer of smartphones and smart devices
2	Ant Financial	45	July 2015	Internet finance company covering mobile payment, cash management and wealth management
3	Meituan/ Dianping	18	January 2016	China's Groupon and Yelp, covering both group buying and consumer reviews
4	Didi Kuaidi	15	July 2015	Dominant taxi-hailing app, Uber's biggest rival in China
5	Lufax	9.6	March 2015	Internet finance, one of the largest peer-to-peer (P2P) online lenders
6	DJI Innovations	8.0	May 2015	The world's largest consumer drone maker by revenue
7	Zhong An Online	8.0	June 2015	China's first online-only insurer
8	Meizu	6.0	February 2015	Smartphone and internet service company backed by Alibaba
9	LeTV mobile	5.5	November 2015	Smartphone unit of LeTV, the internet and video conglomerate
10	Ele.me	3.0	August 2015	Online food delivery service for universities, offices and others

(Data Sources: Disclosures from fund-raising rounds; Approximate valuations)

The Chinese companies' innovative power was demonstrated at the most recent 2016 Consumer Electronics Show (CES) in Las Vegas, which had a decidedly Chinese flavor this year. Of the more than 3,600 exhibitors in the Vegas show, about one-third came from China, up from about one-fourth in the previous year. China's entrepreneurs were bold in releasing new products to showcase their ingenuity, debuting innovative robots, drones, electric cars, virtual reality headsets, elegant looking Android smartwatches and TV sets with the latest true-to-life imaging technology.

Whereas the innovations from Chinese start-ups wowed the CES crowds, China's giant tech companies were also busy launching their new products and research strategies.

Lenovo made headlines at the 2016 CES with news that it aimed to make a $500 Android device with built-in Google spatial perception technology. It seemed that Lenovo would be the first to bring that particular technology (Google's Project Tango) to consumer smartphones later this year.

Meanwhile, the internet and video conglomerate LeTV supplied "an internet brain" to Aston Martin, the trendy British luxury sports car brand that is associated with the legendary secret agent James Bond. LeTV and Aston Martin showcased the first model of their collaboration – an Aston Martin Rapide S that incorporated the LeTV Internet of the Vehicle (IOV) system. The car featured a new concept for the center console and instrument panel, equipped with an HD touch screen. It also incorporated LeTV's latest speech recognition technology, which enabled the car to respond to the driver's orders such as lowering the windows.

Internet-connected and electric cars are considered to be the next key terminal for mobile internet after the smartphones. Related to terms like "intelligent highway", "connected cars" is an umbrella term for the idea of linking increasingly intelligent cars to the mobile internet through a stronger form of Wi-Fi or more robust wireless telecommunications networks. In 2015, China issued a new policy to encourage internet companies to develop electric vehicles. In the past, the biggest hurdle for non-automakers entering the industry had been a stipulation that companies had to possess vehicle production capacity. By allowing companies outside the traditional manufacturing sector to develop electric vehicles, the new policy essentially created a new manufacturing model for the auto industry. In effect non-manufacturers, primarily innovative digital companies, could totally outsource their car production.

China's three biggest internet companies Baidu, Alibaba and Tencent (BAT) are becoming involved in the connected car business. In 2015, in one of the first steps in this direction, Baidu launched a cross-platform (smartphone and in-car system) solution for connected cars called CarLife, based on its digital mapping service, Baidu Maps. CarLife provided users with services including route planning, location inquiries, distance estimations and navigation advice for users to avoid traffic. The company also tested a self-driving car model in 2015 and demonstrated the technology to Chinese President Xi Jinping at an industry expo in Wuzhen, Zhejiang province.

Tencent launched the first smart car hardware, "lubao box" in June 2014, which connected vehicles to Tencent's cloud computing services. The "lubao box" focused on the self-examination of a car's condition (such as fuel consumption). Alibaba, on the other hand, worked to improve the entertainment system in cars by leveraging its extensive investments in the media industry. With its strength in hardware devices and smartphone batteries, ZTE chose wireless charging for vehicles as a point of entry into this new field. For years China has promoted the use of electric vehicles to cut pollution, but the lack of charging stations for any type of alternative energy vehicles has always caused a bottleneck. By making charging wireless, ZTE could solve the biggest headache for both owners and for regulators, and the feedback it received on its venture has been very positive.

Of course, these improvements to cars have thus far primarily involved moving mobile apps from smartphones to vehicles. At this early stage, "connected cars" is more about cars with internet connections rather than cars that are connected with each other and with their drivers and other people. The internet firms may be years away from meaningfully changing the value chain of the auto industry. But their investment in connected cars is set to accelerate in the coming years, and the more revolutionary interaction of car, people and road may come sooner than we expect.

The innovation boom among Chinese companies is partly stimulated by the new innovation ecosystem and partly driven by the need to survive in the competitive global market. The major companies have gradually outgrown the low margin "OEM" or "components manufacturer" image, distancing themselves from competition for rock bottom prices. Instead, they move towards higher price categories in the global market, while upgrading their brands to change the conventional perception that Chinese products mean low price, low quality and poor service.

In particular, the mobile internet market is extremely competitive, and therefore finding new ways of meeting the customers' requirements is critical to commercial success. The Chinese companies are forced to innovate as their profits are squeezed both in domestic and overseas markets. They appreciate the vital importance of innovation and branding in allowing companies to achieve premium pricing, high gross margin and bottom line profitability, which, in turn, can provide the cash flow for further research and development. For that, there is no better example than Apple's dominance in the profit share of the global smartphone market.

Here the case of Apple's iPhone is examined for the last time in this book, and the discussion focuses on the bottom line profitability of Chinese brands and Apple. According to the research firm Canaccord's early 2015 report, Apple (92%) and Samsung (15%) have captured all the profits of the global smartphone industry (see Table 10.2). They collectively

Table 10.2   Profit distribution of the global smartphone industry

Year	Lion's Share of Profits
Before iPhone (2007)	Nokia (67%)
2010	Nokia, Apple, Blackberry (similar share)
2012	Apple, Samsung (50%–50% split)
2014	Apple (92%), Samsung (15%)

(Data Source: Canaccord)

accounted for more than 100% of industry profits because other makers either broke even or lost money. The research firm's data did not include privately held companies such as China's Xiaomi and India's Micromax Informatics, but Canaccord believed that the profits for those companies, if any, were not significant enough to change the industry-wide profit allocation numbers.

Apple's share of profits in early 2015 was remarkable because it sold less than 20% of smartphones but took in 92% of global smartphone profits. Because most Chinese brands (together with Samsung from Korea) are based on Google's Android operating system, it is increasingly difficult to differentiate their products in a highly mature smartphone market. In their high-end products, almost all brands include better cameras and screens, more powerful processors, cooler designs that leverage high quality and innovative materials. To some extent, the smartphone market is beginning to resemble the personal computer (PC) market, where the products are competing in a very saturated market, and most manufacturers struggle to break even. Based on its exclusive ecosystem and branding power, Apple is able to charge a higher price for its iPhones as well as laptops and iMacs to achieve profit dominance.

Of course, the disparity in profits could be partly explained by the different strategies taken by the manufacturers. For example, Xiaomi brands itself as an Internet company that chooses to sell cheaply-priced phones to acquire a large number of users quickly so that it can later focus on more profitable apps and downloads, phone accessories and add-on services. In addition, the Chinese tech companies including Xiaomi believe the global war on smart devices will be decided eventually on a much bigger battlefield than that represented by the smartphone market. As seen in the case of connected cars, all these Chinese players are seeking to tie users into an expanding family of smart devices and internet services.

So far, Chinese tech companies have already proven their mettle by catching up to global rivals in the smartphone and fourth-generation (4G) technology development process. They are now joining a fiercely competitive global race to become the first companies to offer fifth-generation (5G) wireless networks and products to global customers. Many Chinese firms are moving aggressively into the future state of a multi-device and hyper-connected world, which is "Smart 2.0" in ZTE's terminology, "convergence of telecom and IT" in Huawei's, and "all-inclusive ecosystem" in Xiaomi's.

The 5G technology's most visible advantage is its data transfer speeds, which is expected to be 1,000 times faster than that of 4G technology. The high-speed and highly stable 5G services are expected to encompass wireless applications that go far beyond basic internet communication to include driverless smart cars and more. Ultimately, 5G is the infrastructure for the "Internet of Things" (IoT), a loose term used to describe a network of mobile internet, smart devices, home appliances and any physical objects that interact through cloud technology. For example, the faster data transmission rates are expected to provide a constant and reliable stream of real-time street data that is required for driverless cars to function effectively and safely.

Huawei, ZTE and other Chinese tech firms have spent heavily on 5G research, as 5G represents a technological as well as a business revolution. More than 500 Huawei researchers have reportedly been working on the technology since 2009, and the firm is in the middle of a six-year, $600 million 5G research and development program. In July 2015, Huawei CEO Hu Houkun announced that the company planned to finish drafting its 5G standards by the end of 2018 and start commercial deployment in 2020.

Huawei's major rival, ZTE, also launched a 5G research effort in 2009. In ZTE's Smart 2.0 vision, every device – whether smartwatch or conventional refrigerator – is connected to a network, every network – whether highways or cable – is a pipe for objects and information, and every product is customized to individual users based on their unique requirements. According to its own disclosures, ZTE has established eight 5G research centers – four in China, three in the US and one in Europe. Overall, Chinese companies have secured a stronger position in the 5G development process than they had during the run-up to the roll-out of 4G, and China may well play a leading role in setting global standards for 5G technology as a result.

In addition to internal research and organic innovation, Chinese firms also actively acquire research and development capabilities from external markets. As seen in the Baidu/Uber and Lenovo/Motorola Mobility cases, Chinese firms are taking significant equity stakes in foreign firms, and in many cases they are beginning to complete full takeovers. Increasingly, Chinese firms are interested in acquiring cutting-edge technology development by investing in start-ups, especially in Silicon Valley that is still viewed as a key source of innovation and the capital of the mobile internet. Alibaba as well as Baidu and Tencent have collectively invested billions of dollars in these start-ups (see Table 10.3 on recent investments by Alibaba).

As Chinese companies are dealing with the same in their attempts to grow their business as many US companies, their cooperation may lead to promising cross-pollination of tech innovation. As mentioned previously, Alibaba is working with its portfolio company Quixey to innovate in the area of mobile searching. When compared to traditional search engine searches, mobile searches are more opaque and could be

Table 10.3   Alibaba's recent investments into US Start-ups

US Start-ups	Business sector	Amount ($ millions)	Date
Snapchat	Mobile messaging	$200	March 2015
Peel	Smart TV mobile app	$ 50	October 2014
Kabam	Mobile gaming developer	$120	August 2014
Lyft	On demand ride-sharing	$250	April 2014
TangoMe	Social messaging	$280	March 2014
Shoprunner	Members-only e-commerce	$206	October 2013
Quixey	"Deep" search engine for information in mobile apps	$ 50	October 2013

(Data Sources: News Reports and Public Disclosure)

described as scattered. For example, information on a restaurant and its promotion deals is spread over multiple apps for map information, group purchases, consumer reviews and so on. The two companies are now combining their capabilities to develop a "deep search" function to consolidate the information held on multiple apps into one search function so that the users do not have to install and run the individual apps themselves.

It is worth noting that through their investment relationships, the Chinese firms also provide the young companies with valuable insight into China, a market that an ambitious company cannot afford to miss, but at the same time is really difficult to penetrate. For a foreign start-up, it can be advantageous to align with a strategic partner who understands customer behavior, potential competitors, marketing and distribution, and numerous other barriers to entry in the local market. For example, when Tango's gaming and social network business plans to expand beyond the US, Tencent is a formidable incumbent. And, the company that has the best understanding of Tencent other than Tencent is probably Alibaba. As seen in the description of the taxi-hailing market, the player who best understands Alibaba and Tencent and their strengths and weaknesses is Baidu.

In conclusion, in the near future the Chinese market is poised to be a trend-setter, rather than the trend-follower, especially when it comes to next-generation mobile devices and services. One critical component playing into their hands is access to user data, which in the digital era is becoming a significant asset, although it is rarely recorded on corporate balance sheets (sooner or later it must be). With more than half of the 1.4 billion population being internet users, the data in the possession of the Chinese players focused on the consumer market is second to none. It is the oil of the information economy and the source of future Chinese designed products and business models.

In addition to the unrivalled internet user population size, what also makes the market unique is the fact that China is the largest "mobile-first" and "mobile-only" market in the world.

For many people in China, especially in rural areas, their first internet experience is often mobile instead of connected to a personal computer of any type – their engagement with products and services begins the moment he or she starts using a smartphone. For example, as seen in the earlier mobile payment discussions, the lack of a widely-spread credit card system in China means that mobile payment are the "first" and "only" non-cash payment options for a vast majority of users.

As a result of these unique conditions, China's digital market has evolved in a very different way from the Western world, moving more aggressively into mobile or originating in mobile in the first instance. Mobile users can book movie tickets, order wedding services and manage financial investments using their smartphones and are comfortable in doing this too. As illustrated in the Uber China case, new mobile applications can potentially achieve significant scale more quickly in China than elsewhere. Because of the very rich array of mobile apps vying for a space in Chinese people's daily lives, in an extreme case the general public actually believed there was a mobile app providing "thugs for hire". **(See the "Didi Daren" box.)**

Didi Daren ("Thugs for Hire" App)

The imagination of Chinese entrepreneurs seems to have no boundaries. The widely-promoted taxi-hailing mobile app Didi Dache ("Honk Honk" Hail a Taxi) unexpectedly inspired a sensational name for an entirely new breed of service app. By changing the character "che" (car) into "ren" (person), the new app was named Didi Daren. Because "da" in Chinese could either mean "hail" or "beat", the app's name could loosely be translated to "Honk Honk Beat a Person".

After the app became available for download, some users understandably took the name at its face value. Chinese media reported that people used the app to offer themselves as thugs for hire, providing strong credentials such as "a team with diverse capabilities, verified by authorities, and from various professional backgrounds including sports trainers, retired veterans, experienced thugs, wanted fugitives and more".

More confusion was created by *Baozou Big News*, an online Chinese comedy show, which broadcast a skit of a bullied nurse and a harassed schoolgirl who used the app to call for enforcers to beat up the offenders. In the video the offenders were beaten unconscious and the schoolgirl and nurse thanked the app profusely for "empowering" them. Having watched this skit, and having once again taken it entirely at face value, even more people believed that the app was a real service provider for the hiring of "muscle". More alarmingly, to demonstrate that there was a market for this type of service, the app was downloaded around 200,000 times within three months.

Later it turned out that the app was a concierge service created by a tech company whose English name was Joke. Instead of being an "Uber for thugs", the app was intended to help people "hail a person" who might help with errands. The Joke Company used the pun on "Honk Honk Beat a Person" as a way to attract attention in what could be viewed as very effective "guerilla" marketing. In the fierce competition for market share of the mobile internet, companies seek any possible edge to grab the attention of potential users. In the case of "Didi Daren", it seemed clear that it was worthwhile to be audacious.

Before the Didi Daren app was ultimately removed from the app stores as a result of public controversy, many people actually believed that the app was an innovation on thug-hiring. Some internet pundits responded positively, saying that Didi Daren "democratized" the criminal world, because even people with no relationship to a Godfather could find an appropriate "helper". In addition, on the online platform the price was negotiable, service quality could be reviewed and the word-of-mouth reputation could be consolidated with the data held online. Sophisticated and useful to say the least!

More sophisticated reviews linked the Didi Daren phenomenon with new mobile internet-related business models in commercial sectors. They found that the Didi Daren case study illustrated the mobile internet's capacity for revolutionizing service models by cutting out the "middle-man" or "agent". The conclusion was that the traditional service providers would all eventually have to embrace the mobile internet to better serve their customers. When the Joke Company took a free ride on Didi Dache's fame, it is very unlikely that it expected such a profound interpretation of their guerilla marketing strategy.

When Tencent launched its first instant messaging product named QQ years ago, the product was viewed as a replica of the same system on which Yahoo Messenger and MSN Messenger were based. More recently, when Tencent started the new mobile app WeChat, it was compared to Facebook and WhatsApp, because WeChat was first and foremost a messaging app for sending text, voice and photos to friends and family. Today, however, WeChat as well as QQ have evolved into much more complex and multi-faceted mobile platforms that seem only very loosely related to their foreign counterparts.

To satisfy Chinese mobile users' needs, Tencent has built an entire ecosystem of interrelated services around the WeChat platform. Alongside text, video and voice messaging, WeChat users can now shop and make payments, play games, book hotels or flight tickets, order a taxi and do many other things without ever leaving the app ecosystem. The critical component binding it all together is the mature mobile payment system, which makes the integrated services provided by the app more relevant in China than in the US. Another special feature is its voice input capability, which allows users to bypass the cumbersome process of writing Chinese characters on phone screens.

"In the next five years, there will be more innovation, more invention, more entrepreneurship happening in China, happening in Beijing than in Silicon Valley," said Travis Kalanick, the founder of the world's most valuable start-up Uber Technologies at an early 2016 Beijing conference. "We gotta play our A-game in order to compete with the best." Indeed, the planned merger between Uber China and Didi has illustrated not only the fierce competition in this cutting-edge market, but also the potential opportunity for a nimble and fast-growing entrant. Uber's continuing deep involvement with the Chinese market, irrespective of whether the merger will be approved or not, may be a harbinger of more external entrants arriving in China to look for new markets and develop new features, products as well as business models. Backed by the emerging ecosystem of entrepreneurship in China, the story of China is rapidly transforming from the old "Made in China" factories to the younger "Innovated in China".

Bibliography

Agence France-Presse (AFP). "China Web Firms Odds-On Winners With World Cup Gambling", NDTV, 4 July 2014. http://www.ndtv.com/world-news/china-web-firms-odds-on-winners-with-world-cup-gambling-583651

Alibaba Group. "Alibaba Group and Youku Tudou Enter into Definitive Merger Agreement", Press release, 6 November 2015, http://www.alibabagroup.com/en/news/article?news=p151106

Alibaba Group. "Alibaba Group to Ring New York Stock Exchange Opening Bell", Press release, 11 November 2015. http://www.alibabagroup.com/en/news/article?news=p151109

Alibaba Group. "Alibaba Group Generated USD14.3 Billion of GMV on 2015 11.11 Global Shopping Festival", Press release, 12 November 2015. http://www.alibabagroup.com/en/news/article?news=p151112

Arakali, Harichandan. "Chinese smartphone vendors make inroads in India, boost market share" Forbes India, 16 February 2016. http://forbesindia.com/printcontent/42341

Atsmon, Yuval and Magni, Max. "Meet the Chinese consumer of 2020", McKinsey Quarterly, March 2012. http://www.mckinsey.com/global-themes/asia-pacific/meet-the-chinese-consumer-of-2020

Austin, Scott, Canipe, Chris and Slobin, Sarah. "The Billion Dollar Startup Club", Wall Street Journal, 18 February 2015. http://graphics.wsj.com/billion-dollar-club/

Back, Aaron. "Xiaomi's Valuation Backed By More Than Buzz", Wall Street Journal, 22 December 2014. http://www.wsj.com/articles/xiaomis-valuation-backed-by-more-than-buzz-heard-on-the-street-1419241661

Baeder, George. "iPhone 6: Can Apple Survive?", China Global Insight, 24 September 2014. http://chinaglobalinsight.com/iphone-6-can-apple-survive/

Barboza, David. "A Popular Chinese Social Networking App Blazes Its Own Path", New York Times, 20 January 2014. http://www.nytimes.com/2014/01/21/technology/a-chinese-social-network-blazes-its-own-path.html

Barboza, David. "China's Other E-Commerce Giant Follows Its Own Path", New York Times, 26 January 2015. http://www.nytimes.com/

2015/01/27/business/international/jdcom-chinas-other-e-commerce-giant-follows-its-own-path.html?ncid=txtlnkusaolp00000618

Beijing Times. "Jack Ma: 'Web products are not equal to fake products'", 4 February 2015. http://tech.sina.com.cn/i/2015-02-04/01599995576.shtml

Bensinger, Greg. "Alibaba, ShopRunner to Team Up for China Service", *Wall Street Journal*, 7 May 2014. http://www.wsj.com/articles/SB10001424052702304655304579548343863161338

Bezerra, Julio, et al. "The Mobile Revolution: How Mobile Technologies Drive a Trillion-Dollar Impact", Boston Consulting Group (BCG) Perspectives, 15 January 2015. https://www.bcgperspectives.com/content/articles/telecommunications_technology_business_transformation_mobile_revolution/

Blackwell, Richard. "Imax sits back and watches China's cinema appetite grow", *The Globe and Mail*, 24 July 2014. http://www.theglobeandmail.com/report-on-business/international-business/asian-pacific-business/imax-sits-back-and-watches-chinas-cinema-appetite-grow/article19760900/

Bloomberg News. "Apple Looks for Big Screen Boost as IPhone 6 Plus Hits China", Bloomberg, 17 October 2014. http://www.bloomberg.com/news/articles/2014-10-17/apple-looks-for-big-screen-boost-as-iphone-6-hits-china

Bloomberg News. "Xiaomi Puts a Windfall to Work Beyond Phones", Bloomberg, 16 January 2015. http://www.bloomberg.com/news/articles/2015-01-15/xiaomi-invests-in-startups-by-the-dozen

Boehler, Patrick. "China Venture Investing, Driven by Mobile, Soared to Record Level in 2014", *Wall Street Journal*, 1 February 2015. http://blogs.wsj.com/venturecapital/2015/02/01/china-venture-investing-driven-by-mobile-soared-to-record-level-in-2014/

Boston Consulting Group (BCG). "M&A in China: Getting Deals Done, Making Them Work", BCG Perspectives, 15 January 2015. https://www.bcgperspectives.com/content/articles/globalization_mergers_acquisitions_china_getting_deals_done_making_them_work/?chapter=4#chapter4

Bradsher, Keith. "Chinese Titan Takes Aim at Hollywood", *New York Times*, 22 September 2013. http://www.nytimes.com/2013/09/23/business/global/chinese-titan-takes-aim-at-hollywood.html

Burkitt, Laurie. "IMAX Intends to Get Even Bigger in China: Deal With State-Owned Film Company to Add 19 More Theaters in the Country", *Wall Street Journal*, 21 July 2014. http://www.wsj.com/articles/imax-intends-to-get-bigger-in-china-1405976983

Business Times. "Foreign players net big wins in China", 10 May 2014. http://www.btinvest.com.sg/wealth/wealth-planning/foreign-players-net-big-wins-china-20140510/

Cai, Xiao. "Venture capital switches to online-to-offline deals", *China Daily Europe*, 13 February 2015. http://europe.chinadaily.com.cn/epaper/2015-02/13/content_19576285.htm

Cain, Rob. "China's Movie Industry is Growing Faster Than Any Other Country's Anywhere, Any Time, Ever", *Forbes*, 26 June 2015. http://www.forbes.com/sites/robcain/2015/06/26/chinas-movie-industry-is-growing-faster-than-any-other-countrys-anywhere-any-time-ever/

Cain, Robert. "Studio Report Card 2014: Sci-Fi and Animation Drive Another Banner Year in China", *China Film Biz*, 2 January 2015. https://chinafilmbiz.com/2015/01/02/studio-report-card-2014-sci-fi-and-animation-drive-another-banner-year-in-china/

Caixin. "With Conflicting Data from Research Firms, Who is the No.1 Smartphone Brand in China?", 13 November 2014. http://datanews.caixin.com/2014-11-13/100750728.html

Caixin. "Domestic Smartphone Brands taking up market share from Apple and Samsung", 12 August 2015. http://companies.caixin.com/2015-08-12/100838666.html

Cao, Belinda. "Ontario Teachers Score Big With Bet on JD.com", Bloomberg, 17 August 2014. http://www.bloomberg.com/news/articles/2014-08-17/ontario-teachers-score-big-with-bet-on-china-s-jd-com

Carlton Mansfield. "China O2O Industry Report 2014", January 2015.

Carsten, Paul and Ruwitch, John. "Alibaba, Tencent spend billions in race to be China's one-stop online shop", Reuters, 21 January 2015. https://www.yahoo.com/tech/alibaba-tencent-spend-billions-race-chinas-one-stop-210628658--finance.html

Chan, Connie. "When One App Rules Them All: The Case of WeChat and Mobile in China", Andreessen Horowitz, August 2015. http://a16z.com/2015/08/06/wechat-china-mobile-first/

Chen, Biran X. "Apple's Jony Ive Has Harsh Words for Xiaomi", *New York Times*, 10 October 2014. http://bits.blogs.nytimes.com/2014/10/10/apples-jony-ive-has-harsh-words-for-xiaomi/

Chen, Hao. "Didi Daren APP: People Look for Hooligans", *Xinmin Evening Daily*, 20 April 2015. http://shanghai.xinmin.cn/xmsq/2015/04/20/27429927.html

Cheng, Jonathan. "Samsung's Primacy Is Tested in China", *Wall Street Journal*, 27 October 2014. http://www.wsj.com/articles/samsungs-primacy-is-tested-in-china-1414430128

China Daily. "Promoting China's information consumption", 20 August 2013. http://www.chinadaily.com.cn/business/2013-08/20/content_16907716.htm

China Daily. "E-commerce giants go rural", 9 July 2014. http://www.chinadaily.com.cn/business/tech/2014-07/09/content_17688343.htm

China Daily. "Alibaba spent $163m fighting fake goods" 24 December 2014. http://www.chinadaily.com.cn/business/2014-12/24/content_19158332.htm

China Daily. "Yiwu rides e-commerce wave", *China Daily USA*, 18 February 2015. http://usa.chinadaily.com.cn/life/2015-02/18/content_19616665.htm

China Daily. "Tiny Times sweeps Golden Broom Awards", 17 March 2015. http://www.chinadaily.com.cn/culture/2015-03/17/content_19833105.htm

China Daily. "Uber plans to invest $1 billion in China", 13 June 2015. http://www.chinadaily.com.cn/business/2015-06/13/content_20995575.htm

China Internet Network Information Center (CNNIC), Statistical Report on Internet Development in China (the 35th Survey Report), CNNIC, January 2015. http://www1.cnnic.cn/IDR/ReportDownloads/201507/P020150720486421654597.pdf

China Internet Network Information Center (CNNIC). "Statistical Report on Internet Development in China (the 36th Survey Report)", CNNIC, July 2015. http://www1.cnnic.cn/IDR/ReportDownloads/201601/P020160106496544403584.pdf

China Internet Network Information Center (CNNIC). "Statistical Report on Internet Development in China (the 37th Survey Report)", CNNIC, January 2016. http://www1.cnnic.cn/IDR/ReportDownloads/201604/P020160419390562421055.pdf

China Internet Watch. "China Top 100 Mobile Apps in July", 24 August 2015. http://www.chinainternetwatch.com/14363/china-top-20-mobile-apps-july/}ixzz3lOP8gcQh

China IP News. "China Vows to Step up Copyright Commercialization of Internet Literature", State Intellectual Property Office (SIPO) of the PRC, 12 February 2015. http://english.sipo.gov.cn/news/iprspecial/201502/t20150212_1075602.html

China Money Network. "Coatue Leads $600M Investment in Combined Didi Dache-Kuaidi", 1 April 2015. http://www.chinamoneynetwork.com/2015/04/01/coatue-leads-600m-investment-in-combined-didi-dache-kuaidi-dache

Chu, Kathy and Wong, Gillian. "China Tries to Clean up E-Commerce", *Wall Street Journal*, 1 April 2015. http://www.wsj.com/articles/china-tries-to-clean-up-e-commerce-1427894413

Cieply, Michael. "China Wants Its Movies to Be Big in the U.S., Too", *New York Times*, 7 November 2013. http://www.nytimes.com/2013/11/07/business/media/china-wants-its-movies-to-be-big-in-the-us-too.html

Coonan, Clifford. "China Box Office: Local Sensation 'Tiny Times 3.0' Knocks 'Transformers 4' Off Top Spot", *Hollywood Reporter*, 22 July 2014. http://www.hollywoodreporter.com/news/china-box-office-local-sensation-720189

Coonan, Clifford. "'World's Biggest Entertainment Company' Alibaba Keen to Expand Reach in Hollywood", *Hollywood Reporter*, 28 October 2014. http://www.hollywoodreporter.com/news/worlds-biggest-entertainment-company-alibaba-744459

Coonan, Clifford. "China Box Office: 'Furious 7' Becomes Highest-Grossing Movie Ever", *Hollywood Reporter*, 27 April 2015. http://www.hollywoodreporter.com/news/china-box-office-furious-7-791923

Crew, Rick and Osawa, Juro. "Dianping's Funding Round Lifts App Above US Peers", *Wall Street Journal*, 17 February 2015. http://blogs.wsj.com/moneybeat/2015/02/17/dianpings-funding-round-lifts-app-above-us-peers/

Custer, C. "Rumor has it Meituan-Dianping just raised the biggest funding round ever", *Tech in Asia*, 19 January 2016. https://www.techinasia.com/rumor-meituandianping-raised-biggest-funding

Dai, Tian. "Jack Ma apologizes for remarks on JD", *China Daily*, 9 January 2015. http://www.chinadaily.com.cn/business/tech/2015-01/09/content_19282791.htm

Darrell, Larry. "Cross-Border E-Commerce Flourishes in China", *Bidness Etc*, 26 February 2015. http://www.bidnessetc.com/35670-crossborder-ecommerce-flourishes-in-china/

DDB China Group. "PepsiCo year-end striking campaign 'Bring Happiness Home' is back with an integrated edge revolving around 'Pepsi Delivering Happiness'", Press release, 27 January 2014. http://www.ddbchina.com/press/newsline/2014_1_27_PepsiCo%20-year-end%20striking%20campaign%20Bring%20Happiness%20Home_en.pdf

de la Mercred, Michael J. "Chinese Agency Softens Criticism of Alibaba on Sales of Fake Goods", *New York Times*, 30 January 2015.

http://www.nytimes.com/2015/01/31/business/international/chinese-agency-softens-criticism-of-alibaba-on-sales-of-fake-goods.html

Deagon, Brian. "Alibaba, JD.com Gear Up For China's Top Shopping Day", *Investors Business Daily*, 19 October 2015. http://www.investors.com/news/technology/alibaba-jd-tencent-holdings-prepare-for-online-shopping-festival/

Ding, Peng. "Xiaomi TV Faces Internal and External Difficulties", Sina.com.cn, 14 May 2015. http://tech.sina.com.cn/zl/post/detail/it/2015-05-14/pid_8478692.htm

Dobbs, Richard, et al. "China's e-tail revolution: Online shopping as a catalyst for growth", McKinsey Global Institute, March 2013.

Doctoroff, Tom. "The Confucian Consumer and Chinese Luxury: FAQs", *Huffington Post*, 21 June 2010. http://www.huffingtonpost.com/tom-doctoroff/the-confucian-consumer-an_b_547295.html

Dong, Jielin. "Interview with Xiaomi President: How can a Pig Fly?", *Wall Street Journal* (Chinese), 28 April 2014. http://cn.wsj.com/gb/20140428/DJL114123.asp

Economist. "No profits, we promise: JD, an e-commerce firm billed as China's Amazon, prepares an IPO", 15 February 2014. http://www.economist.com/news/business/21596587-jd-e-commerce-firm-billed-chinas-amazon-prepares-ipo-no-profits-we-promise

Economist. "Mi too: An attention-grabbing Chinese superbrand goes global", 20 November 2014. http://www.economist.com/news/21631909-attention-grabbing-chinese-superbrand-goes-global-mi-too

Economist. "It's a Wanda-ful life: China's biggest property tycoon wants to become an entertainment colossus", 14 February 2015. http://www.economist.com/news/business/21643123-chinas-biggest-property-tycoon-wants-become-entertainment-colossus-its-wanda-ful-life

Fan, Feifei. "Pay-to-play content gains acceptance", *China Daily Europe*, 8 April 2016. http://europe.chinadaily.com.cn/business/2016-04/08/content_24389206.htm

Fan, Feifei. "Global industry body says China at the forefront of 5G technology", *China Daily USA*, 15 April 2016. http://usa.chinadaily.com.cn/epaper/2016-04/15/content_24575240.htm

Frater, Patrick. "Chinese Hit 'Tiny Times' Taps Internet Generation Via Audience Research", 10 September 2013. http://variety.com/2013/biz/asia/chinese-hit-tiny-times-taps-internet-generation-via-audience-research-1200605501/

Freifelder, Jack. "Wal-Mart seeks China growth", *China Daily USA*, 4 September 2014. http://usa.chinadaily.com.cn/us/2014-09/04/content_18549399.htm

Friedman, Alan. "In India, Xiaomi drops flash sales of the Xiaomi Redmi Note 4G", *PhoneArena*, 11 February 2015. http://www.phonearena.com/news/In-India-Xiaomi-drops-flash-sales-of-the-Xiaomi-Redmi-Note-4G_id65896

Fuhrman, Peter. "The Alibaba Death Star – How its Taobao Online Business is Wiping Out Traditional Shopping Malls in China", Linkedin, 27 May 2014. https://www.linkedin.com/pulse/20140527080328-355068-the-alibaba-death-star-how-its-taobao-online-business-is-wiping-out-traditional-shopping-malls-in-china

Gelles, David, Hiroko Tabuchi and Michael J. de la Merced, "Alibaba's American Aspirations", *New York Times*, 23 May 2014. http://www.nytimes.com/2014/05/24/business/alibaba-plans-11-main-online-market-geared-toward-americans.html

Gough, Neil. "Alibaba to Make Movies with Crowdfunding Idea", *New York Times*, 26 March 2014. http://dealbook.nytimes.com/2014/03/26/alibaba-enters-the-movie-business-with-a-kind-of-crowdfunding/

Gu, Wei. "Chinese Malls Enlist Mermaids, Monet to Stand Out", *Wall Street Journal*, 26 June 2014. http://www.wsj.com/articles/chinese-malls-enlist-mermaids-monet-to-stand-out-1403826831

Guo, Mengyi. "The War of Words between Cat and Dog", *China Operation Newspaper*, 25 January 2015. http://tech.163.com/15/0125/08/AGPSTK4C000915BF.html

Guo, Yichuan. "LeTV Mobile CEO's Response: Maybe Xiaomi has no Knowledge of Law", JRJ.com, 18 June 2015. http://finance.jrj.com.cn/2015/06/18094519375221.shtml

He, Wei. "Alibaba mapping a future filled with smart devices", *China Daily*, 12 February 2014. http://www.chinadaily.com.cn/business/tech/2014-02/12/content_17278075.htm

Heng, Shao. "Meet Vipshop, The Highest Valued Chinese E-Commerce Stock", *Forbes*, 26 November 2013. http://www.forbes.com/sites/hengshao/2013/11/26/meet-vipshop-the-highest-valued-chinese-e-commerce-stock/#3db07ca3ea48

iQIYI. "iQIYI Becomes Most Popular Free App in China Apple App Store", Press release, 6 July 2015. http://www.prnewswire.com/news-releases/iqiyi-becomes-most-popular-free-app-in-china-apple-app-store-300108843.html

iQIYI. "iQIYI Announces Paid Subscribers Reach Ten Million", Press release, 3 December 2015. http://www.prnewswire.com/news-releases/iqiyi-announces-paid-subscribers-reach-ten-million-300187500.html

Isaac, Mike, and de la Merced, Michael J. "Alibaba Is Investing Huge Sums in an Array of U.S. Tech Companies", *New York Times*, 31

July 2014. http://www.nytimes.com/2014/08/01/technology/alibaba-is-investing-huge-sums-in-an-array-of-us-tech-companies.html

Jia, Jinghua. "A Strategic Error: Motorola's Return to China", 21cn.com, 26 January 2015. http://jiaweb.baijia.baidu.com/article/43861

Jia, Jinghua. "With Meizu Attacking, Xiaomi in Dilemma", 21cn.com, 29 January 2015. http://it.21cn.com/itnews/a/2015/0129/11/28971295.shtml

Jiang, Long. "Whether bai-fa-you-xi investment product makes sense", *China Investment Funds Newspaper*, 29 September 2014. http://finance.sina.com.cn/money/fund/20140929/034020438401.shtml

Kan, Michael. "Top online pirated video provider in China slapped with fine", *PC World*, 17 June 2014. http://www.pcworld.com/article/2364640/top-online-pirated-video-provider-in-china-slapped-with-fine.html

Kan, Michael. "Xiaomi and Huawei wrestle for all-important top smartphone spot in China", CNET, 29 October 2015. http://www.cnet.com/news/xiaomi-still-leads-chinas-smartphone-market-but-huawei-is-not-far-behind/

KPMG Global China Practice. "E-commerce in China: Driving a new consumer culture", China 360, January 2014. https://www.kpmg.com/CN/en/IssuesAndInsights/ArticlesPublications/Newsletters/China-360/Documents/China-360-Issue15-201401-E-commerce-in-China.pdf

Krishna, R. Jai. "Arrival of Chinese Phone Brands Sets Stage for Price War in India – Low-Cost Handset Makers Challenge Dominance of Micromax, Karbonn Mobiles", *Wall Street Journal*, 8 August 2014. http://www.wsj.com/articles/arrival-of-chinese-phone-brands-sets-stage-for-price-war-in-india-1407493144

Kuhn, Troy. "Alibaba Group Holding Ltd Bolsters Logistics Network", *Bidness Etc*, 28 May 2015. http://www.bidnessetc.com/43836-alibaba-group-holding-ltd-bolsters-logistics-network/

Lannes, Bruno, Weiwen, Han, Ding, Jason, and Ling, Chenkai. "How Retailers Adapt to China's 'New Normal'", Bain & Company, 19 October 2015. http://www.bain.com/publications/articles/how-retailers-adapt-to-chinas-new-normal.aspx

Lau, Alan, Chi, Jayson, Gong, Fang, Li, Lihua and Liao, Nianling. "China's iConsumer 2015: A growing appetite for choice and change", McKinsey & Company, February 2015. http://www.iberchina.org/files/Chinas-iConsumer.pdf

Lee, Emma. "Rural China: The Next Battlefield for Domestic E-commerce", *Tech Node*, 14 January 2015. http://technode.com/2015/01/14/rural-ecommerce/

Lei, Jianping. "LeTV and Xiaomi are in an epic battle to upend the TV industry – here's who's winning", *Business Insider*, 1 July 2015. http://www.businessinsider.com/letv-and-xiaomi-are-in-an-epic-battle-to-upend-the-tv-industry--heres-whos-winning-2015-7

Li, David. "Shanzhai: Open innovation as an invitation to start new brands", China Innovation, Campaign Asia. http://chinainnovation.campaignasia.com/home/articles/shanzhai-open-innovation-as-an-invitation-to-start-new-brands/

Li, Hong. "Marketing to China's Middle Class", *China Business Review*, 6 January 2014. http://www.chinabusinessreview.com/marketing-to-chinas-middle-class/

Li, Keqiang. "Li Keqiang expounds on urbanization", China.org.cn, 26 May 2013. http://china.org.cn/china/2013-05/26/content_28934485.htm

Li, Yan. "Baidu, QVOD fined 250,000 yuan each for video copyright violations", *Global Times*, 31 December 2013. http://www.globaltimes.cn/content/835030.shtml

Lian, Zi, "Alibaba digs 'deep' in mobile search deal, calling it critical piece", *China Daily USA*, 21 October 2014. http://usa.chinadaily.com.cn/us/2014-10/21/content_18780307.htm

Liu, Mingkang. "Internet Finance and Regulation in China", Fung Global Institute, August 2015, http://www.asiaglobalinstitute.hku.hk/en/wp-content/uploads/2015/08/FGI-Report-Internet-Finance-part-I-Main-Report-2.pdf

Liu, Shuangshuang. "2015 China's Box Office Increased 48.7% from the Previous Year", Caixin, 1 January 2016. http://culture.caixin.com/2016-01-01/100895135.html

Liu, Wei. "No room for the Golden Broom?", *China Daily*, 28 February 2011. http://www.chinadailyasia.com/life/2011-02/28/content_61326.html

Liu, Wei. "Chinese stories, Hollywood thrills", *China Daily USA*, 19 June 2014. http://usa.chinadaily.com.cn/epaper/2014-06/19/content_17600977.htm

Liu, Xiaojin. "2015 Tencent Entertainment White Paper Released", Caixin, 23 December 2015. http://companies.caixin.com/2015-12-23/100891707.html

Liu, Zheng. "JD.com on opportunities, challenges in rural areas", *China Daily*, 17 March 2015. http://www.chinadaily.com.cn/business/tech/2015-03/17/content_19828179.htm

Liu, Zheng. "ZTE's new flagship phone to be presented as state gift to UK", *China Daily*, 23 October 2015. http://www.chinadaily.com.cn/world/2015xivisituk/2015-10/23/content_22265870.htm

Liu, Zheng. "Nubia announces first eye-scan smartphone", *China Daily*, 29 October 2015. http://www.chinadaily.com.cn/business/tech/2015-10/29/content_22311578.htm

Luk, Lorraine, and Osawa, Juro. "ZTE Taking Staff From BlackBerry: Chinese Company Looking for Talent to Help With Global Expansion", *Wall Street Journal*, 10 June 2014. http://www.wsj.com/articles/chinas-zte-taking-staff-from-blackberry-motorola-mobility-1402390450

Ma, Rui. "More than messaging: Why you should stop comparing WeChat to WhatsApp", *The Next Web*, 24 January 2014. http://thenextweb.com/asia/2014/01/24/messaging-stop-comparing-wechat-whatsapp/

Ma, Wayne. "Companies Allowing QQ, WeChat Users to Reserve Consoles Days Before Other Consumers", *Wall Street Journal*, 28 July 2014. http://www.wsj.com/articles/jd-com-tencent-to-presell-microsofts-xbox-in-china-1406509872

Macgregor, Luke. "Royal Mail announces China link-up through Alibaba's Tmall", Reuters, 2 March 2015. http://finance.yahoo.com/news/royal-mail-announces-china-alibabas-150713047.html

Madisonboom. "The Birth of WeChat Bees", 21 July 2014. http://www.madisonboom.cn/2014/07/21/hakuhodo-cooperate-with-advertising-school-of-cuc-launch-report/

Manjoo, Farhad. "Alibaba Bets on a Growing Chinese Economy and New Consumers", *New York Times*, 7 May 2014. http://www.nytimes.com/2014/05/08/technology/alibaba-bets-on-a-growing-chinese-economy-and-new-consumers.html

Mathew, Jerin. "Alibaba Plans 'Online-to-Offline' Business with $692m Investment in Mall Operator Intime", *International Business Times*, 31 March 2014. http://www.ibtimes.co.uk/alibaba-plans-online-offline-business-692m-investment-mall-operator-intime-1442617

Mendoza, Menchie. "Alibaba's Tmall Box Office Will Be Netflix and HBO of China", *Tech Times*, 15 June 2015. http://www.techtimes.com/articles/60419/20150615/alibabas-tmall-box-office-will-be-netflix-and-hbo-of-china.htm

Meng, Jing. "Tencent's WeChat bites the advertising bullet", *China Daily*, 27 January 2015. http://www.chinadaily.com.cn/business/tech/2015-01/27/content_19415584.htm

Meng, Jing, and Xie Yu, "WeChat global push slows as user growth plateaus", *China Daily*, 19 March 2015. http://www.chinadaily.com.cn/business/tech/2015-03/19/content_19850779.htm

Meng, Jing. "Shake-up in store for O2O sector", *China Daily USA*, 18 December 2015, http://usa.chinadaily.com.cn/epaper/2015-12/18/content_22743653.htm

Meng, Jing. "Taobao village clusters spreading reach", *China Daily*, 26 December 2015. http://www.chinadaily.com.cn/cndy/2015-12/26/content_22813197.htm

Meng, Jing. "Alibaba to add 200 staff to fight against counterfeit products", *China Daily*, 28 December 2015. http://www.chinadaily.com.cn/business/2015-12/28/content_228-43364.htm

Meng, Jing. "Alipay study: Online payments via smartphones gaining ground", *China Daily USA*, 13 January 2016. http://usa.chinadaily.com.cn/epaper/2016-01/13/content_23071262.htm

Mitchell, Tom. "China to launch $6.5bn VC fund for emerging industries start-ups", *Financial Times*, 15 January 2015. http://www.ft.com/intl/cms/s/0/73f216c8-9c97-11e4-a730-00144feabdc0.html}axzz4AJjmfMqF

Mozur, Paul. "Q&A: Youku Tudou CEO on Alibaba Investment", *Wall Street Journal*, 29 April 2014. http://blogs.wsj.com/digits/2014/04/29/qa-youku-tudou-ceo-on-alibaba-investment/

Mozur, Paul, and Osawa, Juro. "Can Alibaba Taxi App Be a Growth Driver?", *Wall Street Journal*, 16 March 2014. http://www.wsj.com/articles/SB10001424052702303287804579442993327079748

Mtime. "Bullet Screens for Movies: an Era of Watching Movies while Tu-cao?", 21ccom.net, 13 August 2014. http://www.21ccom.net/articles/culture/wenyi/20140813111145.html

Newman, Alex. "China Buys Hollywood Influence with Takeover of Top U.S. Cinema Chain", *The New American*, 29 May 2012. http://www.thenewamerican.com/economy/markets/item/11537-china-buys-hollywood-influence-with-takeover-of-top-us-cinema-chain

Nielsen. "A new era in consumption", 19 June 2014. http://www.nielsen.com/cn/en/insights/reports/2014/A-new-era-in-Consumption-2014.html

Noble, Josh. "Alibaba and JD Online take fresh approach to China food shopping," *Financial Times*, 1 March 2015. http://www.ft.com/cms/s/0/bfaa55da-be4d-11e4-a341-00144feab7de.html#axzz4A0q55VBA

Northeast news. "2014 top ten 'little fresh meat' elected", 12 August 2014. http://amuse.nen.com.cn/system/2014/08/12/012580283.shtml

Olson, Parmy. "Xiaomi May Have a Major Patent Problem", *Forbes*, 29 January 2015. http://www.forbes.com/sites/parmyolson/2015/01/29/xiaomi-patent-problem/#412ae3a522ec

Osawa, Juro, Gillian Wong and Rick Carew. "Xiaomi Becomes World's Most Valuable Tech Startup", *Wall Street Journal*, 29 December 2014. http://www.wsj.com/articles/xiaomi-becomes-worlds-most-valuable-tech-startup-1419843430

Osawa, Juro. "Alibaba's Next Challenge: Making Money from Mobile Traffic", *Wall Street Journal*, 7 May 2014.

http://blogs.wsj.com/digits/2014/05/07/alibabas-next-challenge-making-money-from-mobile-traffic/

Osawa, Juro. "Lenovo Sees Motorola as Weapon in Tough Chinese Smartphone Market", *Wall Street Journal*, 21 May 2014. http://www.wsj.com/articles/SB10001424052702304198504579575132-383470714

Osawa, Juro. "Alibaba Tackles Amazon, eBay on Home Turf", *Wall Street Journal*, 11 June 2014. http://www.wsj.com/articles/alibaba-launches-u-s-shopping-site-11-main-1402469675

Osawa, Juro. "Can WeChat Become a Major Advertising Platform?", *Wall Street Journal*, 9 July 2014. http://blogs.wsj.com/digits/2014/07/09/can-wechat-become-a-major-advertising-platform/

Osawa, Juro. "Is Huawei Eating Samsung's Lunch?", *Wall Street Journal*, 30 July 2014. http://blogs.wsj.com/digits/2014/07/30/is-huawei-eating-samsungs-lunch/

Osnos, Evan. "A New China in 'House of Cards'", *The New Yorker*, 11 March 2014. http://www.newyorker.com/online/blogs/comment/2014/03/a-new-china-in-house-of-cards.html

Ovide, Shira, and Wakabayashi, Daisuke. "Apple's Share of Smartphone Industry's Profits Soars to 92%", *Wall Street Journal*, 12 July 2015. http://www.wsj.com/articles/apples-share-of-smartphone-industrys-profits-soars-to-92-1436727458

Peng, Bo "China is on a fast lane to become an innovative nation", Keynote speech, China Copyright Annual Forum, 15 November 2014. http://ip.people.com.cn/n/2014/1115/c136655-26030845.html

People's Daily Online. "China unveils road map for 'Internet plus'", 29 June 2015. http://en.people.cn/n/2015/0629/c98649-8912583.html

Phillips, Tom. "Uniqlo sex video: film shot in Beijing store goes viral and angers government", *The Guardian*, 16 July 2015. http://www.theguardian.com/world/2015/jul/16/uniqlo-sex-video-film-shot-in-beijing-store-goes-viral-and-angers-government

PricewaterhouseCoopers Zhong Tian. "Banking and finance in China: The outlook for 2015", January 2015. http://www.pwccn.com/webmedia/doc/635585738589999909_bfic_2015.pdf

Qin, Xiaoying. "Why Do the Chinese Love 'House Of Cards'?", *China & US Focus*, 14 May 2014. http://www.chinausfocus.com/culture-history/why-do-the-chinese-love-house-of-cards/

Savov, Vlad. "Can Lenovo save Motorola?", *The Verge*, 30 January 2014. http://www.theverge.com/2014/1/30/5360698/lenovo-motorola-takeover-report

Schwankert, Steven. "Yao Ming to Crowdfund New Financing for California Winery", *The Beijinger*, 5 March 2015.

http://www.thebeijinger.com/blog/2015/03/05/yao-ming-crowdfund-new-financing-california-winery

Schwartzel, Eric. "Box-Office Receipts in 2014: Far From Epic", *Wall Street Journal*, 4 January 2015. http://www.wsj.com/articles/hollywood-tries-to-forget-rough-2014-1420404720

Shanghai Daily. "China's Internet video portals battle piracy", 9 December 2013. http://www.shanghaidaily.com/Business/economy/Chinas-Internet-video-portals-battle-piracy/

Shek, Colin. "The New Empire Builders: China's Digital Conglomerates", CKGSB Knowledge, 22 September 2015. http://knowledge.ckgsb.edu.cn/2015/09/22/china/the-new-empire-builders-chinas-digital-conglomerates/

Shone, Tom. "Hollywood transformed: How China is changing the DNA of America's blockbuster movies", *Financial Times*, 25 July 2014. http://www.ft.com/intl/cms/s/2/60338b6c-1263-11e4-93a5-00144feabdc0.html}axzz4ADYlN3Eb

Shu, Catherine. "Xiaomi and Shunwei Capital Make $300M Strategic Investment in iQiyi, One of China's Largest Online Video Platforms", *Tech Crunch*, 18 November 2014. http://techcrunch.com/2014/11/18/xiaomi-makes-300m-strategic-investment-in-iqiyi-one-of-chinas-largest-online-video-platforms/

Shu, Catherine. "Youku Tudou, One of China's Leading Streaming Video Sites, Launches Its First Hardware Line", *Tech Crunch*, 10 December 2014. http://techcrunch.com/2014/12/10/youku-tudou-one-of-chinas-leading-streaming-video-sites-launches-its-first-hardware-line/

Sina. "Crowd-funding: attending Harvard with 99 Yuan", 17 July 2015. http://edu.sina.com.cn/a/2015-07-17/1100261689.shtml

Sina Caijing. "Interview with Wanda's Wang Jianlin: the former most rich in China facing a 'crisis'", 20 February 2014. http://finance.sina.com.cn/china/20140220/065918273805.shtml

Smith, Geoffrey. "Amazon to launch in Shanghai free-trade zone", *Fortune*, 21 August 2014. http://fortune.com/2014/08/21/amazon-to-launch-in-shanghai-free-trade-zone/

Song, Yongjie. "Is Xiaomi worth $40 billion?", *Xinliang IT/China Daily*, 3 November 2014. http://www.chinadaily.com.cn/hqcj/xfly/2014-11-03/content_12644475.html

Soper, Spencer. "Amazon Opens Store on Alibaba's Tmall for Chinese Shoppers", Bloomberg, 6 March 2015. http://www.bloomberg.com/news/articles/2015-03-05/amazon-opens-store-on-alibaba-s-tmall-to-reach-chinese-shoppers

State Council of The People's Republic of China. "Internet Plus: Premier Li's new tech tool", 13 March 2015. http://english.gov.cn/premier/news/2015/03/13/content_281475070887811.htm

Su, Yi. "BAT entering into Internet Phones: the War of Entry Points Escalating", *Sohu IT*, 22 August 2014. http://it.sohu.com/20140822/n403666271.shtml

Tan, Ming. "Chinese Smartphone Brands' War in India", Caixin.Net, 18 September 2015. http://topics.caixin.com/shoujizhanyindu/

Tencent. "NBA and Tencent Announce Groundbreaking Partnership to make Tencent the Exclusive Official Digital Partner in China", Press release, 30 January 2015. http://www.tencent.com/en-us/content/at/2015/attachments/20150130.pdf

Verot, Olivier. "Top 10 advertising campaigns on Wechat", *Marketing China*, 15 January 2015. http://marketingtochina.com/top-10-advertising-campaigns-wechat/

Voyles, Bennett. "Will China Overtake Silicon Valley?", CKGSB Knowledge, 23 June 2014. http://knowledge.ckgsb.edu.cn/2014/06/23/finance-and-investment/will-china-overtake-silicon-valley/

Wang, Chao. "Why Ant Financial launches an independent APP?", 20 August 2015. http://tech.sina.com.cn/i/2015-08-20/doc-ifxhcvsf0984311.shtml

Wang, Kaihao. "Big plans for tiny times", *China Daily*, 1 July 2014. http://www.chinadaily.com.cn/culture/2014-07/17/content_17810642.htm

Wang, Qionghui. "Alibaba CEO Zhang Yong: Move Beyond the GMV-centered Development Model", Caixin.com, 6 January 2016. http://companies.caixin.com/2016-01-06/100896746.html

Wang, Shanshan, and Mozurnov, Paul. "Alibaba and Others Push to Improve Delivery, on Singles' Day in China", *New York Times*, 11 November 2014. http://www.nytimes.com/2014/11/12/technology/on-singles-day-in-china-a-push-to-improve-online-shoppings-slow-delivery.html

Wang, Yue. "JD.com Invests $700 Million in Chinese Supermarket Chain Yonghui", *Forbes Asia*, 7 August 2015. http://www.forbes.com/sites/ywang/2015/08/07/jd-com-invests-700-million-in-chinese-supermarket-chain-yonghui/#7f225fd47c98

Wang, Yue. "O2O Leads Chinese Startups' Boom and Bust Cycle", *Forbes*, 21 April 2016. http://www.forbes.com/sites/ywang/2016/04/21/o2o-leads-chinese-startups-boom-and-bust-cycle/}55d900718018

Want China Times "WeChat increasingly a sales channel in China", 20 February 2015. http://www.technologynewschina.com/2015/02/wechat-increasingly-sales-channel-in.html

Watson, Mark. "PepsiCo Year-End Integrated Campaign 'Bring Happiness Home'", Advertising@chinaSMACK, 28 January 2014. http://advertising.chinasmack.com/2014/pepsico-year-end-integrated-campaign-bring-happiness-home.html

Wei, Gu. "Alibaba Is Going Hollywood: E-Commerce Giant Seeks a Role in China's Burgeoning Film Industry", *Wall Street Journal*, 19 June 2014. http://www.wsj.com/articles/alibaba-is-going-hollywood-1403190518

Wei, Gu. "Alibaba could Become a Victim of its Success", *Wall Street Journal*, 26 September 2014. http://www.wsj.com/articles/the-peoples-money-alibaba-could-become-a-victim-of-its-success-1411653293

Welitzkin, Paul. "ZTE: New phone is affordable high-end", *China Daily USA*, 15 July 2015. http://usa.chinadaily.com.cn/epaper/2015-07/15/content_21287106.htm

Williams, Trey. "Alibaba wants you to make mobile payments with a smile", *Market Watch*, 16 March 2015. http://www.market-watch.com/story/alibaba-wants-you-to-make-mobile-payments-with-a-smile–03-16

Williams-Grut, Oscar. "There's another Chinese market growing explosively – and Beijing wants to take control before it 'blows up'", *Business Insider UK*, 26 August 2015. http://uk.businessinsider.com/china-regulate-peer-to-peer-and-internet-finance-2015-8

Woetzel, Jonathan, et al. "China's digital transformation: The Internet's impact on productivity and growth", McKinsey Global Institute, July 2014.

Wong, Gillian. "A Glimpse into How Chinese Smartphone Maker Xiaomi Works", *Wall Street Journal*, 18 December 2014. http://blogs.wsj.com/digits/2014/12/18/a-glimpse-into-how-chinese-smartphone-maker-xiaomi-works/

Wong, Gillian. "Alibaba Disputes U.S. Group's Claim It Tolerates Fake Goods on Taobao", *Wall Street Journal*, 14 April 2015. http://www.wsj.com/articles/alibaba-rebuts-u-s-groups-claim-it-tolerates-fake-goods-on-taobao-1428981233

Xiang, Tracey. "Xiaomi's Custom Android System MIUI Has 100M Users", *Tech Node*, 13 February 2015. http://technode.com/2015/02/13/xiaomis-custom-android-system-miui-100m-users/

Xinhua News Agency. "Online vendors bring bite of China to masses", *China Daily*, 30 January 2013. http://www.chinadaily.com.cn/business/2013-01/30/content_16188595.htm

Xinhua News Agency. "China boosts information consumption", China.org.cn, 14 August 2013. http://www.china.org.cn/business/2013-08/14/content_29717660.htm

Xinhua News Agency. "Alibaba helps make China's largest fund", 16 November 2013. http://news.xinhuanet.com/english/china/2013-11/16/c_132893320.htm

Xinhua News Agency. "Wanda, Tencent and Baidu set up joint venture", 30 August 2014. http://news.xinhuanet.com/english/video/2014-08/30/c_133607725.htm

Xinhua News Agency. "China lowers growth target, eyes better quality", 5 March 2015. http://news.xinhuanet.com/english/2015-03/05/c_134041702.htm

Xinhua News Agency. "Entrepreneurs at 3W coffee shop", *People's Daily*, 19 June 2015. http://en.people.cn/n/2015/0619/c98649-8909051.html

Xinhua News Agency. "Uber vows to expand ride-hailing service to more Chinese cities", 9 September 2015. http://news.xinhuanet.com/english/2015-09/08/c_134603282.htm

Xinhua News Agency. "Chinese smartphone supplier ZTE expands basketball sponsorships to five NBA teams", 29 October 2015. http://news.xinhuanet.com/english/2015-10/28/c_134760025.htm

Xinhua News Agency. "China to continue experiencing strong uptake of mobile internet services: GSMA", 24 February, 2016. http://news.xinhuanet.com/english/2016-02/24/c_135127963.htm

Xinhua News Agency. "The global impact of China's 13th Five-Year Plan", 10 March 2016. http://news.xinhuanet.com/english/2016-03/10/c_135175652.htm

Xinhua News Agency. "What is China's 'new economy'?", 16 March 2016. http://news.xinhuanet.com/english/2016-03/16/c_135194608.htm

Xinhua News Agency. "China Focus: Popular Korean TV series draws online paying users", 26 March 2016. http://news.xinhuanet.com/english/2016-03/26/c_135225231.htm

Yang, Jie, and Mozur, Paul. "China's Internet Giants Raise Stakes for World Cup Wagers: Alibaba, Tencent Make It Easier for Fans to Bet Via Smartphone or Computer", *Wall Street Journal*, 24 June 2014. http://www.wsj.com/articles/chinas-internet-giants-raise-stakes-for-world-cup-wagers-1403615258

Yinan, Zhao and Jingxi, Mo. "Li says virtual commerce can benefit real economy", *China Daily USA*, 20 November 2014. http://usa.chinadaily.com.cn/epaper/2014-11/20/content_18950-317.htm

Yoshimura, Midori. "Basketball Star Yao Ming Crowdfunds Napa Valley Luxury Wine Brand, Yao Family Wines, with China and US Distribution", *Crowd Fund Insider*, 5 March 2015. http://www.crowdfundinsider.com/2015/03/63835-yao-ming-creates-napa-valley-luxury-wine-brand-yao-family-wines-with-china-and-us-distribution/

Yuan, Michelle. "Weibo's True Reach Limits Value", *Wall Street Journal*, 17 April 2014. http://blogs.wsj.com/moneybeat/2014/04/17/weibos-true-reach-limits-value/

Zakkour, Michael. "Hollywood Vet Producing TV Shows for China – Viewers and Brands Love Them", *Forbes*, 23 December 2013.

http://www.forbes.com/sites/michaelzakkour/2013/12/23/hollywood-vet-producing-tv-shows-for-china-viewers-and-brands-love-them/

Zero2IPO Research. "An Overview of China's Angel Investment and Equity Investment Markets", March 2015.

Zhang, Ye, "Alibaba, Baidu, Tencent make big plans for annual red envelope giveaway", *Global Times*, 27 January 2016. http://www.globaltimes.cn/content/965961.shtml

Zhang, Ye. "Over 100m people enjoy holiday hongbao", *Global Times*, 25 February 2015. http://www.globaltimes.cn/content/908709.shtml

Zhao, Chenting. "Lenovo Replaces its Mobile Business Management for New Strategies", *China Business News*, 3 June 2015. http://business.sohu.com/20150603/n414329861.shtml

Zhao, Yinan. "Premier meets with group of innovators over coffee", *China Daily*, 8 May 2015. http://www.chinadaily.com.cn/china/2015-05/08/content_20654522.htm

Zhong, Isabella. "Vipshop: The Rising Star of China E-commerce", *Barron's*, 12 December 2014. http://www.barrons.com/articles/vipshop-the-rising-star-of-china-e-commerce-1418374560

Zhou, May. "ZTE aiming for high-end tech", *China Daily USA*, 7 August 2015. http://usa.chinadaily.com.cn/business/2015-08/07/content_21533458.htm

Zhu, Yishi. "Why Alibaba Fears Tencent's Online Incursions", *Caixin*, 25 March 2014. http://english.caixin.com/2014-03-25/100656493.html

Index

Compiled by Marian Preston for INDEXING SPECIALISTS (UK) Ltd., Indexing House, 306A Portland Road, Hove, East Sussex BN3 5LP United Kingdom.